Reedbound

To Doug
A little light reading while you
find your dancing feet again!

Reedbound

A Year on Ireland's Inland Waterways

Best wishes and much love
Giles and Jill.

Giles Byford

Illustrated by Jill Parkinson

Matador
9 Priory Business Park,
Wistow Road, Kibworth Beauchamp,
Leicestershire. LE8 0RX
Tel: (+44) 116 279 2299
Fax: (+44) 116 279 2277
Email: books@troubador.co.uk
Web: www.troubador.co.uk/matador

ISBN 978 1784623 999

British Library Cataloguing in Publication Data.
A catalogue record for this book is available from the British Library.

Printed and bound in the UK by TJ International, Padstow, Cornwall
Typeset in Adobe Garamond Pro by Troubador Publishing Ltd, Leicester, UK

Matador is an imprint of Troubador Publishing Ltd

For Mum and Dad

CONTENTS

River Camlin
Royal Canal
Lanesborough
Barley Harbour
Lecarrow
N
W   E
S
Athlone   Coosan Lough
Ballinasloe
Clonmacnoise
Shannonbridge
River Suck
Edenderry
Dublin
Shannon Harbour   Tullamore   Sallins
Grand Canal
Portumna   River Shannon   Monasterevin   Naas
Lough Derg
Athy
Mountshannon   Dromineer
Carlow
Scarriff   River Barrow
Garrykennedy   Graiguenamanagh
St.Mullins
Killaloe
Not to be used
for navigation!

Belleek

Lower Lough Erne

.Enniskillen

'The Shannon Pot'

Lough Allen

Drumshambo

Upper Lough Erne

Crom Castle

Boyle

Lough Key

Ballinamore

Ballyconnell

S.E.W.*

Leitrim

Lough Garadice

Belturbet

Carrick-on-Shannon

Jamestown Canal

Lough Boderg

Grange

Lough Bofin

Dromod

Roosky

Kilglass

River Shannon

* Shannon-Erne Waterway

MISFITS TOUR 08

PROLOGUE

White-knuckled and queasy-stomached, I brace against our wheelhouse woodwork and watch the wave lift our bow. It pauses, briefly framed by blue, then falls. Whoomph! Our baseplate slams violently down into the white-flecked, grey-green sea. Displaced water surges out and, carried by the breeze, rains down across our windscreen. I can't hear the wiper but, by the time it's cleared the screen, our bow is again framed by blue. I thought it might be a little choppy, but had never expected things to be as rough as this. This is worse than a nightmare, for nightmares end when you wake up, and I am anything but asleep.

All we can do is hang on and hope this steep-waved hell is a consequence of wind meeting tide in the estuary's shallows; that, once we're in the deeper water beyond its bar, our torment will ease. It has to, for I cannot imagine coping with this for the twenty-four hours it'll take us to reach Dublin. And that's just me; what about the stress on the home that Jill and I have spent years building? What's this pounding going to do to it? Will we even make it? And those are thoughts I really cannot cope with. So, to clear my head of panic, I set off to check and check again anything and everything that my imagination sees failing.

The engine is under the wheelhouse floor, which has been sealed shut in case a rogue wave wipes out the wood and glass over it. So, grasping for anything to steady myself with, I go down into the workshop in *Hawthorn's* stern, pull out the steps I designed to slide for this moment, and clamber into the engine bay's noise and heat and smells.

A restored antique Gardner, there's always oil weeping somewhere on our engine. No more than usual? Check. No water or fuel leaks? Check. No unusual looseness or movement? Check. Nothing odd? Check. I can see myself spending the whole voyage in here, just watching and waiting and filling my head with anything other than the state of the sea. But I can't; I need to inspect our stern for leaks on the steering, weedhatch and drive to convince myself we're not slowly flooding.

Back in the wheelhouse crowded with crew and Jill, little has changed. The retreating tide dragging us offshore means England is now a few hundred yards further away, but that's all: Jill's still as ashen, the lads can't hide their concern, and the sea's as lumpy and endless as it was minutes before. Not wanting to look outside, I'm about to start my inspections again, but I don't: jamming myself in the only free corner I force myself to watch the bow rise and slam, and to listen to the discordant orchestra of water, steel and spray for a few minutes. And I try to find the trust I'm desperately seeking.

How different a voyage this would have been if we'd made it when planned a year ago. That is before the near disastrous event in the salt marshes of the Ribble estuary we're now leaving had begun the erosion of the trust our world was built on. The months that followed had left us frightened and fragile, but now we hoped to put all that behind us and arrive in Dublin full of confidence and looking forward to a year exploring Ireland's inland waterways. Or, and this was the least disturbing dark scenario, we'd be calling at some unexpected port. The worst? Well that had to be that our adventure would end in a helicopter or lifeboat ride that would leave us with just the clothes we're wearing.

The bow's still rising, falling, slamming; best I go check those drips…

ORIGINS

'You know, we could live on one of them. That might be fun,' I said, looking at the narrowboats in the marina opposite.

Jill and I were on the Macclesfield Canal at Poynton, enjoying the peace and quiet of the hills south of Manchester where we were living in a rented flat; we were only walking the towpath because the high ground we'd set out for was cloaked in cold cloud. We were discussing our future together, and possible ways of escaping paying rent without committing to the terrifying debt of a mortgage. Perhaps it was the way the light was diffused by the mist and smoke from the narrowboats' chimneys, or the gently dripping near-silence, but the idea seemed both romantic and not unrealistic.

'Perhaps,' Jill replied, before turning and crunching on down the frosty towpath.

Back from our walk, life went on as normal. Jill got up early to drive to Birkenhead, where she worked running a development kitchen for a supermarket supplier, while I tried to drum up interest in the anthropology degree I was studying for. But a seed had been sown, and Jill wasn't surprised to come home one evening to a pile of inland waterways magazines, and me babbling on about how we might just be able to make this happen. By this point I'd read enough to know that all narrowboats were just under 7' wide, so the only thing determining the size of our new home was how long a boat we could afford, or wanted. While it was immediately obvious we wouldn't be moving onto anything flashy, let alone be buying the sort of space we enjoyed in our one-bedroomed flat, there appeared to be boats advertised that we might be able to make a go of. My enthusiasm must have been contagious, as it wasn't long before Jill agreed with me.

Our walks in the hills were replaced by weekends driving around the country to boatyards and brokerages, where we'd walk past shiny vessels being purred over by people older and richer than us. We may have been poor, but our youth made it possible for us to clamber into the distant corners most of the bargain boats seemed to be hidden in. We always left home with optimism and returned disappointed, for it seemed boat brokers' adverts were as far from the truth as the blurb I wrote about student flats in my part-time job at a letting agency. And then our luck changed.

We'd driven to Northwich in Cheshire to visit one of England's largest brokerages. We were returning the keys to yet more disappointments and describing our struggles when the salesman suddenly stopped us and said 'Hang on a minute, I do have this.' Opening his desk drawer, he passed us a brown envelope. It was full of photographs of a rather pretty and seemingly well-kept 55' boat called *Camberwell Beauty*. For once it was in our price range and was being lived on.

'Wow, that looks bang on,' we both enthused. 'We'd love to have a look. Where is it? Have you got the keys?'

'Ah, it's not here. It's miles away in a marina at Poynton on the Macclesfield Canal. I can give the owner a ring if you want?'

After numerous trips to boat yards all over the English north and midlands, to be driving back to Poynton to view a boat that genuinely excited us felt very odd. This feeling intensified when, once we were standing outside *Camberwell Beauty*, we realised we were within a hundred yards of where I'd first suggested living on a boat. Better still was discovering that for once photographs actually portrayed reality and that this boat really was full of life and light. It also seemed more spacious than we'd anticipated, though we didn't then know that its owners, Chris and Kate, had spent the previous day piling all their clutter into the Land Rover parked beside it. We were shown around, and then sat for an hour or so drinking tea and chatting. Jill and I then stood outside contemplating the magnitude of what we were doing for all of two minutes before making an offer.

This being subject to survey meant *Camberwell Beauty* had to be moved to the brokerage and boatyard at Northwich where we'd been told about her. This gave Chris and Kate a last voyage through Macclesfield to Stoke-on-Trent and then the long descent to the Cheshire Plain to say goodbye to their home. It was also a blessing for us as, being midway between Jill's work south of Liverpool and my studies in Manchester, Northwich was the perfect base for us to begin life afloat. Six weeks later we were moving on board.

Jill and I moved on without a lot of the baggage and clutter we'd collected both independently and together. There simply wasn't room for my large music system and hundreds of records, or space in the galley for most of Jill's kitchen equipment. Though, without the 240-volt power needed to run such things, they were all redundant anyway. We had some fixed bookshelves, but our large pieces of art were never going to fit on sloping cabin sides. Fortunately we were too excited to worry about how long the list of things to pass on to others was getting. Why, when we'd never been to one, we thought a car boot sale might be a good idea I'll never know. It was so soul destroying we vowed to give everything away rather than haggle over its value. And we did, much to friends and family, and the rest to charity shops. It was all very exciting. And we hadn't the slightest inkling of what we were doing.

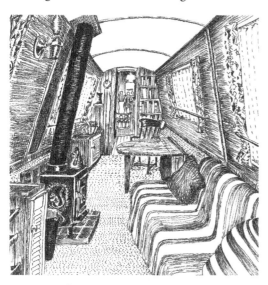

While *Camberwell Beauty* was set up as a live-aboard with both a large solar panel and a wind generator on its roof, living with only 12-volt battery power took some getting used to. As did the 'bucket and chuck it' camping toilet, of which the less said the better. We were lucky to move on in late spring when the days were drawing out and the weather warming. Jill would arrive at the boatyard each Friday to find the engine running and the ropes all but untied, and our home ready to slip out of the yard for a weekend of rural solitude. Longer holidays were spent boating further afield. This was the romance we'd been dreaming of, and much of the reason we, and the many friends and family who came to visit, so loved our new life.

I took to it with vigour, arguably too much vigour as I struggled to retain any interest in academia. By Christmas I'd had enough and packed it in. I soon had two job offers: as a researcher at the BBC, or labouring on the new marina being built just down the canal at Anderton. The BBC were in London, and there was no way we were going there, so I pulled on the overalls and work boots I'd worn through my twenties, and picked up a shovel. It was a decision that filled friends with horror yet, trusting in the sense of feeling blessed on the water and confident all would turn out well, I wasn't too worried. And then came the day a few months later when I decided to replace the tired cover on the front of *Camberwell*: a relatively minor task that was to have major consequences.

Unlike proper, traditional narrowboats, which would have had cloth covers over much of their length, modern steel-cabined narrowboats usually just have a few feet of fabric – a cratch cover – over their front well decks. This gives a handy dry area just outside the doors, adds a little shelter from the worst of inclement weather and offers a little privacy from passing prying eyes. Posh covers had zips, to make going in and out of the boat easy, and PVC windows to let in light. Aside from having neither, our original cover was starting to wear and rip. It badly needed replacing, yet having one made seemed insanely expensive. Fortunately, my history of academic disappointment meant I left school at fifteen to take up an apprenticeship in upholstery. So, and I thought long and hard about this while mixing concrete, carting bricks and driving dumpers, I had some relevant skills. I borrowed a sewing machine, bought some fabric and fittings, and made a replacement cover. It wasn't an easy undertaking – cover-making required different skills from restoring antique furniture – but it must have looked OK, for I was soon getting asked to make covers for boats around us. This gave me the confidence to invest in our own sewing machine and the tools needed to finish cloths properly, and what had been a small spare room and study became a workshop. My timing couldn't have been better for the marina was nearing completion and, without this unforeseen possibility, I'd have been looking for work further afield. It was perfect, and I didn't even need to buy a car.

Quite possibly to prevent me exploding with smugness, fate delivered a sobering blow when we decided to get a dog. Dogs seemed to go with boating, and my being about all day meant we were perfectly set to give one a happy home. We naively imagined ours would be like all the others we saw around the waterways: peacefully content to lie on the towpath, never going far, and generally easy-going company. So when the local paper had a 'Tail of the Week' advert for 'a loveable Labrador cross' we trotted off, benignly assuming the god that looked after our boating world would be spoiling us again. Was he hell! It may have been coincidence that the six-month-old mongrel we went to see was being kept in a dark barn, but my game-keeping brother, who knows more than a thing or two about matters canine, took one look at our new companion, Hobbes, before declaring him a devil dog.

That was possibly a little strong, for Hobbes was never nasty, he was just – and they say dogs are like their owners – obsessed with eating and utterly dismissive of authority. Every time I turned my back he was gone: off to steal food from another boat, the other local marina's tea hut or the public bins. He'd even take himself to the pub to see what was on their menu. I spent so much time wandering round the village cursing his mangy hide I got to know many of the locals. Still young and full of character, we were glad there were enough good moments for us to forgive him his trespasses while we waited for time and maturity to calm him. Fortunately he was a natural boater and, once lifted onto the cabin roof from the stern deck – he soon learnt to jump up and put his front paws on the hatch to make picking him up easier – he'd spend the voyage madly charging up and down, barking at ducks, dogs, walkers and cyclists. Leaping ashore when we got to a lock, he'd pad about sniffing for anything remotely edible. Then, when the roof was level with the lock-side, he'd step back on. He was soon known and loved by many in our community, and we even warmed to him a bit.

Of course, all the time I was playing at being alternative, Jill was still slaving away designing ready meals for supermarkets, something she couldn't imagine spending the rest of her working life doing. And she didn't have to: saving hard and living cheaply we rapidly paid off our debts and Jill handed her notice in. On her last day she entered the factory to be greeted by a boat, carved from topside of beef (only the best for Jill) on the finished line's conveyor belt, and forty hardened butchers saluting and singing *I am sailing*. Once home, Jill made a sign advertising our skills, the qualities of which were plainly evident on the front of our own boat; we gave away the car and set about seeing if we really could make our way as waterborne itinerants. We'd been living aboard for just two years, and our lives had taken a direction never imagined when we gave up bricks and mortar for steel on water.

Our sense of feeling blessed blossomed over the next few months. We knew we were chancing our arm setting off with just a few quid and a full fuel tank. But what could we lose? We'd more than enough skills between us to earn the little we needed to live on, and if things got really desperate £100 and a fortnight would get us back to friends and work in Cheshire from anywhere on the English waterways. As everyone seemed to be always telling us, we were indeed very lucky buggers.

We'd often be boating before breakfast, usually with Jill walking Hobbes down the towpath, and we'd plod along for a few hours before calling it a day in the early afternoon. If possible we'd pull in somewhere quiet and rural, far from madding crowds and teeming traffic. The waterways were busy, and working from the boat meant we got lots of the little jobs – the missing fixings, damaged zips and minor tears – people otherwise put off dealing with. While they were not big payers, we didn't need many hours work to put food on the table and diesel in our tank. The only real crisis was when our old engine and gearbox began to show signs they were nearing retirement while we were on the river at Cambridge. A few weeks spent labouring for a friend bought second-hand replacements, which I fitted in a fortnight. That worked out well, as our new engine was much more powerful and we now flew along larger waters.

Over the next few years life developed a pattern: we'd winter amongst friends and guaranteed work around Anderton, and then head away each spring to wander at will, returning in late autumn. While *Camberwell Beauty* seemed cramped to live on at times, her width was perfect as we could travel the entire English system without being restricted by the narrow canals of the English midlands that limited anything wider than us to either northern or southern waters; her length was also ideal, for anything more than 2' longer and compromises would have denied us other routes. Even just a few hours a day at walking pace was enough to cover a lot of water each season, and we divided the country into annual routes: one year we'd go south to London, Bath and the rivers Severn and Avon; the next, south and east down the River Nene into the East Anglian fens and drains; or across the Leeds and Liverpool to the Yorkshire Navigations, with a return run up the Trent. On arriving back in Cheshire we'd buy a banger of a car we could afford to give away in the spring. The English waterways were ours to play in, and we knew we were happy and blessed.

Unfortunately, while living and working afloat was as close to perfect as we could have hoped, the lack of space became increasingly frustrating. The problem was the size of our workshop: every morning we had to move work in progress and jobs we'd finished onto our bed, and cutting out cloths in such constricted space involved shifting furniture and a demanding degree of gymnastics. In the evening everything had to be moved back. The very nature of taking on work at short notice meant we needed to carry a lot of stock and, despite increasingly ingenious solutions; we'd long run out of storage. Even if that hadn't been the case, our narrowboat's low ceiling meant I couldn't quite stand upright, and consequently suffered with back pain. While there was never a single moment of major crisis, we slowly accepted we couldn't carry on as we were. Once again, Jill and I started to ponder how and where we might live.

The longest narrowboat you can navigate the full English waterways system on is only 2' 6" longer than the one we already had, so buying another would have been a pointless exercise. There was the option, as generations of working boatmen had done and hotel boats still did, of towing an unpowered boat, a butty. If we used the butty for making covers, we'd have the benefit of separating work and home, but at the expense of needing to operate each single lock twice. The butty would also have to be steered and, after thousands of hours spent sat together on *Camberwell's* stern with Hobbes in front of us, neither of us liked the idea of travelling apart. We briefly considered moving ashore. Yet, even if we could find and afford somewhere we liked, we'd either be looking for new careers or driving to the waterways several times a week. Then there was a bigger picture still, the fact that the waterways we'd initially known were fast changing, that further complicated our futures.

We'd moved onto *Camberwell Beauty* at a time when interest in the English waterways was soaring and, while we had many reasons to be grateful as the influx of new boats and moorings had made our business successful, the more crowded the canals became the less pleasure we took boating them. We were witnessing more bad-tempered exchanges at locks, the days of mooring in solitude seemed to be ever scarcer and the sense of relaxed wellbeing we'd once found so charming wasn't what it was. We weren't the only ones noticing this; it often came up in conversations with boating friends, as did the notion we might one day leave England to make a living on the European waterways. Even if we never went, building a boat unsuited to a possible future abroad made no sense at all. And that meant the only vessel we could imagine next was a Dutch-style barge capable of crossing the salt waters between our present and our possible futures.

HAWTHORN

Nothing about finding our second boat, or more exactly someone to build our second boat, made us think our luck on the water had deserted us. Indeed, after one very odd day in Yorkshire, we were utterly convinced we weren't just lucky, but blessed.

While it's possible to buy a boat so completely finished all you have to do is step on it and start cruising, you can also buy the basic steelwork – the shell – and then fit an engine, windows, insulation and interior yourself. Always intending to go down this route, we'd driven across the Pennines from our winter base in Cheshire expecting to give a boat-builder a deposit. Yet when we got there he refused to take the money, and said he was only going to build finished craft in the future. Given we'd rung the day before and discussed what we wanted, we left dumbfounded and disappointed, and drove away in a car full of angry expletives to call on boating companions moored nearby. There, over the inevitable cup of tea and a piece of calming cake, we were asked if we'd spoken to another boat-builder. We knew the man mentioned as we'd been admiring his own boat just that summer but, never imagining we'd be able to afford one of his creations, we'd never researched what one would cost. A phone call proved that notion wrong, and brought an invitation for us to visit his yard on our way home that afternoon. That this builder was much better established and respected than the one we'd been rejected by hours earlier, left us in the highest of spirits. It seemed fate had again looked after us, and we'd found our very own dream-maker. All we had to do now was decide exactly what shape and form this dream should take.

While not as pricey as a finished boat, we knew buying a shell and completing all the work on it ourselves would take a lot of time, energy and know-how, and still wouldn't be what anyone would call cheap. We didn't mind; in fact far from it: we'd been around boats long enough to know what worked well, we had no end of skills and we were excited about the prospect of designing and constructing a home to last a lifetime ourselves. The crucial thing was to get the basics right.

Given our desire to separate work and home, the obvious thing to build was a barge with a cabin astern of the wheelhouse that we'd fit out as a workshop, rather than the conventional bedroom with an en-suite bathroom for guests. The much larger space forward of the wheelhouse would be fitted out as open-plan living quarters. The boat-builder's standard shell was 57' 6" long. It was big, indeed huge after the cramped confines of *Camberwell Beauty*, but we added a further 2' 6" to the rear cabin to make the workshop as large as possible. This meant we wouldn't be able to boat on a couple of Yorkshire's broad canals, but we weren't going to spend the rest of our lives being cramped on the chance we might one day want to go to Wakefield. As with most people's Grand Designs our ambitions kept creeping up and, unable to see the point of building a boat to last a lifetime but compromising on its engine, we set about looking for the Rolls Royce of diesel engines – a Gardner.

With Gardner no longer in business, we were a couple of decades too late to buy a new engine but, with original spares still available and the skills needed to put one together not yet lost, it was still possible to restore second-hand units to as-new condition. The extra expense over a conventional modern engine would be returned over time by the frugal fuel consumption the Gardner's low revs and tight tolerances would deliver. Even if they didn't, we valued the comfort that being powered by a Gardner, renowned for never breaking down or giving trouble, would be worth one day on a rough sea or flooded river.

Assuming that finding and getting such an engine restored was going to be a difficult task, we were delighted to hear the boat-builder had several. Better still, they weren't in his yard but already with an engine-restorer we were promised was the best in the business. Learning he was happy to sell us one was great news and, biting the bullet and determined to only have the best, we then added to the order by asking the boat-builder to install both it and the hydraulic drive system we intended to use. I'd changed the engine and gearbox on *Camberwell* and, while restoring a vintage engine was beyond me, installing one wasn't. Yet it wasn't my trade, and I wasn't willing to take on the stress of worrying that I might, perhaps unknowingly, compromise something crucial.

All we needed now was a name and, after months of consideration and head scratching, we decided to call the barge after a tree long associated with good luck and hope. Our new home would be *Hawthorn*.

The scale of our financial commitment was such that we knew we were going to have to work like never before. Which meant, rather than wandering about trusting to fortune, we'd have to take a mooring and buckle down. Once again we fell on our feet when we were offered a spot on the Bridgewater Canal as the only live-aboard (we'd worked in marinas with lots of boats being lived on and found the politics loathsome) on a short linear mooring – basically the non-towpath bank – just south of Warrington. There was no power or water, but the secure fence did mean we could take our eyes off Hobbes for a few minutes without then losing hours looking for him. Even better news was that there was also room for *Hawthorn* to join us when the shell was finished in eighteen months time. All we now needed was lots of work, and once again fortune smiled on us: within a few weeks we'd filled the next year with promised orders.

'There's your boat,' said the builder, pointing to a pile of flat plates, angle iron and square sections on his workshop floor. It seemed unlikely that such a solid mass of steel could somehow be cut and bent and welded together into something that wouldn't just float but would look beautiful while it did so. Though, as our fortnightly visits soon revealed, it didn't bother the builder and his team: by our third or fourth trip our new home was taking shape, and it seemed massive. We'd clamber in, wander about, poke and prod a bit while discreetly trying to grasp the magnitude of what we were doing. Knowing from our own experience that by far the easiest customers to work for were those that trusted us, we left the builder to do what he thought best and assumed this meant we got the promised best of everything. There were some items we had to be involved in – the positioning of portholes and hatches for instance – but for us *Hawthorn's* build consisted of not much more than delivering cakes or biscuits and discussing any relevant details. Confident that we were being royally looked after, it was all very relaxed and fun.

Finally, in February 2005, after the builder had seen it off from his yard by telling us 'That's the nicest shell we've ever built and I hope you're going to do it justice,' a low-loader and crane delivered *Hawthorn* to a boatyard on the Bridgewater Canal. To our surprise – we had asked but he was confident all would be well – the boat-builder didn't attend the launch. While we were never

going to break a bottle of champagne on the bow, we happily opened a few to share with the gang of friends who'd braved the weather to join us. The party didn't last long – the day was too cold and we had too much to do for that – and when gloves were handed out it wasn't for warmth but to protect hands unaccustomed to handling the concrete bricks we'd had delivered for ballast. The following day, not without more than a little stress, we moved *Hawthorn* the dozen or so miles to our mooring.

We'd delayed our build by six months to take advantage of spring's better weather and longer daylight hours, and cleared a few weeks of cover work to concentrate on getting *Hawthorn* weatherproof and hopefully almost habitable. We didn't have a workshop, or any covered space outside *Hawthorn*, so to be moving into *Hawthorn* by the middle of June was nothing short of extraordinary. That was the week of my 40th birthday, with an appropriate party now best remembered for Hobbes getting drunk: every time he passed the drip tray on the beer barrel, he emptied it of dregs. He ended up so pissed every time he tried to scratch his ear with a hind leg he fell over, and we all fell about. Put out by everyone's laughter, he passed out in the shade and snored late into the evening.

When *Camberwell Beauty* was sold a few weeks later, we watched her stern disappearing down the canal, and then turned away from our past and got on with building our future. We'd moved into a barely started space that still needed years of woodwork, wiring, plumbing and – here I was spoilt for Jill did all of it – painting and varnishing to finish.

Impatient to see how *Hawthorn* went on the deeper water she was designed for, and itching to have a break after years of work and fitting out, we took a few months off in the summer of 2006 to cross the Pennines to Yorkshire's larger waters. This being the first time we'd taken *Hawthorn* anywhere further than our regular local runs for water and pump-outs at our friend's chandlery, Thorn Marine, in Stockton Heath an hour away, just how hard it was to get a deep-drafted barge through the shallow Leeds and Liverpool Canal was a real shock. Yet the moment we gained the deep water of the River Aire and *Hawthorn* suddenly went and steered as she was designed to, it was all well worth it. Unfortunately our joy only lasted the two days it took to get to the tidal River Ouse, where we pushed a little harder. After only half an hour, with a smell of charred wood and hot metal, and our engine oil temperature twice what it should have been, we pulled into slack water. Our engine bay was so hot we were convinced something would catch fire if we carried on, so we removed as much panelling as possible between the engine and the stern cabin, opened the roof and stern hatch and finished the run as gently as possible.

Both the engine-restorer and the boat-builder assured us all was as it was meant to be, though the boat-builder did come out to add an oil cooler and to stop water leaking into our stern cabin through the steering system. Neither fix was particularly successful, and we made our first sea voyage – across the Wash from Boston to King's Lynn – with panelling removed to keep the engine bay cool, and with so much water leaking through the steering that our bilge pump ran continuously. Everyone put the heat down to our having a large dry exhaust, but our problems didn't stop there: the hydraulic drive motor was so far out of line it knocked the stern tube packing out in less than twenty hours and its grinding could be heard on the bow. To our great disappointment, the boat-builder seemed to have no interest in putting any of this right, and what we'd thought was a happy and trusting relationship soured as we got on with fixing things ourselves.

Returning to Cheshire, we put the boat into a dry dock and, with the help of a friend, cut out and rebuilt the drive, found a way to stop the water leaking through the steering and installed a specialist 3" thick exhaust bandage to prevent the heat from the exhaust cooking everything. Just to make doubly sure there was nothing amiss with the engine, we paid its restorer to service it. He departed declaring it 'as sweet a running engine as I've ever built'. Relieved to find all was well, we settled back into our old routine of fitting out and working. Having to sort so many things wasn't the best end to a great summer, but we'd learnt a lot. Not least that the immediate future we'd planned simply wasn't going to happen.

LIMITATIONS

Change without any sacrifice is a rare thing and, given *Hawthorn's* size, we'd always known that the moment *Camberwell Beauty* left our lives would be the end of our runs through the Midlands and summers in London or on the Kennet and Avon Canal. The only way we'd ever visit the south of England again would be by making the long and exposed run round East Anglia's coast to the Thames estuary. We knew that was probably going to be a permanent transition, so we planned to spend several years working in England's northern broad-beam waterways, with winters in Cheshire and summers in Yorkshire and on the East Anglian waters. Like a lot of great plans, it was perfect in theory but, as we quickly found when we went for that cruise as a break from fitting out in 2006, doomed in practice.

The problem was the Leeds and Liverpool Canal. We were looking forward to enjoying the scenic run across England's spine to the River Aire in Leeds on a canal we knew well from our travels with *Camberwell Beauty*. Enjoy it? We barely got through it. We'd already got a hint of what was coming on the last few miles to Wigan, but above the town it felt as if we were dragging an anchor. Quickly realising

that we were too big and deep to get along as we'd done in our narrowboat days, we soon found each day just a long, hard grind. The lock-free twelve miles east of Skipton took eight hours, and then we were hard aground for thirty minutes just short of Bingley's staircase locks. Jill and I pulled *Hawthorn* down to the

waiting keeper with ropes, and were both relieved and alarmed when he told us we'd been lucky as an overnight downpour meant the water was four inches deeper than normal. At least the complexity of using Bingley's five-lock staircase meant we had a keeper to help, and his locks were in perfect condition. Which was not something we could have said about those we'd been through getting that far.

Over our years on *Camberwell* we'd been through hundreds of wide locks and, even when travelling with another narrowboat, had usually only used one gate of each lock's top and bottom pair. The problem with *Hawthorn* was the need to open all the gates right back into their recesses, and we often had to clear rubbish from behind the less-used gates. Other than sodden mattresses, the floating stuff was relatively easy to deal with, though the sunken shopping trolleys and bicycles took more effort to fish out. Even once we'd cleared the rubbish, these less-used gates were often reluctant to fully open, and when they did some were so rotten they had to be treated with great care. It was a slog, and we thought we'd come unstuck when one lock gate in the middle of Blackburn started to fall apart. Seeking help we rang British Waterways and half an hour later a van drew up, and three workers climbed out.

'You've bust it,' one of them claimed.

'Have we hell!' There was a bit of an argument and, fortunately, we were allowed on our way. Once clear of the top gates, we looked back to see the failing gate being padlocked in place and taped off. Narrowboats could still use the remaining working gate but, had we been below the lock, that would have been the end of our boating for weeks.

Issues with rubbish weren't limited to the locks, and here again we were so much worse off in *Hawthorn* than in *Camberwell*. The canal hadn't been dredged in years, and our depth and width meant we were dragging through silt untouched by narrowboats and cruisers – the canal was designed to take loaded working boats but it was now so shallow they'd never get through – and this meant we caught all the sunken debris. What little momentum we had was lost while I grubbed about through the weed-hatch clearing the propeller of plastic bags, clothes and bits of rope. We finished our worst rubbish day with four full bin bags, and one very large and heavy rug. Getting that off had been hard work, though not as hard as the fully armoured motorcycle jacket we picked up in Burnley. Life would have been much easier if only I could have seen what felt like a leather octopus knotted round our propeller and shaft. I couldn't see as far as my elbow, let alone the knife in my hand, through the filthy stinking murk I was up to my shoulder in.

We could cope with the rubbish, the dodgy lock gates and the narrowboaters expecting us to get over when we were barely floating in the middle of the canal. That was all doable, but we didn't want to spend weeks stuck in Blackburn, Burnley, Nelson or Leeds (where another lock gate had been almost impossible). And we'd been lucky: the dry summer closed the canal for weeks, and we only got back to Cheshire after it had been brimmed by a dramatically wet September fortnight. Fearful of getting stuck, we began to accept that *Hawthorn* was too large a boat to regularly use the canal. We determined to cross it just once more. Had we wanted to go straight to France, Holland or Belgium to spend our days drinking wine and eating cheese, the long-term consequences of finding the Leeds and Liverpool Canal all but unusable wouldn't have been significant. But, while we both expected to make that move at some point in the future, we first wanted to do something only possible from Cheshire. We wanted to go to Ireland.

I don't know why, but Ireland's inland waterways somehow seem to slip under the radar of the English boating public. And we'd probably have ignored them ourselves if it hadn't been for a friend who lived just up the canal from us. Roger had motored his own barge to Dublin and spent several years on Ireland's canals and rivers before boating back. We'd bump into him now and again – quite literally the day the guest steering his barge clipped the bridge we moored next to and slammed into *Hawthorn's* stern – and whenever we did he'd push Ireland as an ideal destination for a first foreign adventure. Given Roger was a surveyor and knew more about boats and boating than pretty much anyone we knew, we listened carefully. And then agreed: after all, Dublin was no more difficult to get to than London, the Irish were famously welcoming, and we'd be spared the daunting task of having to quickly grasp a foreign language. All this had been discussed while we were building *Hawthorn*, and Roger had called on occasion to offer advice about our home's seaworthiness. Yet we hadn't planned to go until we were thoroughly tired of boating in England and had restored at least a little savings. Now, seeing that it was going to be a case of sooner rather than later, we began to make plans.

Guessing it might help if we knew something about Ireland, we took a holiday there in the summer of 2007. The pretext was to look at inland waterways, but we weren't very serious: we were there for a week and only got a brief glimpse of the River Shannon as we motored across it at Athlone. We also saw a short length of the Royal Canal: badly needing to walk Hobbes after a long ferry ride and getting completely lost in Dublin, we'd seen the canal signposted from the main road we were on. So our holiday in the west of Ireland taught us nothing about its rivers and canals, but we enjoyed the landscape round the rented Connemara cottage and liked the people we met. While we could have stopped at the Shannon on our way back home, we didn't bother. Our minds were made up, and there'd be time enough to see all we wanted when we got there the following year.

Once back to the reality of finishing *Hawthorn*, Ireland seemed a long way away. Fitting out was now a case of heads down and press on. The last trims and tidies we thought would quickly fall into place seemed to take forever, and every dry day was spent outside, machining and shaping the wood we fixed and oiled when it was wet or dark. Thankfully, once all the solid oak and teak, the curved bulkheads and soft rounds of cupboards and porthole liners were completed in early 2008, the effort seemed well worthwhile. Finishing was a shock and a surprise, as was actually building a home as lovely as the one we'd imagined. Desperate to be boating again, and excited by the adventure of going to Ireland, we soon pushed off. While we had a leaving party, we kept the payment on the mooring going, and assured everyone we'd be back the following year.

Roger's professional skills were now called upon to write the Letter of Seaworthiness our insurer demanded before extending our cover to such serious salt-water work as the Irish Sea. Given we'd seen him several times over the build, and had always listened carefully to any advice he offered, we knew this wasn't going to be a problem. What we weren't prepared for were the pages of notes Jill made as he advised us on the realities of what was needed: the boarding up and extending of engine room vents, fitting jackstays so it would be possible to go to the bow while clipped to a safety harness, strapping down the wheelhouse against rogue waves, upping the power of our navigation lights, fitting various bilge pumps and all manner of minutiae we would never have considered. It was daunting, but Roger was so full of enthusiasm it sounded like he might want to make the crossing with us. So I asked him, and was promptly told 'I'd love to, but I'd only be sick.' He also suggested we leave from Tarleton and the Ribble Estuary just outside Preston rather than Liverpool. Not only would this put us north of the shipping lanes, we could wait for a weather window on the canal without suffering the high expense of a coastal marina. That advice alone paid Roger's small fee many times over.

Dawdling to Tarleton we called at a friend's boatyard and then stopped in the countryside west of Wigan for a few days. After spending a fortune more than we'd budgeted on *Hawthorn* and not having a clue if we'd have any work in Ireland, we took on any jobs we were offered. Leapfrogging our way north and west from job to job reminded us of how things used to be, except now we had the space we wanted to cut and sew in and went to bed without a battle with mounds of cloth. There was no rush: we couldn't leave until the sea was calm and we couldn't be too long at Tarleton waiting for the weather without falling foul of the authorities for overstaying. We were in no hurry to be gone, and all was well with the world. And then it wasn't: Jill's father fell ill, and everything stopped.

Clearly there was no way we were going to leave the country with Noel in such poor health, but putting *Hawthorn* close to where he lived on the Suffolk coast so we could visit and help care for him, was not going to be easy. The Norfolk Broads were the closest option, but our barge would be a big ship on already crowded waters and the logistics of getting there were daunting. We'd have the long haul on the Leeds and Liverpool we were already avoiding, several days on the Yorkshire navigations, a run up the River Trent and then east through Lincoln to Boston. And that was the easy bit: the run from Boston to Great Yarmouth on the North Sea round the east coast of England, was far from simple, and would only be possible in the best of weather. If we did go we knew we'd never return this far north and west, which meant Ireland would never happen.

Fortunately we'd not yet done as we usually did when heading away after a winter and given away our car. So we did what normal people do and drove up and down as often as possible through March. Noel had been frail on a number of occasions, and we assumed it was only going to be a matter of time before the hospital got him sorted and home. We even still hoped he'd be fit enough to come and visit us in Ireland when we did get there. Yet it wasn't to be. Stunned with grief and shock, come mid-April the only thing we were organising was his funeral.

FIRE!

Unsurprisingly, we returned north without much enthusiasm for the challenges of the Irish Sea and learning our way in another country. For a couple of weeks we dithered about returning to our mooring at Warrington and relative normality, and then Jill declared we'd go to Ireland. Not having been on deep water for a couple of years, all we now needed to do was to give *Hawthorn* a fast run to make sure all was well after the work we'd done on our cooling and drive since 2006. With friends just over an hour's boating away in Preston, plans were made to meet the following Saturday. That date was the tenth anniversary of our having moved onto *Camberwell Beauty*, something we took as both a curious coincidence and a good time for a fresh start.

Just listening to the gentle, rolling idling of our Gardner engine while we waited for it to warm up felt good. As did dropping our lines to start slowly making our way down the long line of moored boats. As usual we chatted to a few of the folk on them.

'Mind if I come for a ride?' came a request from a barge beside us.

'Not at all!' we replied. We barely knew the chap, yet he was local and, with the day's run being tidal and possibly tricky, having him along wasn't going to do any harm. He grabbed his life jacket and jumped on just as we were entering the lock. A few minutes later we were pushing into the swirling brown silt of the inrushing tide and enjoying how *Hawthorn* felt when working properly – something we'd forgotten in all our ditch crawling.

While the change of pace and scene were both good, the main purpose of the run was to see how hot the engine bay got now that I'd lagged the dry exhaust in a 3" thick specialist bandage. Hopefully helping things were the newly installed vent and 7" fan capable of forcefully expelling hundreds of square feet of air a minute.

With everything feeling fine, I gradually eased the throttle further open. We were beginning to get on now and, as the mud flats and marshy greenery beyond them slowly receded, the water piled ever harder against *Hawthorn's* bow and we caught and passed some of the narrowboats that had left before us. We reached the River Ribble without incident and turned east for Preston. Now heading inland, the river ahead noticeably narrowed, but looking west down the estuary and out into the distant Irish Sea created a tight knot of nerves in our stomachs. And that was only looking at it: neither of us wanted to contemplate how we'd feel when that view and the challenge it offered would be over our bow and not our stern some time soon. Not that it mattered now: the important thing was making sure all was well, and just to be certain I opened the throttle as far as it would go. We were only a couple of miles from Preston's docks, and we were really flying. And then everything went horribly wrong.

It was our guest I felt most sorry for. One moment he was happily chatting away while he steered us up the broad and sunlit river; and the next the wheelhouse was full of smoke, and I was bundling him sideways off the wheel. It wasn't a time for niceties: he appeared to have frozen, and all that mattered was closing the throttle, stopping the engine and lifting the engine board he was standing on. I think he ended up with his back against the port side door. I don't know, and at the time didn't care as fear and adrenalin kicked in. The smoke was frightening enough but I'd left our dinghy uninflated and the life raft we'd bought for the Irish Sea crossing was nowhere accessible, which meant if we had to abandon ship we'd have to get into the water. As the engine stopped, I raised the board over the engine bay a couple of inches. When only smoke poured through the crack, I opened it fully.

Coughing and gagging at the foul air swirling round us, we peered into the blackness below. Bright blue and green flames were visible the far side of the engine. The acrid smoke was the melting of the rubber coatings of hydraulic pipes that these flames were licking. Terrified they might fail and hot oil would further fuel the blaze, I grabbed the wheelhouse fire extinguisher and leaned in over the engine. Off balance and with streaming eyes, aiming wasn't easy. I pulled the safety pin and squeezed the trigger. Nothing happened.

'Get the one from the galley, Jill!' She was gone in an instant, and almost back before she'd gone. Powder roared out, the flames died back and … what the hell?

As the smoke cleared I was able to see the supposedly fireproof exhaust bandage appeared to have caught fire: there were smouldering wisps rising from a crater in it. What? Oh God no! As I watched, flames started appearing through the extinguisher powder. Talk about an improbable nightmare: not only had the fireproof bandage caught fire; it seemed impossible to put out.

Sod messing about with extinguishers! 'Fill the kettle Jill!' Several very long seconds later, the kettle was handed from Jill to frightened guest, and on to me. I emptied it into the flames. And out they went, and out they stayed.

Looking around we were grateful to see the tide was full and we'd only drifted a hundred yards in the two or three minutes of panic. And the presence of one of the narrowboats we'd just charged past meant we weren't as alone as we'd felt. Its skipper was wise enough to keep his distance, but not outside shouting range.

'Are you OK?' drifted across the water.

'We think so,' I hollered back, 'though we'd be grateful if you'd follow us to the lock in case we're not.'

I started the engine and we slowly made the last half mile to Preston's harbour. Our badly shaken guest departed, and the friends we'd earlier arranged to meet for what was meant to be a jolly day arrived. As hosts, we were supposed to be the ones ensuring everyone had a good time, yet Jill and I sat mutely thinking about how close we'd just come to losing not just the home we'd spent five years creating but also the business that funded it, and pretty much everything we had. Yet we knew we'd been lucky: if we hadn't tried the engine flat out for a couple of minutes we would have caught fire on the Irish Sea on our way to Dublin. Even on a tidal river, with Preston and a helpful boater both close to hand, we'd been terrified. What if the same thing happened in the dark miles offshore, with the floor sealed down and taped shut in case the wheelhouse flooded? It didn't bear thinking about. Not that I spent a lot of time pondering what might have been: I was much too busy trying to work out how a fireproof bandage on a professionally restored and installed engine could ignite.

SLOUGH OF DESPOND

If we'd been in a bleak place when setting out to Preston, it was nothing like the abject misery we felt as we returned to Tarleton the following morning. We made that run at low revs, with the inflated dinghy towed behind us, and the wheelhouse doors open to try to remove the bitter smell of burnt rubber. Poor Jill, already mourning her loss, wasn't even able to busy herself with the technical aspects of working out what had gone so badly wrong. So much for our tenth anniversary of boating and a fresh start.

While Jill struggled to find something to take her mind off our what had happened, I searched the Internet looking for explanations. I also emailed our engine-restorer to say what had happened and to ask advice. He replied promptly and sympathetically, though he didn't have a clue and, having now retired abroad, wasn't able to visit to seek one. What we could do was get our fire extinguishers tested. They, including the one that had failed, were all within date and supposedly sound. We replaced most of them, added a couple, and made a note to do as the supplier suggested and occasionally turn each extinguisher upside down and give it a gentle tap and shake. This, we were assured, would keep it in top condition.

In amongst the many odd replies to the dilemma I'd posted on an Internet forum was a suggestion I should check the engine's exhaust to make sure it was correct for our engine. So I did, and found that our Gardner had been trying to breathe out through a system so restricted it was a miracle it ran at all. Already in a foul mood, I rang the boat-builder. He wasn't very sympathetic. In fact, on hearing I'd been exchanging mails with the engine-restorer, he said: 'I'm surprised; he didn't reply to any of the mails I sent when I had problems with my engine.'

'What? You've had problems with your engine? The one you said we could have for *Hawthorn* if we wanted as all your engines were the same and perfect?

Surely it occurred to you, indeed it must have as you'd tried to fix them, that we too were having problems? Weren't our lives and wellbeing, and quite possibly the lives and wellbeing of innocent others, even worth the price of a phone call?' As if our mood wasn't dark enough, discovering the man who'd built our home – a man we'd liked, trusted and considered a friend – had chosen not to pick up a phone to warn us we might be in danger was as dark as it got. Or so I thought at the time.

At least ours was 'one of the nicest running engines' our restorer had ever built and, as he had pointed out, all that was needed was for me to rebuild the exhaust and all would be well. So I did; and it wasn't. It sounded better, in fact it sounded lovely, but the moment we took it out onto the tide to see how it ran we knew we were in deep trouble: far from running cooler, it now ran so hot that the cables mounted above the exhaust manifold melted! Seeing them start to sag and drip, we turned the boat and went back to the lock. We'd been out just eleven minutes.

The restorer suggested I call in a couple of his mates, so we did. They fiddled for a few hours, then left saying they couldn't find anything amiss. We were long overdue some good news, and in a way our being close to where Gardner engines had been built was that. With genuine, factory-trained experts to seek advice from locally, I took my pick and rang one, Walsh Engineering, and explained our situation. They asked who'd built our engine and, after a short silence where someone was clearly working out how to tell me bad news, I was told they'd just fixed our boat-builder's engine. It seemed his fuel pumps were worn out, and the symptoms I was describing suggested the same issue. Having paid a large extra sum precisely because our engine's fuel system had to be rebuilt to new spec when we bought it, I doubted that.

But then, what did I know? Within two days of them visiting to remove our fuel pump and much of our fuel system, Walsh Engineering were ringing to say it was knackered. They emailed a report, which I emailed on to our restorer. He never replied. It seemed when it came to building *Hawthorn* we'd been either unlucky or careless with the men we'd placed our trust in.

Once fitted with new pumps and injectors, the engine was fired up. Wow, what a difference: it now ran like a massive sewing machine, smoothly and right through the rev range, without the vibration and rough edge its restorer had always blamed on our hydraulic system. Having already given the outside of the engine, and anything they could get to without pulling things apart, a good going over, the engineers now listened carefully for any tell-tale knocks or rattles.

Short of stripping it down and starting again, the best we could hope for was that they were right when they reported that all seemed well.

At least we now knew why we'd caught fire: an unlikely combination – too much fuel, a poorly designed exhaust and the wrong silencer – had forced unburnt diesel into the fireproof bandage. In a way we were lucky to have caught fire, as if we hadn't the over-fuelled engine would have eventually done both itself, and possibly us, serious harm.

The engineers then pointed out some other failings in the way the engine had been installed. Given I'd already done the exhaust and had replaced the boat-builder's solid engine mounts with modern rubber and steel units the year before, by the time I'd replaced the molten cables, and sorted out the fuel lines, I might as well have installed the bloody engine myself.

We'd lost a month and several thousand pounds finding and fixing the issues, but at least when we now took to the tide *Hawthorn* felt like a different boat. The only thing that appeared to need attention was one slight drip from a hydraulic coupling.

I'd rung the hydraulic drive supplier, John, to find out what to do, and of course the way our luck was going meant I had to replace the whole pipe. So off it came, and up the road I went to a local supplier. I was half way out their door with the new one when it occurred to me to ask what pressure it was rated to.

'Same as the one you bought in,' replied the fitter who'd made it.

'And what pressure's that?'

'165 bar.'

'What! Are you sure?'

'I am,' he said; 'it's a bog standard two-wire hose, and its rating is stamped on the hose wall.'

I'd no idea what was going on, but I knew we were generating pressures way in excess of those the hose was rated for. So I rang John again. He listened, groaned, uttered a few choice expletives about our boat-builder (who'd been sent all he needed to do the job properly and even then had been on the phone to John several times) and then told me the pressure relief valve on the system was set to 260 bar. Which meant that if something – a large branch or one of the pallets we'd seen on the tidal Ouse when boating to York – jammed the drive when we were at high revs, a hose would fail long before the relief valve kicked in. If that happened, gallons of hot oil would spray out. There was also the far from minor point that, with no drive to steer or stop with, we'd be entirely at the mercy of momentum, wind and flow. God only knows what, or who, we might destroy if that happened.

'Bloody hell John! We've made tidal runs on those hoses!' I gasped.

'You've been a lucky boy so far,' he replied, before adding 'Your boat's a death trap; you shouldn't move until the hoses are changed.'

I remember that phone call well. That was the time I sat in the engine room and wept.

Once again I rang the boat-builder, and once again was fobbed off with some old blarney that it wasn't their fault. By now I'd spoken to a solicitor several times, so I was confident he was wrong, but what the hell: we'd discuss that once all our problems were sorted. If the boat-builder was uninterested, the same couldn't be said of the much larger business that had fitted the hoses: the moment they heard that the Trading Standards Authority were involved, they couldn't sort our problems fast enough. Of course the original hoses were boxed in, and getting to them meant tearing out yet more sections of finished workshop. Hopefully, though, that was that, so just to make sure – and now completely spooked and utterly distrustful of anything our builder had installed – we paid John to send a fitter to check the drive was now correct. He pronounced it safe, though possibly a little under-cooled. At least we could go boating again.

The weeks since the fire had opened our personal Pandora's Box were spectacularly grim. We might have coped better if the start of our nightmare hadn't been losing Jill's father, but what followed made grieving for him difficult, and spiralled down from there. While it kept me busy in mind and body for weeks, poor Jill didn't know what to do with herself: she could only take the dog on so many long walks, and it's only possible to do so much cooking. Fortunately, for I'm a comfort eater inclined to balloon in times of stress, we had plenty of visitors to help consume the treats she baked.

Seeing how our worst of times brought out the best in people was a wonderful thing. What we were going through was common knowledge in the local boating community; people we'd previously known only vaguely would call to see if they could help. 'You can,' I'd say, handing them a plate full of cake and putting biscuits in their pockets. One local couple, Don and Elaine, had particularly good reason to be interested as they lived on a barge not only built by the same man as ours, but powered by an engine from the same restorer. While concerned our issues might one day be theirs, it soon became clear they were as worried for us as they were for themselves.

Even before we'd learnt he was a qualified marine engineer, Don's beaming smile, ponytail and constant need to wear shorts meant he was the kind of man we'd automatically be fond of. Now retired, he called in most days to offer advice and see what he could do to help, and we were always pleased to see him. As was Hobbes, for he never came without a treat or two for him, and sausages and cheese always seemed to be appearing on the floor of Don and Elaine's barge whenever we visited. Their basic caring decency probably kept us sane and, sensing the moments we really did need to step back, we'd be invited to eat with them, or they'd take us up the pub. It was Don who put me in touch with Harry. A highly skilled and intelligent man with a lifetime's experience of boats and engines, Harry lived by the lock. He was another godsend, and another recipient of cake.

Most of the conversations I had with Harry involved working out why *Hawthorn* wouldn't do the 7 knots we'd wanted and been promised when we ordered our shell. Harry's answers involved complicated mathematics, and I'd then take the propeller off, and drive it into Oldham. Here another friend worked his dark arts of heat and pressure to change the propeller's pitch. Unfortunately the boat-builder had installed the drive shaft out of centre, which meant we couldn't change the propeller's diameter. After trying every possible variable we could alter within the space this imposed, we accepted 6 knots was our limit.

Believing our problems were at an end, we set about getting some of the cost of correcting their shoddy work back from the boat-builders. We'd documented everything we'd been through, kept receipts and engineers' reports, and been to both Trading Standards and a specialist solicitor for advice. So we knew we were on very firm legal ground and, while it took a brief and bad-tempered exchange of emails for the boat-builder to see the light, he soon agreed. We were disappointed not to get an apology, but at least, after ten weeks of hell, we could now move on. Once again we began the wait for the spell of calm weather needed to get us to Dublin.

Then the phone rang. 'You need to have a look at your steering,' said the caller.

REALITY BITES

I knew all about our steering, or at least thought I did, as our first ever run down the canal had been ruined when *Hawthorn* refused to respond to the wheel. We ran onto the bank, into trees, and even went straight on when trying to drive the stern round at the first junction we came to. Fortunately we were on an empty canal in the middle of winter, and the only people we scared were ourselves. After initially putting this down to the alien art of steering with a wheel and not a tiller, and our incompetence with such a large and deep-drafted boat, we eventually realised the problem was that the steering was slipping. It was a problem the boat-builder would have seen and sorted in a matter of minutes, but he was in Yorkshire, and I'd foolishly left all our tools on *Camberwell Beauty*. Fortunately I was able to borrow some spanners from the owner of a canal-side house and, after adding some temporary packing, we made the remaining seven miles to our mooring in half the time the first three had taken. A few weeks later the boat-builder did visit to add a larger washer.

The steering had since leaked on the tidal runs but I'd stopped that with a mate's help when we were in the dry dock in 2006. Our caller, another owner of a barge built in the same yard as *Hawthorn*, was adamant the design of the steering was dangerous: the collar that turned it wasn't keyed on and if it slipped the emergency steering failed with it. He'd had so many problems with his own he'd ripped it out and rebuilt it and was now involved in a battle with his insurance company and our boat-builder.

If we'd been told this a year earlier, we'd probably have rung our boat-builder for a chat, been told the guy was off his rocker and then dismissed it. But not now, oh no, no way. Jill and I sat in mute disbelief surveying the wreckage of our plans for what seemed the umpteenth time that summer. And we were done. Not having the energy to take on another major job, we turned the boat south and, hugely relieved we'd kept it on, headed slowly back to our mooring near Warrington.

We'd left there full of hope and excitement, so to slink back with heavy hearts and uncertain futures wasn't a happy time. Things got so bleak we even discussed ripping out the workshop and refitting the stern cabin as a conventional en-suite master bedroom, and flogging *Hawthorn*. But where would that leave us? We couldn't consider selling the boat without fixing all the problems first, our income and freedom were predicated on life afloat – and we still couldn't afford to buy the sort of space ashore we would want to live in. So we got on with cover making, and waited to see how things settled.

Stitching boat covers together is pretty mindless and while I worked my thoughts were largely engaged with the problems boxed in beneath me. Our sewing machine sits beneath the window in the stern of the boat, and from where I sat it was easy to watch the canal and towpath. Passing boats and dog-walking friends gave my day a bit of colour, but what I really wanted to see was *Womble*: the little blue barge used to collect rubbish, owned and worked by Roger's brother and our friend, Paul.

Rubbishing along the canal was only Paul's part-time job; the rest of the time he worked on other people's boats. Given we didn't know a better welder or mechanic, it wasn't surprising that he was always busy, or that we sought his help whenever we needed to fix *Hawthorn's* issues. Over the years we'd been at Warrington it had become a habit for Paul to pull alongside when wombling, throw a handful of the countless balls he'd pulled out of the water ashore for Hobbes, and then come aboard for lunch. In the winter, frozen from being outside (and there are few colder places than on an open boat), he'd hug the Rayburn while the kettle came to a boil. In kinder seasons we sat outside with mugs of tea chatting. We valued his opinion highly, and now when Paul arrived he usually found me clutching a list of questions and desperate to discuss all manner of technical detail.

A delightfully generous soul, he didn't appear to mind and, while Jill made him a brew, we'd chat about what needed to be done to make *Hawthorn* safe. The steering was the highest priority; we also wanted to re-engineer our weedhatch as it wasn't deep enough and its locking mechanism was already bending. Having seen just how quickly a boat could sink with an open weedhatch, this was something I wasn't prepared to live with. The hydraulic oil needed more cooling and, in one final push to make our drive as efficient as possible, we decided to cut out and then rebuild the stern tube our boat-builder had installed off-centre so we could fit the largest and most efficient propeller possible. Getting the materials together for these jobs took several months; then, in February 2009, we set off to spend one, and we were adamant it would be only one, final week in a dry dock.

We got stuck in while the dock was still draining. While Paul did his thing on the drive and propeller set-up, I took a spanner to the steering mechanism, freed the rudder and then carried it up to the workbench for Paul to come and weld the new assembly on. I then turned to the weedhatch extension. Weight and bending were not concerns with the new kit which, in a characteristic act of extreme generosity, was a present from another friend, Seamus. It was so solid it could have had Chubb stamped on it.

I knew we were going a little mad but, after what we'd been through, the only way we were ever going to be content with *Hawthorn* was to go completely overboard, and this included sorting the extra cooling for the hydraulic oil suggested by the visiting engineer the previous summer. So holes were drilled in the side of the hull, and Paul welded the pipes I'd made up over the winter along the swim. This more than quadrupled the cooling's volume. I then installed a fancy digital thermometer with three remote senders so we could easily and constantly monitor the temperature of the exhaust, hydraulic oil and engine room. At best this gauge would only be the bearer of good news; at worst we'd know something was wrong earlier than we would without it.

Needing to get our work approved and signed off to satisfy our insurance company, we then waited for the surveyor to visit. He duly arrived, drank tea, ate cake, poked around, drank more tea and chatted about what we'd done and been through. Then, just as he was leaving, he happened to see the old steering mechanism resting where I'd left it on the dock's workbench.

'What the...?' he asked.

'That's what we took off,' I explained.

He was as stunned by the poor quality of its engineering as Paul had been when I first took it off. What was meant to be an accurately machined taper appeared to have been cut with an angle grinder, and crudely dressed with a file. Being a quiet, gentle creature, Paul had walked away shaking his head. The surveyor's reaction was a little more animated and, despite my saying it didn't matter any more as we'd binned it, not to mention he'd already been paid, he insisted on recording the abomination.

We now needed a charge in deep water to make sure all was well, and we weren't going all the way to Tarleton. The only other option, the Manchester Ship Canal, involved a fair bit of expense and a lot of paperwork; but having no tide to contend with reduced a lot of stress, and starting in the city made it easy for Paul to come with us. We joined the canal early one morning in the middle of Manchester and then ran *Hawthorn* hard all the way to the boat museum in Ellesmere Port. The only rest the engine got was while we waited in each of the four vast locks – in which *Hawthorn* looked like a child's toy in a bath – needed to lower the canal from Manchester to the flat lands of the Mersey Estuary west of Warrington. These were all in the first half of the run, and the fully open throttle wasn't touched for the last fifteen miles.

After a few minutes early in the run fettling with the hydraulic pump to get the pressures just right, we monitored instruments and the newly installed thermometers to make sure all was well. Electronic gizmos are one thing but by far the most crucial gauges were our own senses and, with the engine and drive looking, sounding, feeling and smelling right, we arrived at the museum with beaming grins. *Hawthorn* hadn't quite achieved 7 knots, but we now knew she'd run happily all day every day at 6.

How nice it was not to worry about *Hawthorn's* set-up and to be able to enjoy spending a couple of hours being shown around the museum by Paul. A member since its inception, his knowledge was as encyclopaedic as his enthusiasm was contagious. We wandered round barges and boats, sheds full of ancient marine engines and the cottages restored to how they were when the basin was busy transiting goods and materials between the English Midlands and ships serving the empire. We only stayed a night and, with the Ship Canal something a lot of local boaters were keen to experience, made the return run the following day with more friends on board. Now confident we had the boat we'd always wanted, once again our thoughts turned west towards Ireland.

THE IRISH SEA

'OK?' asks the man with the windlass.

I nod. His arm slowly swings. The lock rack clacks. And *Hawthorn* starts to drop. With all the strappings across the wooden cabin roof lights and wheelhouse, the plywood covering the two opening portholes, the boxed-in engine vents and the inflated dinghy beside the emergency life raft atop the rear cabin, our home looks so different: somehow compromised and out of her comfort zone. My dry mouth, sweaty palms and sense of tension – close to panic – confirm I'm out of mine. How fuddled I am is soon made clear when a voice beside me gently states 'You'd better get on, mate.'

On? Oh bugger! I'm still standing on the stonework, and *Hawthorn's* now descended several feet. I drop onto the cabin roof praying that when I step ashore it's going to be onto Irish soil, and that the step is not from a lifeboat or helicopter. Jill stands beside the wheelhouse door looking more than a little troubled. Nervous? We aren't nervous. We're bloody terrified.

With the many phone calls organising crew, the long hours preparing *Hawthorn* and all the lying awake at night, our imminent departure had taken on a surreal quality of intense nerves and apprehension that racked up as leaving drew ever nearer.

The first crewmember to arrive was Sid. A qualified pilot we'd stayed in touch with since crossing the Wash with him in 2006, Sid would look after the navigation and VHF radio. To our delight Paul had joined us though, while he knew *Hawthorn's* mechanics well, we hoped his skills and knowledge wouldn't be needed. And then there was Don, who'd just kissed Elaine goodbye and stepped off his own barge onto ours. Don was such a sound and sensible soul we knew his presence could only be positive.

As Tarleton lock emptied and *Hawthorn* sank towards the salt, the small gang of friends who'd come down to wish us well stood and chatted on the lock-side.

And then they'd gone: off to put their arses against the lock beams. A thin chink of light split the dark and dripping wood in front of us. It steadily broadened, and then the lock gates fully opened. It was time to go. Somebody, just who I didn't note and can't recall, put the boat in gear. And somebody steered us onto the tide.

The one thing I was conscious of was pushing the throttle fully open, letting the engine settle at 1300 rpm, and then easing it back to 1150. If all went well – that is if our engine and drive held up to the strain of by far the longest and hardest task we'd asked of it – the next time we touched the throttle would be in Dublin. I'd prepared the engine thoroughly and, as I cleaned it, checked its oil and water and apologised for any pain when I nipped its nuts with a spanner, I'd kept telling it 'You're the most reliable, solid diesel engine ever built. You're as good as a Rolls Royce! It's time to prove it. Or we'll get a Ford.' So it knew what was coming.

While a thing of beauty, an idle engine is just a cold assembly of bolted-together machine shop parts that is never going to reply. Now, running and warm and animated, it could answer, and we carefully listened to the echo of its contented purr from the salt marshes for the first couple of miles down the tidal creek, and then slowly stopped intentionally listening. Its even cadence would now be monitored subconsciously; it would take only the slightest hint of a miss or a murmur for all of us to instantly focus on it. I hoped it would remain in the background. It needed to, for we soon had other concerns.

By the time we were approaching Lytham St Annes at the mouth of the Ribble estuary, *Hawthorn* was starting to rear up on the incoming swell, and then dropping with a bang into the hollow behind it. Ignoring the violence wasn't easy, but we had to focus on Lytham's picturesque Victorian skyline to find the White Tower marked in our pilotage notes. And it had to be the White Tower, not the white dome on the Boys' Grammar School. Missing that marker would make it likely we'd miss the Hole in the Wall where, now it was devoid of large ships and the dredging needed to get them to Preston, the river punched its own wild way through the sea defences once containing it. With the tide full that wall was now submerged, though precisely where, and by how much, we couldn't be certain. All we knew was that somewhere in the grey rolling swell south west of us lurked the deep-water route we needed to take. Ironically, given we'd only just started, finding it was the hardest bit of navigation on the whole run, and only possible by lining up the White Tower with a second transit point of a cardinal marker north of the old ship channel. It was just visible in the distance north west of us.

We watch the view beyond the marker slowly change from sea to land, to pine-woods and golf courses, and then the Lytham sea front of grand hotels, pubs and tourist shops. And then we see the distant bright white tower is above the rusting guano-stained marker in the foreground, and we shout to Sid to put the wheel hard down. *Hawthorn* swings to port, and Sid grins and points to his GPS screen: he's mapped the route while sitting in the comfort of a British Rail carriage on his way to us from East Anglia, and he's chuffed to find he's correct. This is good news as from here on, whoever's on the helm will be guided down a highway – it appears as a road on the GPS screen – to the next marked waypoint.

While Sid watches his route, I watch the depth gauge screen. *Hawthorn* has a fancy Forward Looking Sonar (FLS) unit that tells us the depth ahead of the boat, and I'm concerned it will suddenly reveal we're running into shallower water. If it does there'll be some very nervous moments, for we can't see the gap in the submerged wall and have no idea how much we'll clear it by. The depth remains constant, and then gradually gets deeper. We've cleared the sea defences and are now in the channel scoured through the sand banks by the freshwater river at low tide. We've reached the Irish Sea. We should be relieved to get through the hole without any added tension, to relax and settle down for the long, boring run ahead of us. But we aren't relieved, and nobody thinks boring is likely to be a suitable adjective for what we're about to endure.

It doesn't matter how well prepared your boat, or how efficient, skilled and happy your crew: take a barge to sea in the wrong weather and you're in for a miserable time. Knowing this, and keen to catch one of the rare moments when the Irish Sea resembles a millpond, Sid, Jill and I had spent weeks studying forecasts for a suitable window, only to watch approaching high pressures falter in the Bay of Biscay or east Atlantic. Finally seeing a promising forecast in late May, we'd set about readying *Hawthorn*. Prematurely it seemed when, rather than holding for the first week of June and the motorcycle racing of the Isle of Man TT as we expected and hoped, the length of the predicted calm kept shortening. On the morning of our departure we were left with a likely window of just thirty-six hours. Long conversations with Sid followed. He was keen to go but, as he pointed out, the decision was one I needed to make. Tarleton being some miles from the open water, there was no way of physically seeing what the sea was doing, so I'd paced up and down, and rung the coastguard. The forecast sea state was Force 3 and, while not as calm as we'd have liked, nothing that *Hawthorn*, or our insurers, couldn't or wouldn't handle. The hope was that we'd leave onto calming seas as the high was building, and be in Dublin long before it was gone.

But rather than boating out onto the innocent-sounding 'wavelets' and scattered 'whitecaps' of a Force 3, we were now faced with something much nastier: certainly a high Force 4 or possibly even a low Force 5 with 'moderate waves of some length'. Nobody suggested retreating, for we'd all boated enough to know that the sea on our bow was nothing to what it would be on our beam – rolling in from the side – for as long as it took us to turn. It was rough, and bloody scary, and we had no choice other than to bear it grimly for as long as it lasted.

Grasping anything solid to keep our balance, we stood watching the bow rising, falling, slamming; the juddering hull and white-lipped horizon the exhausting opposite of our millpond wish, and the windscreen wiper's constant chase of breeze-blown spray a metronome of our misery. We'd have been nervous as hell in any barge in this sea, but in our own with our troubled mechanical history? It wasn't surprising I was having the 'God, I hope I did that up properly' moments we'd naively paid our boat-builder lot of money to try to avoid. Unable to relax and needing to be busy, I kept pulling out the wheelhouse steps to get into the engine bay without lifting the floor, and checking the engine. And then I'd put them back and check everything else my paranoid mind kept throwing up as a source of imminent disaster.

'You're going to have to have a rest from that, Giles!' shouted Sid on one of my rare visits to the wheelhouse. 'The stench of hot metal and oil is making people gag, and we can rely on gauges to tell us what's happening.'

'Ah come on now Sid, surely you know how much better it is to deal with early symptoms than it is a full-blown trauma? And that's what the gauges will be harbingers of if something has gone wrong.'

I probably didn't shout harbingers, and my language may well have been coarser, but I was stressed, as was Sid. We were both right, and soon came to a compromise where the checks would still happen, just not every two minutes. This was fair enough as I knew I was using concerns about the engine, drive, steering and weed-hatch to displace the bigger issue outside, and the last thing we needed was tension amongst the crew.

By now Jill had gone a peculiar grey colour, and she couldn't go below without instantly being sick. Her need to both see the horizon and remain occupied meant pretty much the only thing she was able to do was steer, whereas I didn't want to look at the sea at all. Not that I could have stayed in the wheelhouse if I'd wanted to: we'd designed it for two adults and a dog to be comfortable in, and what spare space we normally had was filled with a bearded, capped or pony-tailed sailor type. So I went forward, down the six steps into the galley, passed the saucer-eyed dog in his bolted-down bed and sat on the strapped-down sofa. While I was no longer looking at the violence of the rising, slamming bow, there was no hiding from the noise. The din was terrific, and not just of steel and salt water colliding: the interior we'd built was groaning and creaking, and I was soon as obsessed with concerns about our fit-out as I was about our engine.

I couldn't stop thinking about the story Sid had told us about a pilot taking a narrowboat across the Wash. He'd jumped on, asked if all was well, and immediately departed into a sea a bit like ours – that is, rougher than expected. Both the pilot and the narrowboat's skipper stayed outside by the tiller as they pitched and rolled around and over the Wash's notorious shallows for several hours. Finally arriving in the shelter of the river approaching Boston, a cup of tea was suggested and the boat owner went below. He returned a couple of minutes later to ask 'Would you mind drinking your tea from a saucepan? It's just I haven't any mugs left.' As the pilot was to see once they docked, broken mugs were the least of the owner's concerns as the interior of the boat looked like vandals had run through it: all the crockery was smashed; books, furniture, even the flat screen television, were randomly piled on the floor, and all was littered with food once stored in the galley cupboards. Their doors now hung half on, half off. It was the only time that pilot took a narrowboat on that run.

That image of carnage had remained with us, and we'd spent three days trying to ensure nothing similar happened in *Hawthorn*. Working out just how to keep everything in place, without permanently wrecking our finish, had been a bit of a challenge. With plenty of screws, elastic rope, webbing, assorted ironmongery and tools in the workshop to play with, we'd slowly worked our way through the long list we'd prepared with Roger's help. Cupboard doors were secured, lengths of dowel were added to the bookcases, drawers were strapped shut and all our art was taken down, bubble-wrapped and put in the bath. Being solid teak and home made, and thus both deeper and squarer than commercial moulded baths, there was lots of room for more. So we took the art out, and in went as much crockery and glassware as we could fit, with towels and bedding as packing. The art went in last; then, suspecting our luck might just see them opening and flooding the lot, I cable-tied the bath tap handles shut. By this point we were getting more than a little paranoid, and anything and everything we could imagine moving was either fixed, strapped or stored.

We soon found we'd not been paranoid enough: within minutes of clearing the estuary I'd had to dash about lashing, screwing and wedging items we'd never thought would move in place. The hardest thing to fathom was the door into the toilet. It had never opened by itself before, but now we couldn't keep it shut. Banging about on the high seas not being a time to be delicate, I wedged it closed with one of the battens we had ready for emergencies. This worked, though it did mean anyone going to the toilet would have to move it, and then hold the door from within or risk embarrassment.

Fortunately, the one item we'd always been concerned mustn't move – the cast iron Rayburn we used for heat, cooking and hot water in the winter – showed no signs of going walkabout. I'd mounted it on a steel plate bolted into the floor bearers, and butted the oak floor boards up against its base to stop any chance of it creeping. Roger suggested we added the additional support of a lorry strap over it and then under the floor for the crossing, and this I'd duly done. It was genuinely worth worrying about as it weighed nearly half a ton and if it were to break loose and start rolling round we'd never be able to lash it down. Even if it didn't sink us, at best we'd be left with a home fit only for kindling.

Boaters are famously superstitious, and there was one item superstition made me constantly check. Mounted low down on the woodwork behind the Rayburn we've a picture of a bony goblin clambering out of a split in the woodwork. A friend able to sketch out ideas while they were being spoken – he worked as an artist in the advertising industry – had drawn it in all of ten minutes the previous autumn, when we were joking about all our problems being down to an unseen and malevolent spirit moving about our home. Even as a raw sketch it had power, and once

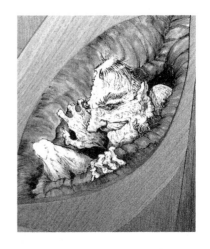

coloured and finished it was a fine portrayal of wickedness. Jill painted the background behind the figure the same tone as the oak it was mounted on, and I'd made a frame resembling the large knots seen on old tree trunks. It's easy to dismiss such notions as nonsense of course, but we'd not had a problem since trapping the bugger in his portal and we always joked that seeing the frame empty would be the moment to panic. Now, with my head full of potential mechanical gremlins, I was relieved he was still there, grinning his nastiness and unable to harm us.

Don's stumbling, surface-grasping transit through the galley was a welcome interruption to my mental masochism. There was not a hint of self-pity at what he'd become embroiled in, and I was interested to see he was buzzing, almost high, on ozone-fuelled adrenalin. I couldn't help but feel lucky to have him along, but then I knew Don would be sound. For ours wasn't the first barge we'd taken to Dublin together.

A strange thing happened while we were at Tarleton in 2008 dealing with *Hawthorn's* unhappy innards: another barge destined for Ireland turned up. Living memory only recorded one barge – Roger's in the late 1990s – going to Dublin from Tarleton in decades, so two arriving together was quite a coincidence. Even stranger was that the barge with crew, *Hawthorn*, wasn't fit to go, while the other was perfectly able to, but only had a skipper. It was all very odd, and I was asked if I'd help out. After checking that Don was also wanted and willing, we'd both agreed to go. At the time I'd needed a break from sorting *Hawthorn's* issues, and knowing the skipper had brought the boat up the coast from the south of England, assumed he knew what he was at. If nothing else we thought it would be a bit of a laugh, and I hoped the experience would prove valuable.

From the moment Don and I got on board to find all sorts of electrical kit needing attention, we began to wonder about the wisdom of what we were doing. Everything seemed a little chaotic, frantic even, but this only added to the sense of adventure and the sea was forecast to be calm. So we just got on with it, and while I steered down the estuary Don rewired and got the VHF working, and the skipper charged about getting his home ready for the sea. Still, we had our doubts and, if we had gotten ashore for a pint when anchored overnight off Lytham St Annes while waiting for the morning tide, Don and I might well have talked ourselves into going AWOL. If some light-fingered soul hadn't nicked the tender's oars we'd have gone, and might well have refused to row back. Doing a runner would have been a mistake, for what followed taught us far more than we'd anticipated.

We left Lytham at dawn, into a day so dull the sea and sky merged on the horizon, making us the centre of a vast grey bubble. With no distinguishing marks, sun or conventional magnetic compass to steer by, and on a sea so calm there weren't any waves to judge direction from, we tried to use the compass facility on the GPS. The trouble is that set up this way a GPS shows where you're coming from not where you're headed, and then with a huge delay. The skipper was quite good at reading it, but Don and I were hopeless: left to our own devices we wandered way off line, would then over-correct – and then over-correct again trying to return to where we should be. We wandered around the sea as if drunk and, once we'd folded down the canvas canopy over the barge's rear deck, our meandering wake was clearly visible astern. Coming up from below, the skipper would glance at it and frown. Then, while Don and I giggled and winked like naughty schoolboys behind him, we'd get another demonstration of how it should be done. We couldn't master it, and couldn't see much point when there are much easier ways of using a GPS. In the end our despairing skipper agreed, and set his up with the highway system we preferred. At least his crew could now keep a straight line, but it was keeping a straight line that was so nearly the undoing of us.

We were some way west of Holyhead when night fell and, without a star or moon in the sky or a light to be seen, it got really dark. Wanting both to enjoy the beauty of being on a calm sea at night, and to improve our visibility should a ship approach from anywhere other than directly ahead, we left the canopy down. It was magical, and we'd have missed seeing the sea thick with huge jellyfish if we'd enclosed ourselves. It was while we were shining a torch over the side to try to work out how many layers there were of them – they were densely stacked as far as we could see – that we became aware of lights on the horizon ahead of us. Among the bits of kit I'd brought with me from *Hawthorn* were our marine binoculars, and I used the compass in them to take a bearing on whatever it was in the dark distance.

While our skipper went through books trying to figure out if we were approaching a gas platform, a working minesweeper or a ship with divers beneath it, I kept taking bearings, and noting their consistency. Given we were only getting along at about 5 knots, it was baffling how quickly the lights, which looked nothing like conventional navigation lights, were closing in on us. And then the penny dropped, and our skipper grabbed the wheel and turned hard to starboard. Two minutes later the churning white bow wash and blazing halogen-lit decks of a large ferry doing at least 20 knots ran straight through where we would have been. It could have been a modern *Mary Celeste* for all the people we could see on it. We were left bobbing in its wake, watching it motor into the distance. Don and I were both certain it had no idea we were there. Even without any of the other moments, those few minutes realising just how insignificant and vulnerable a barge is at sea made the trip well worthwhile.

How easy it had been to be frivolous and fancy free when crewing for someone else. To mess about with a hunting horn bugling away for a laugh: a laugh that faltered on learning it wasn't a trinket and would be needed for real if it got foggy. It was a lark, an adventure, a bit of bonding Don and I would be remembering and reliving for years to come. Now, looking at the waterproof grab bags prepared in case we had to abandon *Hawthorn*, we realised just how much being on your own vessel changed things: how, aside from a few small personal items, we were risking being left with just the clothes we were wearing, a little money in the bank and a very damp dog. And that's if a disaster went well. Even if *Hawthorn's* mechanical history had been perfect and the sea glassy calm, our stress levels would have been high. Now, with all the worries of the past and present, Jill was having such a rough time the lads left her on the wheel for hours just to keep her busy. While not feeling sick, I skulked below not wanting to look out the window. Why on earth did we put ourselves through this when it would have been easier, and cheaper, to crane *Hawthorn* onto a lorry?

Over the years we had moved about the rivers and canals of England the only time we'd taken either narrowboat or barge out of the water was in dry docks. And, given we left and returned to the water in exactly the same place, I'd grown to see our travels as one continuous thread winding over and through both geography and time. To me it seemed only natural to view our decade of English wanderings as sparse thin lines for the rarely travelled margins, with thicker, interwoven lacings on the routes we used more often. I'd always imagined that these lines would one day extend into estuaries and then out from the shore across the seas to distant destinations, and it was these imaginings that fuelled our desire to build a seaworthy barge. This continuity mattered: moving *Hawthorn* by crane, lorry and ferry would shatter how we saw the world, so we were determined to keep to our plans. The interesting thing was that the only people who didn't think us mad were those who knew what they were talking about – Roger, Paul, Sid and Don etc. Occasionally someone would understand our point, but for most the idea of actually welcoming the vulnerability of risking all, and engaging with the wildness of the sea, was just too extreme. So we ceased to point out that sanity is subjective, stopped justifying our actions or starting 'O ye of little faith' conversations, and just repeated 'La la la la' internally once the negativity began.

Since our wheelhouse had filled with smoke the previous May, we'd been struggling to recover our faith that we were always going to be happiest living on the water. Believing that had been easy when everything that happened to us had been relentlessly positive ever since we'd found the right boat in *Camberwell Beauty*. It wasn't long after I chanced making my first cover that Jill was able to join me and our wandering lifestyle suited us. When we built *Hawthorn*, the seeming long-term security of our futures had come so easily we'd never doubted we were doing the right thing. It would be a little extreme to suggest we'd been through a long dark night of the soul over the last year, but we did hope the act of faith we'd made by setting out on the adventure of crossing the Irish Sea would bring the greatest gift on arriving in Dublin: restoration of our confidence in *Hawthorn* and in our lives afloat.

We'd done all that was possible to make the voyage a success. *Hawthorn's* wheelhouse bristled with antennas, including the very latest electronic radar reflector we were assured would make a rowing boat appear as big as a ship on a radar screen. That it worked was easily checked with the coastguard, and we were relieved to hear them say how clearly they could see us. Another antenna was connected to the AIS (Automatic Identification System) unit whose screen would show us the position, speed and direction of any shipping in our area and, we fervently hoped, would give us a bit of notice that trouble might be heading our way. We'd had all this kit the previous year and, right up to the *Mary Celeste* moment on the skipper's boat, I'd wondered if I was being a little over-cautious. I didn't now: though, just in case we had to speak to ships or shore, we had a number of VHF radios, including a waterproof hand-held model. Given it was packed in a grab bag in readiness for a disaster of such scale we had to abandon ship, I hoped we'd never need to use it. If we did, it would be from the life raft strapped across the rear cabin. Until we learnt, rather bizarrely, that shipping lines classify life rafts as hazardous luggage and charge a fortune to carry them, we'd planned to hire one and ferry it back after the trip. So we'd bought our own, which had been a large expense but, given we intended to return from Ireland and then make other sea crossings, another one that would pay for itself over time. We genuinely felt we'd done all we could to make sure we were safe: we had all the kit, a fine crew – and Sid.

While this was Sid's first trip to Ireland, we knew he'd delivered numerous barges across the North Sea and English Channel and our insurers were delighted when we told them he was coming. We knew Sid could deal with trouble, go into strange ports and even manage a lifeboat rescue if the worst came to the worst. Indeed, the day after he'd seen us back to Boston from King's Lynn, he'd headed up the east coast on another barge, only to run into unexpectedly rough seas that stirred the sediment in its fuel tanks. (This is the most common reason barges break down at sea and why I'd vacuumed our fuel tank dry, refilled it with clean fuel and fitted filters that could be changed without stopping our engine.) The sediment had clogged the fuel system, it was getting dark and the lifeboat was called to tow the barge in. Just seeing what the current sea state meant, I knew rolling about in an unpowered barge in a Force 6 was not something I'd handle well.

Skulking below doesn't make the time go any faster, yet going into the wheelhouse doesn't help. There's nothing to suggest the sea is getting calmer as the bow continues to lift and slam, and the windscreen wiper is still needed. We're neither short enough to ride over individual waves nor, and it would have eased things, long enough to straddle several. It feels so rough because each wave is rolling under our pivot point before the bow has met the one following it. Which means the stern's being lifted as the bow is falling, hence the nastiness of the slamming. I watch for a bit, even briefly take the wheel. Then I remember from that first crossing with Don just how important steering is to breaking the boredom, how slowly turns on the helm come round and how badly Jill needs the focus holding the wheel brings. I hand it back. A brief conference is held and we agree we're doing okay: the sea remains on the bow, the engine and drive are behaving and everything below is holding together. Sadly the coastguard's weather reports on the VHF don't promise much relief, though neither do they forecast increased unpleasantness. The biggest problem is that time seems to have somehow slowed down – so much so that looking at a clock only brings despair.

With no room in the wheelhouse, I beat a retreat. Keen to show me the paper chart he and Sid have been recording our position on with neat (well, as neat as they could manage in the conditions) pencil crosses every hour, Don joins me below. The tide's influence can be clearly seen in the distances between their marks. We're now at low water, and the marks are about to dramatically compress together as the flood tide starts to take back our earlier gains on the ebb.

The turning tide arrives as the light gradually fades. Such is its force I don't have to look at instruments to be aware of it. I can feel its weight pressing into the bow in the very gradual change in the engine's sound as its load increases. When I do go up into the wheelhouse, I stand on the top step, brace myself and look around. Other than instrument screens and the background glow of our navigation lights, it's pitch black. We've been parallel to the high ground in North Wales for the last seven hours; its dark smudge now has bright specks scattered across it, and we assume the glow southwest of us is a seaside resort. Imagining its chippies, dodgems, boozers and bingo, the people enjoying a normal Thursday night, it's easy to reflect just how otherworldly our own experience is – but this only lasts as long as it takes someone, probably Sid, to work out the lights are a nuclear power station. With the inrushing tide slowing us to a crawl, we grow to hate those lights over the four hours we spend punching past them. They're only finally subsumed when the sun rises while we're passing north of Holyhead.

We've been at sea for fifteen hours and it's as rough now as it was at Lytham St Annes. Nobody has eaten or slept, and it's not surprising there's an air of exhaustion about the place. Yet there is good news, not least that we're well past the halfway mark of sixty-three nautical miles (seventy-two statute), and have turned the few degrees south needed to point directly at Dublin. After using the dawn light to make a thorough check that all is well, I return to squatting on the sofa. Once again Don joins me. We're discussing how we might just make it, when I'm suddenly conscious of water running past my feet.

What the hell? This just doesn't make any sense: if the bilges were full the water would be coming through the floor boards, and then only if both the 24- and the 240-volt pumps have failed. This being the sort of scenario that made us delighted Paul was with us, I shout up to him that we've an issue. It doesn't take long to work out the water is running under the jammed-shut toilet door. As the only through-hull fitting in that section is the sink drain, and it's both turned off with a sea-cock and 18" above the waterline, I find this both very odd and deeply worrying. Opening the door, we try to make sense of what greets us: the water's flowing over the top of the toilet bowl which, given there's no external connection on it, is as mad and unlikely as having a fireproof bandage catch fire.

At least it's easier to deal with: turning off the boat's water pump stops the flow. I turn the pump back on, and the flow returns. There's a collective sigh of relief as we realise all that's happened is that the filter sand that gradually accumulates in boat tanks (we'd all seen it on our own boats) has somehow buggered up our bog. The water in both the taps and the toilet had gone a muddy brown colour after the bow started to be thrown about, and we guessed our issue was caused by grit in the toilet's solenoid valve. The good news is the few minutes panicking have everyone wide awake. There's also been a change in conversation: for what seems like the first time in days, there's something to talk about other than where we are and how much longer we're going to suffer.

At least we are able to converse about how we felt. Poor Hobbes has spent the whole trip lying in his bed pretending to doze. His water and food are beside him on a non-slip mat, but both are untouched. Which is a good thing, for he's struggling to stand on the varnished floor, and he has yet to take advantage of the cabin corner we've grassed over with a chunk of Tarleton's bankside to serve as his toilet. Jill and I were laughing about how he'd be the last of us to pee on English soil when we put it down, and now we are glad we did as we could not risk putting him on the roof as we'd done on our shorter sea crossings. Knowing the voyage would be hard on the lad, we had discussed a compromise where Jill would take the ferry with him. That wasn't going to happen when we realised our not having a car would mean he'd be on his own in a cage, something we both knew he'd find more stressful than crossing with us. Besides which, he's a dog and he will be fine.

We've been crawling westward for eighteen hours before the news that, finally, there's something solid ahead of us is shouted down to me. 'Hooray!' I think, and rush up the stairs to see what the joy's about.

'There,' says Paul, pointing directly ahead and handing me the binoculars. Taking a steadying lean against the wheelhouse's woodwork, I'm just able to make out two pencil-thin outlines. I know what they are: they're the chimneys beside Dublin Bay Don and I remember boating out of the dawn towards on the previous year's run. The only downer is we know how tall they are, which means we know far away they are and just how long reaching the shelter beside them is going to take.

If our intention had been to push the limits of both *Hawthorn* and ourselves, we'd have ordered the sting in the tail the last few hours delivered. In theory the wind was now offshore and the sea should have started to get calmer. To our dismay not only does it gradually get rougher, it slowly backs south to run parallel to the coast. All the time the bow had been slamming directly into the waves we'd been praying it would stop yet, as we begin to roll from port to starboard and back again, we all wish it hadn't. It's horrible and now, being very close to shipping lanes and huge ferries, there isn't the room to take it on the bow and tack into the port. Bloody hell! To be so close and then be put through this seems cruel, certainly too cruel for me to watch. I soon return to the solitude, aside from Hobbes that is, below. Returning to the wheelhouse an hour later I'm relieved Ireland is fast approaching. We're nearly there, and we're soon going to have to speak to Port Control. Thank God we've Sid to do all the talking: the last thing we need is to go through a similar experience to the one Don and I endured on our previous delivery run.

You don't just blithely run into busy shipping lanes and through a port without first talking to Port Control on the VHF. You call them up, tell them who you are and where you're going, and let them guide you through. Or, as it nearly turned out when Don and I crewed for the barge skipper, not. On that occasion Dublin Port Control made it very clear they'd no idea who the hell we were or where we'd come from, and that they definitely hadn't been told to expect us by Waterways Ireland. Not helping was how our skipper's exhaustion left him struggling with the protocol involved in using the radio. Port Control left us hanging in the bay for half an hour while they decided what to do with us, and then insisted we go to somewhere called Dunleary. What or where that was we'd no idea – the only other harbour we could see was spelt Dún Laoghaire, which we were reading as 'Dunlahair' – and it took several more confused VHF calls to sort out the muddle caused by our lack of linguistic skills. Then, out of the blue and for no apparent reason, Port Control suddenly granted us a reprieve, though only as long as we could get through the port in twenty minutes. Being on the wheel at the time, I pushed the throttle fully open, and we motored in as fast as the barge could manage.

While belting past docked ferries had been good fun, the weird radio conversation wasn't. Determined to avoid going through anything similar with *Hawthorn*, I'd rung Dublin Port Control before leaving Tarleton to tell them we were coming, and now we were here it will be Sid, who holds an international VHF licence, on the radio. We're almost in the shipping channel when Sid calls them up. It's over thirty hours since he's had any sleep, yet there's no hint of exhaustion when he speaks to them. Whatever he's said there's no ambivalence about how he's said it, and there's a murmur of relief in our wheelhouse when we're welcomed by a warm Dublin voice telling us to head straight in.

By now we're near enough to be able to see individual houses on the high headlands north and south of us, and cars on the beachside road at the edge of the bay. We're so near, but the waves continue to pile into our port side, and Don's holding Jill's hand. Finally, against the port's cranes and a skyline now crowded with Dublin's taller buildings, we're able to make out the pepper pot tower of Poolbeg lighthouse. We know it stands at the end of the breakwater we need to pass to reach smooth water, yet the last two miles and twenty minutes take forever. And then we're level with the lighthouse, and all is suddenly calm. Smiles of relief abound. Jill hugs Don, and I hug Hobbes. We're almost there.

The only remaining obstacles between the haven of Grand Canal Dock and us are a low bridge and a sea lock. While Sid calculates the air-draft needed to clear the bridge, Don, Paul and I set about stripping any antennas mounted on the wheelhouse, and Jill tries to ring the lockkeeper. Our phone won't connect to a network, and neither will Sid's or Paul's. Fortunately Don's does; unfortunately nobody answers. Which leaves us fearing we're going to miss the lock, which can only be used when the tide's in, leaving us to spend the next twenty-two hours on the river. If we had to Jill and I would cope; Hobbes on the other hand is another matter: he's been ready for the longest pee of his life since he first got the scent of land, but we've dropped the turf sod overboard while still in the bay, and the idea of having to get him up a high stone quay without his bladder bursting is too much to consider. Success comes on both counts when we don't hit the bridge, and when the second number Jill has – for an Assistant Inspector miles inland – brings the cheering news help is on hand.

For some strange reason it's important for the crew that I steer the last few yards. I'm too relieved to have made it, to see Jill returning to something resembling a healthy colour (doubtless she thinks the same of me), and too grateful for the crew's help to care. It doesn't feel right when others have done all the work, but they insist, so I take the wheel. The really big moment is easing the throttle back, which I do with massive relief that the engine's behaved so perfectly. The din of the past day subsides, and we all relax. Possibly too much, for Port Control must monitor upstream of the bridge with cameras, and the moment we head for the quayside they're on the radio telling us the river is out of bounds and that we're to moor off the dumb barge below the lock immediately to our portside. Having a jolly up the river being the last thing we wanted to do anyway, we're happy to oblige.

There's little flow hampering our approach. A burst of reverse nearly stops us, Paul drops our bow rope over a cleat, and Don lassoes one from our stern. They tie us off. I grip the engine stop, pause to thank it for being such a star and, with a big grin, pull it. The silence in the wheelhouse feels spectacular. We've made it.

DUBLIN

We're not really big on ceremony but, for obvious reasons given all we've been through and all it means, I'm determined to really savour the moment of stepping from *Hawthorn* onto Ireland. And then, as the filling lock brings our gunwale almost level with the lock-side stonework, Hobbes barrels past, leaps ashore and begins the longest pee of his life. That his leg is cocked against the bollard our rope is round causes much amusement, and the smile on my face when I do step ashore is there for a reason I'd never imagined.

'I'd be taking that down if I were you,' says the lockkeeper gesturing towards the Red Ensign on *Hawthorn's* stern just before we leave the lock. Conscious of what it might signify I'm happy to stow it away and leave it stowed until we return to international waters. My saying as much grates with Sid, so I spend my first few minutes on Irish inland waters arguing with a fellow Englishmen about what that flag symbolises. I'm about to go downstairs to put on my 'I'm a Republican!' T-shirt, when we both realise just how ridiculous we're being. We're both exhausted, but not too tired to smile at our differences.

At the far end of the large basin we go under a bridge into a much smaller space. It's full of mooring jetties which, other than two small cruisers, are all empty. We'd wanted to be surprised by Ireland, and it's certainly surprising not to find a vibrant live-aboard community in a city we know to be very expensive to live in. The lockkeeper has driven round, and he takes our ropes and gives us a key for the security gate. And now we really are done, and everything can be switched off, and everyone can rest. Don, who's as meticulous about cleanliness as anyone I've ever met, promptly lies down on a jetty splattered with seagull shit and falls asleep in the sun. Hobbes joins him, while Paul and Sid take the more conventional options of bed and couch. Jill and I are still rather too wired to switch off and, with our mobile phone now working, we spend the next hour telling family and friends where we are. As we saw no point in worrying people when they were helpless to change anything, this is the first many of them know of our leaving. Needless to say promises to visit are instantly made.

Given the bed he's chosen, Don doesn't doze for long, and while he and I sit outside chatting, Jill cooks the first hot meal anyone has eaten in thirty hours. The food is wonderful, but the only thing on my mind once we've eaten is to get away from *Hawthorn*. And I want a pint of Guinness.

To my surprise, this suggestion goes down rather well. Knowing we need life, noise, a bit of clatter and chatter, we walk past rows of empty chintzy bars, and head into the sort of pub a cultured Scottish drinking buddy of mine claims he taught me how to find. He'd have been impressed: people come and go with cheerful greetings and shouted leavings, there are bouts of singing, and the two men laughing and joking at the bar beside us seem to fall in and out with each other every few minutes. Best of all nobody seems to notice or care about us, and the Guinness is good. The beer has done its job; we sleep for sixteen hours.

Lingering somewhere short of wakefulness, I lay in bed taking in the restricted view of the outside world afforded by our porthole and wondering where we were. All I could see were the ubiquitous materials of gentrified waterside property: glass and chrome, cleaned soft bricks and stainless steel. We could be in London, Leeds, Manchester, Bristol or any one of countless similar docks that money has been thrown

at over the past two decades. The only really novel thing was that I was looking through a porthole glass thick with salt, and I remembered the exhausted elation of yesterday – and that we were in Dublin.

The shock of where we were really began to sink in once Don and Paul had wished us all the best and set off for the ferry soon after breakfast. Knowing we wouldn't even be in Ireland without their friendship made their leaving painful but, and we only had to glance at *Hawthorn* to see this, self-pity and loneliness were going to have to wait until we'd stripped the sea-going extras and washed the salt from our home. This took a couple of hours, and then we started emptying the bath and boxes, rehanging our art and removing the straps and screws that were now such a nuisance. Seeing how nothing we've built has moved, or even cracked, brings relief. Which leads me to the strange place of having to admire our boat-builder's skill with steel, for even the slightest movement of his work would have left our interior in tatters. And then the phone rang, and Paul asked if they could return.

It wasn't that he and Don loved us too much to leave. Far from it: they'd run into a complete arse at the ferry desk refusing to let any foot passengers on board, even the booked and ticketed ones like our crew. So they came back and – how apt this was – until they left in the evening hoping there was someone rather more personable behind the ferry's check-in desk, the four of us spent the day putting our home together again. The only interruption was a visitor, Mark, from the navigation authority, Waterways Ireland (WI).

To license a boat on inland waterways in England you need to provide the authorities with all manner of paperwork. So, terrified we'd arrive in Dublin without some crucial piece of paper and then have to go through all sorts of nonsense, I'd written to ask what was needed long before we set out. So now, and I'd printed the email in readiness to argue, I was going to find out if we really did only need €126.

Apart from another cup of coffee, that was all we had to provide. Which was as nice a surprise as to find Irish officialdom happy to sit down and chat with us, let alone that the licence fee included mooring, which we were used to paying £1000 a year for. The only thing was we couldn't stay in Dublin, as mooring there was not permitted. This was so rigidly enforced we were told if we hadn't arrived at the start of a Bank Holiday weekend we'd now be readying to leave the following day. It seemed the only exception was while the rally was on in early May, which the two boats beside us were the broken-down remnants of. It didn't matter, as we'd no intention of staying in Dublin. In fact, within a couple of days we were raring to go.

The high pressure we'd missed in our crossing had now arrived, and Dublin was baking. Even the Irish Sea was now flat calm though, knowing we were going to be better off in the long run for having survived a beating, we didn't mind that. Neither did we really mind that the basin we were moored in had become a swimming pool for local youths. The problem, or delight depending on your wishes, was the water was deep enough to be leapt into from as high on its surrounding structures as the bravest chose to climb, the security gate was but a token, and the jetties swarmed with dripping lads. While never threatened or intimidated, we both feared we'd become an object of interest at some point. The thing was we couldn't leave until WI had the canal above us ready. This usually took forty-eight hours, but then we had to wait another day for police divers to remove a body. Which isn't what you want to hear when you're already very nervous.

While intentionally ignorant of pretty much all Irish boating, concerned that getting to Dublin and not being able to get any further would be a really stupid thing to do, I'd asked about boating from the city to the Shannon on the Internet forum of the Inland Waterways Association of Ireland (IWAI). While saying we'd physically fit through the canal, the thread soon included a number of postings about how rough getting in and out of Dublin could be. Dublin being a large city, this didn't surprise us; the only downer was we couldn't do as we always did when faced with something similar in England. There, in the hope of getting through dodgy areas while the stone-throwing and abuse-calling types were still abed, we'd usually start our boating at dawn. With Dublin's locks all padlocked, and only lockkeepers having keys, our movements here were restricted to working hours.

The canal left the basin through a low-arched bridge in one corner. There was no towpath on this section so early one morning, before the first screaming bathers destroyed the peace, we walked Hobbes round the back lanes to find it.

'Bloody hell!' I exclaimed, looking into the water above the lock. 'It's shallower and more rubbish-strewn than the Leeds and Liverpool!' My only hope was the water's crystal clear quality might be deceiving us about its depth so, just to check, we lobbed Hobbes in. Actually that's not true: while Hobbes loved to swim he very rarely went into the English canals for fear of not being able to clamber out up their sheer sides. Seeing the Grand Canal banks sloped into the water at a gentle angle, he'd rushed in, and our problem was getting him out. Our initial perception about the depth was confirmed when the canal's saucer shape allowed him to wade a yard from the shore. And when he did swim into the middle his feet stirred sediment below him. Our hearts sank as the water clouded: if what we were looking at was indicative of the entire canal, we knew getting to the Shannon was going to be a nightmare equal to any we'd suffered in England. A mixture of curses and biscuits finally brought Hobbes back, and we returned to *Hawthorn* with a wet dog, heavy hearts and a sense of ironic gloom. The only reason we'd come to Ireland when we did was to avoid the known difficulties of the Leeds and Liverpool Canal, yet what we'd seen and heard now promised a very slow run, with lots of pauses to clear the propeller of rubbish, and heaven knows what incoming from youthful locals.

OUT OF DUBLIN

According to both Mark and the guidebook he'd kindly lent us, the bridge in the basin's corner is the lowest on the Grand Canal. So we took the wheelhouse down before leaving. Folding it flat gives the major bonus of bringing our steering out into the world and it's as liberating an experience as leaving a car for a motorbike. With the sun already throwing sharp shadows long before we set off, we hoped it would be as much fun.

The first surprise is just how much we miss the bridge by – *Hawthorn* glides under it with several feet to spare – and the second is how short that glide is: the moment our bow enters the gloomy space beyond the bridge, we grind to a halt in a dark and narrow passage between high stone and brick buildings. The water is black with disturbed silt and garnished in blanket weed. Looking at it we know this is the soup from hell, and the first lock remains out of sight round a distant bend. *Hawthorn's* flat keel is now buried in silt and with no water to work with we can't motor through it. Neither can we drag the boat along with ropes, as there's no towpath. Paul may have departed, but his presence is still felt when I realise our only hope is the keb he gave us when we moved from narrowboat to barge.

A keb is a rake. Well it is of sorts, if you can imagine a four-pronged fork of the type usually used to dig a garden, but with the prongs bent at ninety degrees and a very, very long handle – ours is 16'. We'd usually use it to clear rubbish from the canal but it also came in handy when *Hawthorn* got stuck to the bottom. Now taking ours from the roof, I lower the handle into the water and push it down. It sinks several feet before I feel enough resistance to walk against. The joy of the angled tines is I can push against the rake with my belly. I make a few feet along the gunwale, and then have to recover the pole and start again. The silt stinks, and every time I pull the pole out it comes up running with wet sludge and weed, which drips all over me. Despite the shade I'm sweating, and wiping my brow with a fouled hand soon gets the silt in my eyes, down my face, and all over my shirt. Conscious the office buildings beside us are now filling with people, I can't help but wonder what the suited workers in their clean and air-conditioned world make of the filthy cursing creature just a few feet away. I guess they think me a little mad. I can't deny I might be, but I'm still way too sane to want to swap my world for theirs.

The one hundred filthy, stinking yards to the lock took over an hour. The same lockkeeper who helped us off the Liffey five days earlier, Stephen, was waiting.

'Where the hell have you been?' he asked with a laugh as he saw the state of *Hawthorn* and me.

'Struggling like hell to get through all the muck below the lock! Please don't tell me the rest of the canal is like that!'

He then pointed out that the level we were on – which included both the small basin we'd moored in and the larger one beyond – was a good 18 inches below full. It had been dropped to let rally boats with air-drafts higher than ours pass under the low bridge. So we didn't need to take down the wheelhouse, and normally wouldn't have struggled in the shallows. Now all we wanted to do was climb the seven locks over the mile and a bit of canal ahead of us. That, we'd been told, was as far as we were going that day.

At least our walks with the dog meant we knew how slow the going would be above the lock and, after our start to the day, just making progress, any progress, under power not pole, was a relief. The locks came thick, but not fast: there was not enough water for speed, and trying to go faster than tick-over brought all the rubbish in the canal onto the propeller. Where it stayed until, despairing at our lack of momentum, I let *Hawthorn* drift and, head down in the weedhatch, sweated and swore while clearing it.

I wasn't the only one swearing for, as we were approaching the 5th lock, a little old lady started screaming at me from the towpath. Eh? People started to look and listen, and one of the watchers explained the woman thought we were going to kill the brood of ducklings swimming in front of us. Ah! OK! At least all I now needed to do was explain we'd passed thousands of ducklings over the years without harming any and the rucking would stop. Oh no! Not a chance!

She completely lost it and a tirade of abuse swept our way. When we got to the lock Stephen was roaring with laughter. It seemed the woman was a well-known local character, and the moment he saw her he knew what was coming.

While the first few locks were in an area dominated by businesses and modern office buildings, we were amongst rows of Victorian artisan cottages by the 7th lock at Portobello, and the feel of the waterway was very different. The mile and a bit from the basin had taken five hours and, other than the usual lock-side watchers and our daft duck-lover, we'd been left well alone. After rebuilding the wheelhouse we put anything on the cabin roof that might go walkabout, or be thrown into the canal, out of temptation's reach, and settled down for what was looking like being a long and noisy evening and night.

Traffic roaring along the road the far side of the canal wasn't the problem: the problem was our being adjacent to a jetty and narrow strip of mown grass in a spell of fine weather. It wasn't that busy when we arrived, yet as the day drew on it got ever busier. By late afternoon both jetty and grass were in the full sun, and both steadily filled with people. The edge of the canal being so shallow meant there was a gap between *Hawthorn* and the jetty. It wasn't much, but it was enough to create a bit of a break between our private world and the public one beside us. This stopped our gunwale becoming, as I was sure it would have done otherwise, an obvious and tempting bench. Despite this we knew it would only be a matter of time before our close proximity proved too tempting a diversion for someone. As with the abuse from the old woman, when someone did clamber aboard it wasn't what I expected.

Sensing movement behind me, I looked up to see a girl standing on our stern. When I asked what she was doing her reply seemed to be something about drowning herself. As her accent was almost unintelligible, I wasn't certain that's what she said. Struggling to grasp her dialect all I could say was 'I'm sorry. You'll have to say that again.'

It seemed her feller had called her a slag, which he'd regret when she was dead.

Seeing I was dealing with a rather peculiar case of teenage histrionics, I changed tack.

'You need to be careful. The water's only three feet deep so I doubt you'll drown, but it is full of rat's piss.'

'Rat's piss?'

'It's full of it. In fact the most likely thing to kill you if you do go in is Weil's disease. So if you do get flu-like symptoms after your dip I'd suggest you tell your doctor you've been in the canal.'

As I suspected, she really didn't want to drown, and the boyfriend's arrival on the bank beside us implied her attention-seeking tactics were working. True love re-established she returned ashore and, after forcing a space amongst the bodies on the jetty, they sat down to celebrate life together with a huge bottle of cider. I looked at Jill and laughed. 'How weird was that?'

I didn't laugh at half two in the morning when, with most of the revellers long departed, footsteps clumped above our heads. 'Bloody hell fire, here we go again!' I thought, getting off – knowing this would happen I hadn't got into – the bed and firing a 'And you're bloody useless!' at the dog as he watched me pass without moving more than his eyes. Two lads of student age were sat on our bow lockers and, judging by the cans between them, they were settling in for a long session.

Being boarded in the middle of the night isn't a rare event in cities, and asking people to leave is something I've become reasonably good at. The knack is to start gently, and then crank it up if necessary. Or, as I found one night in the middle of Manchester when I climbed out *Camberwell's* side hatch stark naked (they scarpered!), out-weirding people if needed. So I started all posh and polite.

'Excuse me lads, but my wife and kids are trying to sleep just below you there.' It seemed a good beginning and, while Jill and I are not married and don't have kids, appealing to people's better side couldn't do any harm.

'Gosh! Oh, we're terribly sorry.' What was it with Dublin? Even the late-night boarders were so different! Either they were wise to my tactics and having their own laugh, or they were genuinely very well spoken. Gently picking up their beers they stepped softly ashore. They were so polite and gentle I felt guilty turfing them off.

Before leaving us at Portobello, Stephen had arranged for a colleague to meet us at 8.30 am by the first of the twelve locks we were going to have to climb to make the safety of the countryside the following morning. That first lock was two miles away, so we allowed two hours to get there. Which meant getting up at 6.00 am.

We arrived half an hour early, and 8.30 came and went without any sign of the promised help. Tired and stressed and knowing that the day ahead would be in the parts of the city people had suggested might be challenging, we just wanted to get going. We had various windlasses that looked like they might fit the Irish lock mechanisms, but they were useless without the key to the padlocks on the chains holding them shut. So I probably wasn't my most graceful when, considerably later than arranged, help finally arrived in a blue WI van. The keeper parked it, pulled two racks to get the lock filling, and then came down to introduce himself. His name was John, and he wasn't late: the man who was meant to be helping us was sick so he'd been sent instead. It didn't really matter, all that mattered was how John took his tea – and to set about getting out of the city as fast as possible.

The first locks were a double – the top gate of the lower lock is also the bottom gate of the upper – and with Jill helping we were soon on our way. The next was a short distance above the first and, being a single lock that John was able to set ahead of us, we were quickly through that. It was still fairly early in the morning and, other than commuters waiting on the tramline station a hundred yards away, there was nobody about. The water's deep and clear, and we make good progress. Three locks down in less than half an hour: things were looking up.

Such foolish optimism was soon negated. The 4th lock, another double, was just the far side of a road bridge, and chained and locked beneath its arch and out of reach of meddling hands, were two weed-cutting boats. Not being John's section of canal he didn't know they were there, and he hadn't got a key. While he started ringing round to get them moved, Jill put the kettle on. As it was nearly an hour before another van arrived, we had plenty of time to drink our tea and chat to John and, wanting to have our own windlass, I asked him where we could get one.

'Windlass? What's a windlass?'

'The lump of metal you use to open the lock racks with John. The thing beside you on the grass there.'

'That's a lock key.'

'A lock key?' That's different. I've only ever heard them called windlasses in England. Not that it matters what you call it, what matters is where we can get one. Any ideas?'

It seemed his lock key came from the yard. No matter: we'd get one at the first chandlery we came to. I was in the process of learning that the Irish use stretch rather than pound for the length of water between locks when another van pulled up and men jumped out to shift the weed-cutters. While they did I practised using my new word by asking how long the stretch above the next double was. John told me the next three locks were all close together.

'That's great news, John. We'll soon be through eight of the day's twelve. We're making better progress than I'd ever hoped.'

'Eight locks? No, we've just done two, and there are four more immediately above the bridge. That's only six.'

'Six? But two of them are doubles, so surely that's eight locks?' I was getting a little panicky for fear there were lots of doubles ahead of us, and he was about to announce the Irish only counted double locks once. Which, of course, he did, and we soon learned we had fifteen 'English' locks to do that day. I sat scratching my head and wondering: if the Bingley five-rise locks were in Dublin, would they only count as one?

We moved *Hawthorn* into the double lock, and while it was filling a tirade of abuse calling into question our parentage, our nationality and the fitness of *Hawthorn* as a vessel for boating the Irish canals was hurled down from the bridge. 'Bugger, it's begun, ' I thought. 'Oh well, best deal with it.' I looked up, and sighed with relief. A familiar beaming face was poking over the bridge's parapet: it was only Stephen having a bit of a laugh. He'd come to help John, and the company was welcome.

And so on we went. Leaving the semi-detached homes and entering an area of industrial estates and warehouses, we soon found ourselves on our own as, unable to drive along the towpath, Stephen and John took to the roads and alleys to meet us at the next lock. In anticipation of feeding our helpers, Jill had got *Hawthorn* well stocked with bacon, eggs and sausages and, given we were starting to get hungry, she was about to offer the lads a breakfast bun each. There was no need: when we arrived at the 5th lock John generously handed out freshly made sausage sandwiches he'd collected from a café en route. Our offers of payment were waved away.

The towpath beside us was being upgraded from a broken rutted track to a smooth asphalt cycle-way and, while the lock was filling, a cement lorry drove down the towpath towards us. It blocked the lockkeepers' vans in. The driver soon made it clear the only way he'd let the vans past was if John and Stephen fought him. Which wasn't going to happen. So that was another delay, another fifty minutes for the kids to yawn themselves awake and head out to play at the locks still above us.

While waiting, Jill and I sat in the hot sun looking at, and through, the startlingly clear water *Hawthorn* was floating on. John now impressed us with his local and historical knowledge and our delay became a lesson in how the canal was built as much for bringing fresh water into the city as it was for carrying goods. He said it's still very clean but, thinking about the body fished out of it a couple of days ago, I was not inclined to fill the kettle. Now in his stride, John went on to tell us about the canal and Guinness and then waved his arm over all the new developments around us and told us that this was all undeveloped until a few years ago. While he was a mine of information, my greatest delight was seeing the cement lorry leaving.

According to all we'd heard, the 10th was the lock most feared. The sun was beating down, and our lost three hours mean it was the early afternoon before we approached it. Expecting to see hundreds of youths, we were relieved to find none. Begging John to pull as many racks as possible, we hoped to be gone without getting caught. We got close, so close, but we didn't quite make it: three lads arrived just as the lock was nearing full and our gunwales were the perfect height for them to walk straight onto our home from the hole in the fence beside us. We weren't naïve enough to have any valuables out in any city, but I had pushed the dog below and closed the doors fore and aft of the wheelhouse as the boys approached.

'Have a sweet,' I suggested offering the packets we had on board just for this moment. The lads looked at me as if I was more than a little odd, but they accepted a bag each.

'Give us a look below Mister,' the oldest, and obvious ringleader, pressed through a mouthful of sugar.

'I can't I'm afraid. The dog will eat you and even if he doesn't it's not my boat and I'm under oath to the owner not to let anyone into it. He'd be pretty pissed if he found you even here.'

So they sat, chewing and gassing away to each other for the short journey to the 11th lock. And then, to our immense relief, once it was full they got off and started to walk back. We watched them carefully. 'I bloody knew it!' Reaching down they picked up stones. 'Bugger! Here we bloody go!' And then it occurred to me they hadn't seen Hobbes so, as they were turning to throw them, I shouted 'Chuck them and I'll set the dog on you!' It was enough to make them pause. Their eyes met my glare, and the stones were dropped.

John, who was standing beside us at the lock, smiled. 'You're lucky,' he said; 'there are days when there are hundreds of them!'

The last stretch was wide, shallow and full of weed and rubbish. It was hell to get through, and we tried everything we knew to keep *Hawthorn* moving: easing the throttle right back to tick-over just brought us to a halt, yet trying to drive on soon had the propeller fouled. That last mile took nearly two hours.

Even when we did get to the 12th lock there was a sting in the tail when the racks in the gates were opened a little early. Hundreds of gallons of water poured onto the bow and crashed against the cabin bulkhead. The steel shutters and a canvas cover, which had kept the Irish Sea at bay, proved inadequate, and our bed got soaked. On another occasion we might have cared but, as the lock filled and *Hawthorn* rose, all we could see ahead were trees and meadows. Sod the bedding! We'd made it!

Hobbes, who'd been downbeat and low for days, clearly sensed our elation. Shedding years, he exploded up the grass towpath in a frenzy of glee, tearing in and out of the water as he went. Jill and I stood laughing at him, tears rolling down our faces: we'd been relieved to get to Dublin after the nightmare crossing, but it was only once we were in the countryside beyond the city that we felt we could relax.

THE GRAND CANAL

The hours and days that followed our emancipation from the terrors of sea and city were so laden with gifts it was hard to keep a perspective on just how much, and how quickly, everything changed above the 12th lock.

After waving John and Stephen goodbye, Jill and Hobbes set off down the towpath while I followed in *Hawthorn*. The idea behind their walking was we'd only go just round the corner and then call it a day, and then we'd found the going easy and, enjoying the greenery and birdsong and wanting to get some distance from the city, gone on for an hour. When we did stop it was only because we'd arrived opposite the comforting familiarity of a long line of moored live-aboards. Which was the perfect ending to our boating day.

Sitting in the sun relaxing on *Hawthorn* that evening, we watched as people gathered in and about boats beside us. This was familiar, and all we now needed was to see a circle of deck chairs round a BBQ to really feel we were in England. But the far bank was overgrown and shaded, and probably harder to dance on than the sunlit barge roof to which bottles, instruments, lanterns and candles were passed. Soon the air filled with laughter and music, which we vicariously indulged in. Of course we were the watched as much as watchers, and it was only a matter of time before a tall lean young man set out in a canoe to see what we were about.

Declining a beer, he introduced himself and we chatted for a bit, during which our absence of any plan and our utter ignorance about Ireland, the Irish and Irish waterways became very evident. He listened and then, just in case we got in trouble somewhere, offered a name, Eric, and a phone number. Eric wintered at Hazelhatch, but he'd left a few days earlier to go sailing on the Shannon.

'Sailing?' This was getting really novel: a live-aboard that could be sailed was either a tiny dwelling or something much more exotic.

'He's on a Dutch Barge with mast and sails. You'll see both it and him at the midsummer rally in Shannon Harbour. I assume that's where you're heading?'

We told him we weren't, and wished him well as he paddled away.

It was a passing comment, but his mentioning a rally was probably our greatest gift since coming to Ireland. Always having run away from any gathering of boaters, let alone rallies that might have hundreds of people at them, our instinct was to carry on as we always had. Yet that was in England, and as the evening went on we reconsidered our instinctive rejection of anything so formal, and began to see there might be good reasons to go, not least as it would mean taking two weeks over a journey we'd expected to make in four days. Slowing right down and taking our time could only be a good thing, so it wasn't a hard decision to make. In fact nothing appealed more at this point than remaining where we were for a day of rest and recovery.

Getting up early the following morning I rang John to say we'd had a rethink, and to ask if it would be all right if we delayed for twenty-four hours. It was, though John was most insistent that he'd bring groceries down to us as we were miles from the nearest shop. I assured him we'd survive; though he only really seemed to relax when I pointed out we still had the makings of the breakfast we intended to give him and Steven.

Despite our thinking we'd made it clear we weren't about to die of starvation or neglect, the day after our sabbatical John arrived to meet us at the 13th lock with bread, milk, a carton of orange juice and a tin of dog food. He'd even had a lock key – still warm from welding and wet with paint – made for us. Perhaps there was some cultural element I was missing but, as with the sandwiches he'd bought in Dublin, he again refused any money. His generosity knowing no bounds, before leaving he gave us the name of a horse and the race it was in, and suggested a trip to the bookies in Sallins would be profitable. While I knew I wouldn't back it, watching him leave I couldn't help but wonder if it might be possible to live in Ireland on gifted groceries and bookies' losses.

Once we'd arrived amongst boats in Hazelhatch we assumed we'd regularly be passing long lines of them, even marinas full of them, all the way to the

Shannon. So it was odd, particularly odd given the boats at Hazelhatch were so tightly packed, that in the six miles from there to Sallins we passed just one, and that was moored and looked like it never moved. Not that it mattered: the water was deep and free from rubbish, the stone bridges arched and pretty and the landscape of hedge-lined meadows and gently rolling pasture surprisingly similar to Cheshire. We pottered gently on, and approached the next lock looking forward to enjoying the independence of being able to do it ourselves. No need: we arrived to find the lock gates already open for us, and the lockkeeper, Martin, sitting on the lock beam with a big smile on his face and his legs merrily swinging.

While we'd stopped before passing any moored boats at Hazelhatch, the shallow canal and overgrown banks meant we couldn't do this when we got to Sallins. So we boated through, and while we did a man clambered off his own barge and walked beside us offering help. Introducing himself as Gene he was soon aboard and, after the inevitable cup of tea, extending his help to driving me to fetch a bottle of gas. I'd expected this to be straightforward, so to find the two bottles we'd brought from England were worthless once empty was a bit of a shock, as was the price of starting again with Irish bottles and an Irish regulator. This was a pain, for it looked like we'd be carting four bottles about for the next year.

That evening the weather broke, with rain as intense as the heatwave preceding it. So we stayed in Sallins another day: talking to Gene about art and poetry and trying to catch the drips coming through the roof-light in our saloon. It had dripped very occasionally in England, but this Irish rain seemed to have a particularly slippery quality that let it easily find its way through previously watertight joints. I laughed about this with Gene, and then confessed I suspected the cause was a combination of Irish Sea salt and hot sun. Hopefully it would seal again; if not then we had the tools and wherewithal to make a canvas cover. When we left the following morning Gene came down to bid us farewell, clutching a piece of paper he pressed into my hand. There were two names and phone numbers on it. I had to smile: while the first was a Ted, the second was Eric. Whoever this guy was, it seemed fate was steering us towards him.

Just beyond Sallins we crossed the River Liffey on a wonderful stone aqueduct. We should have stopped to explore round it, but I'd made the mistake of ringing the lockkeeper to say we were on our way. He was now waiting, as I feared he would be when I worked out we'd have to average 4 knots to be on time. Programmed by our middle-class English upbringing that being late was the height of rudeness, rather than stopping to take in the river's dancing clarity and swift pace, we crossed the aqueduct with only a leap onto the towpath to glance over the bridge parapet. It was a silly rush, and totally unnecessary: once again we arrived at a lock to find Martin swinging his legs and smiling.

Despite having only just crossed the Liffey, a couple of hours, three locks and three miles later, *Hawthorn* was on the canal's summit. As canal summits go the Grand Canal's isn't as obviously dramatic as many of the English summits we'd crossed; though while it doesn't have a tunnel, long views or a deep and darkly dripping cutting, it does mark a significant change: the neat pastures and clipped hedgerows bordering the canal east of the Grand Canal's summit felt like Cheshire, yet, when we emerged into the open west of it, we were somewhere much wilder, and sedge grasses and barbed wire had replaced the lush meadows and green borders we'd become accustomed to since leaving Dublin.

It was some transformation, but then it didn't occur to us that we'd arrived on the very eastern edge of Ireland's boggy centre. All we could see at the time was that we were a long way from anywhere: the towpath was so overgrown we doubted it was ever walked, and the chances of meeting anyone or having a conversation seemed as remote as the location. Or so we thought when we drove mooring pins into the soft, dark-soiled bank and called it a day.

'Bloody hell Jill, there's a boat coming. That's a first!' I said watching the bow of what looked like a small barge in the distance behind us. It slowly drew nearer, and we had a proper look. Guessing its size at about 9' beam and 40' length, we took in the conventional shape of the bow and cabin, but the stern arrangement of a sloping canvas cover off the back of an otherwise open half wheelhouse was unlike anything we'd seen anywhere. The chap at the wheel stuck his head through a gap in the canvas and smiled.

'Hello!' he said.

'Indeed hello!' we replied.

And then he said something that really flummoxed us. He asked 'Are you up for putting a cover on the back of this?'

By now the little barge was passing us, so I walked down our gunwale to finish the conversation and to quickly take in what might be possible. It looked more than a little awkward a job, and we'd need to have a much longer conversation, but I could see no obvious reason why not.

'We could. But where and when I've no idea.'

'You're going to the rally I presume?' he replied, his voice getting louder as his boat drew away.

'Yes.'

'I'll see you there then. Have a good run and enjoy the canal. Goodbye.'

To have such a conversation with the first moving boat we'd seen in Ireland was more than a little surreal, as was our realisation that it was now evening and, other than the chap who'd just passed, the only people we'd spoken to were Gene and Martin. The silence and solitude were striking, and we were still just half an hour's drive from Dublin. While we hadn't expected this, the odd thing was that, even when the opportunity to stop and chat was presented, some odd English reserve kicked in. There weren't many opportunities, but just the following morning we passed up a chance we'd later kick ourselves for ignoring.

Below the lock at the summit's western end, where we had our first conversation of the day with the lockkeeper, we boated through our first Irish boatyard and only the third cluster of boats since leaving Dublin. This was Lowtown and where we'd have left the Grand Canal's mainline and turned south down the branch canal to Athy if we'd been heading for the River Barrow. As always when passing moored boats *Hawthorn* was at tick-over and, with them two abreast with slack in their mooring ropes, there was a bit of movement and banging. Suddenly a hatch swung open, a head and torso came out and we were subjected to a long, bright-eyed stare. 'Here we go, ' I thought. 'We're about to get our first bollocking for going too fast! ' Preparing my usual arguments about being unable to go any slower, I waited for the moans to start. And then, as we drew level, a smile split the man's bearded face and he waved at us.

'Hello from *Blackthorn*, *Hawthorn*!' came a call, as his waving arm now gestured towards where the name of his own boat was painted.

By now we were passing him.

'There's another *Hawthorn* out on the Shannon. When you see it say hello.'

Even though meeting the other *Hawthorn* seemed as likely as meeting Eric, I shouted back 'We will! Thank you!' We were only ticking along, but already out of range of conversation. After a last wave the man disappeared inside Blackthorn, and I concentrated on keeping *Hawthorn* in the centre of the narrow channel between the swinging craft. We were soon in the wilds again, and I was soon wishing I'd stopped just to see what might have followed. And we should have done: just a few months later it was announced on the IWAI forum that the skipper of *Blackthorn* had died, and I watched the thread fill with posting after posting of condolences and stories about the man's boating life. How easy it is to be wise after the event, to look back and regret exchanging just twenty odd words when we had all day – all week if we wanted – to spend with one of the great characters of Irish boating.

Used to being on canals with water the colour and texture of stewed tea, finding the Grand Canal's gin clear brought the unanticipated bonus of making it seem we were boating on an aquarium, and we took turns on the bow watching the large shoals of roach, bream and perch swim ahead of the boat. For a few hundred yards it would feel as if *Hawthorn* was herding them, then some strange instinct for home would see the shoal shoot back between our hull and the reeds. This really suited the killers of the piscine world, the pike, who lay still in the weedy margins ready for any prey unlucky enough to come within range; for death and dinner to combine in a flash of tail and a snap of teeth. Given such efficient calorie consumption it's not surprising pike are the largest fish in Irish waters. We were both so fascinated by this marine world it wasn't rare for Jill to be watching them from the bow while I kept the wheelhouse doors open to look into the water either side of us. We weren't the only ones watching the fish for, and we'd always delighted in their iridescent flash, we passed kingfishers every mile or so.

Even when there weren't fish or birds to watch, the canal bed provided plenty of interest: for such a rural and empty landscape the quantity of old tyres, gardening and household equipment, bits of metal, road signs and traffic cones that slid slowly under us was a surprise. A huge bottle-jack smack bang in the middle of the canal near Allenwood was the strangest sight. It must have weighed several hundredweight, and could only have fallen from a boat, as throwing it that far from the bank would have taken strength surely beyond even one of the descendants of the legendary Irish hero Cúchulainn.

It may have been we'd spent too much time looking down, or that we were lucky enough to experience it on a perfect evening, but the shock of the view across the Bog of Allen from above the lock at Ticknevin when we arrived there was considerable.

Seeing this bog marked on our map, I'd expected a landscape similar to those Jill and I used to wander over on our Sunday morning excursions in the Peak District. For us bogs were treeless swathes of sheep-grazed grass and heather, studded with boulders and the occasional rocky outcrop. In comparison to those hard high spaces, the Bog of Allen's gently undulating gorse and bracken seemed soft and welcoming. My greatest surprise was seeing so many ash, alder, birch and hazel trees. They were scattered individually and growing in

clumps and larger bramble-bordered copses. The air was full of bird song, and when the breeze blew it felt as if the bog breathed with a leafy rustle. The only track we could see across it was our watery road. At sunset it took on a beautiful burnished copper glow and a sense of natural calm and peace descended. Even Hobbes, who would usually wander and bark at that time of day, just lay at ease beside the boat. In awe of the space and moment we were in, I suggested we should boat only an hour a day and take a week to cross it.

'That'll be nice,' said Jill, 'though you're going to be a lot lighter by the time we get to Tullamore as there's not much left on board to eat.'

So, guided by the lockkeeper's local knowledge, our first night on the Bog of Allen was spent moored outside a housing estate in the small town of Edenderry rather than in the back of beyond. At the end of a short branch canal we'd have otherwise ignored, the town had all the stock we needed for the coming days of solitude, and we managed to have a long conversation, the longest by far for many days, with the owner of the part-restored barge we were moored behind. It wasn't a particularly busy mooring – just the odd car came and went from the houses beside us – but compared to the next four nights we spent in the middle of nowhere, it was positively frantic.

With too many people in too small a space and too many engines in too much haste, much of England seems to suffer from crowds and the relentless rumble of traffic. This meant that when we boated there we would go out of our way to stay in the quietest spaces we could find. English waterway guides being based on Ordnance Survey maps meant potentially silent spaces were sometimes visible long before we reached them, and we'd plan our travels to exploit anywhere that looked remote. Not that we'd often have these spaces to ourselves, for canal towpaths being so easily accessed meant walkers would ramble past individually or in small family groups. And even without walkers, there were other boaters.

When we'd started boating with *Camberwell Beauty* there seemed to be an unwritten agreement that, if possible, you didn't moor too close to a boat that had obviously tried to acquire a little solitude. As the canals got busier this decorum seemed to slip and, when we'd stop early and alone, come the evening we'd have boats just a few feet either side of us. We knew this was getting out of hand when people stopped using their own mooring pins and put their ropes around ours. Only Hobbes thought this a good idea, as he'd be through their boat stealing food while they were still tying knots. We could tell from people's reaction to him what sort of company we'd gained.

There was no danger of walkers and boaters being a problem on the Bog of Allen. For here the closest humanity came to intruding was the glimpse of a distant tractor or the fleeting sight of a car on one of the canal's occasional bridges. At night the starlit sky touched the bog's dark blackness, and the canal became bright with reflected light. But the nights were never silent: there was always, and I suspect always is and always will be, a distant barking dog. God it was wonderful – though, as we found on one of our short runs, even in daylight and sober it's a space that could mess with your head.

'Jill,' I whispered loudly, not wanting my voice to carry beyond the wheelhouse, 'what or who the hell is that?'

'Where? Where am I meant to be looking? What are you on about?'

'There! Standing against the hedge by the overflow!'

'Crikey! Don't stare! And don't you even try and take a photo.'

I didn't need to take a photo to remind me of what I'd seen, and was still watching as carefully as I could without being too obvious. Beside the overflow stood a small, stooped figure dressed in the strangest assortment of rags, fertiliser sacks, string and wellington boots. She, and I'm pretty certain it was a woman, was the peat-brown colour of the bog, and she neither moved nor acknowledged our presence. Where she came from we hadn't a clue, as there wasn't a dwelling to be seen. Discreetly glancing back a minute later, she was still standing there, still watching us. Even on *Hawthorn* in broad daylight it was an odd couple of minutes, and I could only imagine how far I'd have run if Hobbes and I had met her on the towpath when I walked him in the dark of night.

After several days of unbroken greenery, to come round a corner and see a vast swathe of brown in the distance was a surprise: a surprise that turned to shock when we got close enough to see the brown was piled peat. We would have boated on, but we couldn't until the lifting bridge carrying a narrow-gauge railway line across the canal had been opened. Given the traffic of boats on the canal we were astonished to see the bridge moving as we approached. We were in the middle of nowhere so I wasn't surprised when the man operating it came out for a chat.

Not so long ago in England, there was a campaign that using Irish peat on your garden was as harmful to the planet as releasing refrigerants or using aerosols. And that was about a few grow-bags of tomatoes, or enriching the soil around your lettuces, so to hear that the sole purpose of the railway line snaking into the distance across the bog was to shift vast amounts of peat – though I soon learnt that in Ireland peat used as fuel was called turf – in order for it to be dried, and then burnt in a power station furnace, was quite a surprise. The scale of this operation was clearly visible in the miles of huge rows of cut peat south of where I was standing. So much for my joshing with Jill that these were the potato sets of the giant who'd thrown the bottle jack in the canal at Allenwood: what we were seeing was an industrial process of open-cast mining. I only had to listen to the bridge operator for a few minutes to realise that my perception that the Bog of Allen was a truly wild space was naïve in the extreme. As if to compound the strangeness of the moment, round the next bend three dozen English – and they were sat beside their cars so we were sure of this – fishermen grumpily lifted the huge poles they were using to fish just inches from the far bank. And that made me think of my father who's logical mind always wondered why pole fishermen didn't sit on the other bank with very short rods.

Just drifting suited us, but we were both quite happy when six locks, three keepers and two hours saw us arriving in Tullamore the following morning. We moored in the almost empty harbour on the outskirts of the town, and then walked into its centre. This took all of two minutes, which surprised us as Tullamore looked enormous on our road map. On our way back we called into the local WI office to get our own copy of the Grand Canal guide we'd been so kindly lent by Mark (we left his in an envelope for internal post to return) and to buy the Shannon boating guides we'd be needing shortly. Arriving back in the harbour we were greeted by the owner of the boat moored behind *Hawthorn*. We explained what we were up to and about, and then he disappeared into his cruiser for a minute before reappearing with three brand new map books of the Shannon and Erne system. Produced for the hire companies on the river, they were a much larger scale and easier to read than the folding laminated charts we'd just bought. Once again our offer of payment was dismissed with a wave of a hand. The only condition attached to our having them was to enjoy the water.

Despite the appeal of local shops, pubs and people, we were keen to return to our gentle pottering and we were on our way again the next day. Within half a mile of leaving the harbour we were back amongst rural greenery. The scale of Irish towns was something we were going to be a while getting our heads round, as did what greeted us a few minutes later.

The only other time we've seen cattle in a canal, the towpath beside them was full of firemen, policemen and farmers trying to get them out. Not here: here the farmer drove them in and it occurred to us we must be at one of the cattle crossings that someone on the IWAI forum had mentioned we might scrape across on the way to the Shannon. Watching the way the cows, and these were big cows, had to swim most of the canal's width, I was pretty certain we weren't going to be poling our way over it or asking the farmer for a tow from a tractor. It was all a lot more fun than that, and we sat on the bow enjoying the spectacle of dripping cattle making their way onto the lush green pasture beside us. Once the way was clear we drove through the churned water. We didn't hit anything. We didn't have to go far west of Tullamore to be in countryside every bit as remote as we had seen east of it and, now becoming attuned to the relaxed pace that attending the rally had imposed on us, we weren't long looking for a spot to spend the rest of the day in.

As much for the sheer joy of boating as for being in a hurry, we'd often boated long days in England: making the run from London to Cheshire in a little over a week, and East Anglia to Cheshire in less than two, was fun, but it meant getting up early and left little time to do other things. While we'd arrived in

Ireland with no itinerary or idea of what to expect, we were both determined that we were going to slow down and see what having time to be creative led to. For Jill the answer was almost instantaneous as she picked up a sketchbook and pencil and started to draw the world around her: within a few minutes of our mooring just beyond the cow crossing, she was off down the towpath back to the jackdaw-nested castle we'd just passed. Less sure of what to do with my time,

I got out a fishing rod and fished inexpertly for a couple of hours, and then I went in and wrote a blog about the last couple of days. When finished I posted it with the others on the page I'd created on our business website. It was a bit of fun, and certainly easier than writing countless emails to the friends and family interested in how we were going. We were finding our feet, and every time we met someone or were helped on our way by a lockkeeper, we seemed to learn something of interest.

Take the lockkeeper, Alan, who lived beside one of the two locks at Rahan. He was the eighth generation of his family to have kept the lock and, judging by the happy flock of young children at his front door when we got there, hopefully not the last. The presence of his family and kitchen didn't stop him accepting a cup of coffee, which he drank while standing just inside the wheelhouse door. Well I say drank, and I say standing, but neither is strictly true: his stories were so funny he spent much of his time bent double with laughter, and most of his coffee splashed onto the floor. Giggling along both with him and at him, we spilt our own coffees, and were very soon glad the floor was varnished not carpeted. Which was a good thing, for being bothered about something so trivial would have ruined the pleasure of hearing about life, and lives, on the canal. It was from Alan we learnt of the engineering wonders needed to carry a canal across a bog, and how vulnerable to sudden disaster this made the Grand Canal.

The bog's liquid qualities were very evident when we drove mooring pins into it, as each sledgehammer blow travelled through the ground below our feet, but Alan's tale of the night of the major breach in the winter of 1989 was something else. As Sod's Law would have it, the breach was in the long section across the Bog of Allen, and of course it had to fail at night. When it did, Alan was one of the many waterways workers called from far and wide to see what could be done. Parking half a mile from where the bank had failed he could hear the tools in the back of his van jiggling, and he'd stepped out to feel the ground beneath his feet shaking and to hear the roar of tumbling water in the dark distance. Knowing there was nothing to be done, the unnerved workers stayed well back and watched as best they could by torchlight.

We'd been aware of the embankments carrying the canal across the bog below Ticknevin, but that a length had been rebuilt relatively recently escaped us. As did the notion that constructing a canal across wet bog land would be such a difficult feat it would take fifteen years and be considered, at least by those that know these things, one of the wonders of the canal-building age. Jill and I were much too accustomed to the less subtle drama of huge aqueducts and long tunnels to have considered the embankment special, or to imagine that what we'd dawdled across in a few hours had taken so long to build.

Even repairing the canal after the breach had taken a year, and that was just one short section and using diesel-powered diggers and dumpers. Hearing this was a shock, for both Jill and I were suddenly aware that if it burst in a big way again while we were west of it, we'd be facing the dilemma of either breaking our declaration not to crane *Hawthorn*, or be boating back to England from Limerick on the Shannon estuary. Leaving from Limerick would mean we'd have to get all the way round Ireland's west and south coasts just to start back across the Irish Sea, and those shorelines were exposed to the full force of the Atlantic Ocean. I only needed to think about that for a few seconds to dismiss it: there's adventure, and then there's downright foolhardiness. There was, of course, the third option of staying longer than the year we intended. As long as the canal remained open none of this mattered, but it was briefly troubling to know that just one small slip in an embankment would leave us unable to get back to England.

A breach was most likely to happen during, or soon after, a prolonged spell of wet weather when the canal was brimmed with water. While this seemed unlikely in mid June's bright sun and blue skies, given Ireland's famously damp climate, this was something that surely had to happen regularly. And thinking about the canal brimming with water reminded me to ask Alan about the absence of any bye-washes at Grand Canal locks.

The simplicity of bye-washes is that the canal's levels are self-regulating: once the summit is full, the water tops a little weir, and then runs round the lock in a stone channel – the bye-wash – into the level below. This in turn fills, and exactly the same process happens at the next lock, and the next level, and so on all the way down to the canal's lowest point. As long as the weirs aren't blocked, and there aren't any leaks in the canal – both of which are easily checked by walking along it occasionally – no labour is ever needed. It's a simple arrangement that's proved perfect for hundreds of years, and something we were used to seeing everywhere we'd boated. So how were the levels here regulated?

'Some water runs through airholes into the locks, but if there's a lot of water to be lost we lift racks,' came Alan's reply. Racks are used to control the paddles that let water in and out of the lock; we were perfectly used to using them when putting boats through, but had never heard of their being used to set levels. Then Alan pointed out that there used to be a time when every lock had a keeper, and the keeper was on call 24 hours a day for 365 days a year. So why bother going to the expense of building bye-washes when there was already a man regulating the water in each level day in day out for nothing? This made sense in a historical perspective, but what about now?

It turned out that the only reason we weren't seeing racks pulled at the moment was the weather was uncommonly dry. If we'd been on the canal the previous summer we'd have had an entirely different experience: then there had been so much rain there were times all the racks on the canal locks had to be opened, which meant it ran like a river. With so much water needing to be moved, and a responsibility to keep people, their property and land safe, a controlled breach in a safe spot had been considered seriously enough for a digger to be placed ready to tear a bank out if needed. This state of high alert had lasted forty-eight hours, and Alan worked all of them. Perversely, hearing this didn't make me think of Alan's exhaustion; it made me consider the beaming happy brood of children we'd seen at his door. For Alan had earlier pointed out that his home was built into the embankment with the bedrooms on the lower floor, and when lots of racks were open the house trembled and the roar of falling water could be heard through its foundations. How odd that must have felt, and how strange for his children to grow up thinking it was normal to lie in bed with their house gently shaking around them.

We could have happily listened to Alan for hours and, as long as he could put off cutting grass or maintaining his lock, might well have done had not an extraordinary event occurred while we were still on jetty below his lock: our conversation was cut short by the arrival of only the second moving boat we'd seen in nearly two weeks.

For some reason this boat was called *4B*, and we were left wondering why anyone would call a boat after a pencil. You wouldn't get away with that in England: there boats were named *Kingfisher* and *Heron*; or were jokes like *Onion Bargee*, *The Mutt's Testes* or *Minced Moorhen*, or combinations of owners' names with Marjorie's and James's boat becoming *Marjam*, Ian's and Alf's *Alfian* and Wanda's and Kerry's... What was *4B* about?

Having put the boat through the lock, Alan came back down to spill more coffee. He told us that *4B* was a former working barge; many such barges were numbered and lettered rather than named. They were traditionally referred to as *canal boats*, not as barges. Most of those still afloat were the M boats his forebears had predominantly helped through the locks he now worked: M showed that they were motor-powered and owned by the Grand Canal Company. The boat that had just passed, *4B*, had been a Bye-trader's boat (hence the B): it operated on the Grand Canal but was not owned by the Company. Alan suggested we'd see a lot more of these converted boats at the Shannon Harbour rally.

We used the few minutes head start we gave *4B* to thank Alan, and then set off to see if the few hundred yards between us would get longer or shorter. To our amazement – we'd never caught anything in *Hawthorn* on the English canals – two miles and an hour later we were closing in and, much as we were used to doing in our normal world, *4B's* crew came out and offered to let us past. While the excitement of passing another boat on a canal was tempting, we knew we were only going to go a little further before stopping and, truth be told, we were only a tiny fraction faster. And if we had passed we'd have missed being in the perfect place to see how Irish bargees clear their props when *4B's* steerer put his boat in neutral, pulled his shirt over his head and clambered down steps welded onto the rudder in just his shorts. He then stood knee deep in the water, and reached down to pull the rubbish and weed off the prop. That his legs and shorts got wet was probably no hardship in the heat of a June day, but I had to wonder how much fun it was in the depths of winter. Perhaps that was when one of the watching teenage sons was press-ganged into action? We followed in their churned wake for a few minutes before calling it a day.

After miles and miles of flat country, long straight runs of canal and endless vistas of bog, the sudden change in landscape below the lock at Glyn made a welcome change. Here willow, alder and ash trees had been left to hang low over water full of reed and weed. It felt more like a small river than a canal, and we'd never seen as many fish, moorhens, coots and kingfishers. It didn't matter that this was the shallowest stretch we'd boated since the cut into Sallins, as going slowly meant we had more time to take it in, and once again we took turns at fish-watching from the bow. The mile to the next lock at Belmont took us an hour, and we almost regretted getting there. As ever, the keeper was waiting.

'That has to be the loveliest stretch of water on the whole canal,' I gushed.

'Really? Most people moan like hell about the lack of water and the weed,' he replied, gently closing the lock gate behind us.

Belmont, the 33rd lock, was the first double since the 13th back at Hazelhatch, and its keeper, another Alan, was in no hurry. He pulled half a rack and stood chatting to us for the twenty minutes it took the top lock to drain, and then we moved into the lower lock and repeated the same gentle descent. Below the lock we all drank tea, and we quizzed Alan about the walk to the local post office where we hoped our mail from England had been delivered. Walk? There was no need to walk! Alan would be going through the village en route to putting us through his next lock, and he'd be happy to call and collect it for us. Which was more than fair play, and another reason to keep the kettle warm.

The landscape above Belmont lock had just been a teaser, for below it we found ourselves looking down a long straight length through yet more bog. Not that it mattered, we'd only a couple of miles and Alan's last lock to go and we'd be in Shannon Harbour. I'd be lying if I said we weren't apprehensive about going to a rally, but after so much solitude we were rather craving the energy of a crowd.

THE SHANNON
HARBOUR RALLY

After the solitude and silence of our gentle dawdle west through the Irish midlands, we were looking forward to arriving in what we expected would be the hustle and bustle of Shannon Harbour. So it was rather ironic that when we did get there it was on foot, and then only to stand on the road bridge above it and shake our heads in dismay on seeing the wide basin below and west of us

solid with all manner of different boats – barges, steel and GRP cruisers and even older wooden vessels. There wasn't a cat in hell's chance of getting *Hawthorn* moored in there. We walked on past the derelict hotel, the restored Harbour Master's House, the two dry docks and the WI workshops and crossed the lock at the other end of the harbour. Below us in the distance we could see the canal's last lock, but the banks between it and us were as densely packed as the harbour behind us. At least we now knew where all the boats we expected to see on the Grand Canal were: they were all, and there must have been twenty times as many here as we'd passed since leaving Dublin, packed into its last mile. Thankful that we'd pulled in when they started, we headed home to make our casually tied lines a little more permanent.

I was banging in mooring pins so we could get our ropes from off the bushes, and properly sorting out the gangplank, when a WI van pulled up beside me. Jason, the last Grand Canal lockkeeper, leaned out its open window. He's younger, leaner and quite possibly more direct than many of his colleagues.

'What the hell are you doing all the way up here?' he asked.

'We've walked down and wandered round and there's nowhere near a space big enough for us anywhere else.'

'What do you mean no room? There's loads of room! Come on – fire her up. I'll get you sorted.' And he'd gone, down the track in a cloud of dust. Jill and I looked at each other and shrugged. Although we couldn't imagine where he planned to put us, we chucked our ropes back on board and gently motored on behind him.

Half an hour later, with Jason saying he was confident the owners wouldn't mind, we were moored outside two big barges above the lock at the end of the harbour and, knowing he wouldn't walk down our gunwales and was a cautious pain when crossing boats, making sure Hobbes could get ashore. He could, and after all our worries this spot was perfect, not least because it was the far side of the canal from the rally's centre, which meant we would be able to bolt to shelter if socialising proved too much, and being beside the lock meant we could discreetly watch boats coming and going. Once again, as when Alan brought our post down that evening, WI's lockkeepers were spoiling us.

Something about the way everyone, including Roger while we were still in England, had spoken about Shannon Harbour meant that Jill and I were under the impression it was a sizeable village or small town. So we were surprised to find it a hamlet with a pub selling groceries. Not having bought anything other than the same essentials this pub sold since leaving Tullamore, this was a blow. Still, we'd come into the bar to find that out, so we couldn't leave without having at least a pint. It was good, better than good, probably even the best I'd had anywhere. Needing to check, I had another, just to make sure and all that. I then pointed out to Jill that the next day was my birthday, and I ought to have a pint for that in case something happened overnight and I couldn't get in the following day. Eventually emerging, blinking, into the sunlight a lot later than we'd expected, full of Guinness and carrying half a dozen large duck eggs, I spent the walk back to *Hawthorn* trying to convince Jill it was possible to live on eggs and stout alone.

It was an argument I was never going to win, so my birthday treat was a trudge down three miles of narrow lanes busy enough with rushing traffic for us to wish for footpaths. Reaching the town of Banagher, we took a wander along the High Street, at the bottom of which a fine bridge spans the Shannon. The river was much bigger than we anticipated so far inland, and the number of navigation markers we could see made us suspect it might be tricky to navigate. Wandering round the back of the town's harbour, we noticed a walk marked along a disused railway line. There was a stile, and a narrow muddy track along the top of the embankment, and the lie of the land made us suspect it was the same disused line we walked over near Shannon Harbour. While I was determined to follow it back, Jill was a little more cautious and suggested we check in the Tourist Information Office we thought we might have passed.

Retracing our steps, we found the door with the Tourist Information Office sticker on it. It looked more like a house than any Tourist Information Office we'd ever been in, and this feeling only intensified when the door opened into a corridor. Seeing and hearing no one, I shouted a greeting rather than go straight in. Silence, so I shouted once more, and a voice in the distance called me in. Leaving Jill with Hobbes outside, I did as I was told. At the far end of the corridor was a room with two women sitting at one desk.

It was immediately obvious that this wasn't the sort of tourist office dealing with hundreds of people fighting to book hotels or enquiring about walks each day. In fact the women seemed completely thrown by my presence and my question 'Would it be possible to walk back to Shannon Harbour from Banagher on the railway line?'

They didn't know for certain, but they did think some people walked the Banagher end of it. Having seen the stile and the muddy footprints, I assured them I too thought that was the case.

'But can we walk all the way to Shannon Harbour?'

I expected a map to be brought out, even a booklet of local walks to be forthcoming. But no, all we got was a very cautious suggestion it should be possible. This became less cautious when one of the women remembered someone she knew sometimes walked her dog along the line.

'Sure it'll be grand!'

It was, well it was for the first half a mile or so. And then the footpath dwindled out, and we were forced to find our way along through nettles, briar and scrub along what was now a high embankment. Weighed down with the big rucksack full of shopping and sweating like hell in the heat, it was only my determination to reward all the effort already invested that made me press on while trying to justify continuing to an ever more doubtful Jill.

'Listen: isn't that traffic on the road we can now hear? We're nearly there. It'll be worth it. Just a few more min… Oh! Bugger!'

The embankment came to a dead stop, dropped down a 30' high brick wall to where a stream connected the swampy land either side of us, and then started again in another sheer brick face. If only someone hadn't nicked the bridge once spanning the void we'd have been fine.

We started to walk back and, if we hadn't seen a lad getting the cattle in from the fields for milking, we would have completed the retreat all the way to the river and Banagher. The lad could only have been about ten, so we were impressed with how well he dealt with the shock of two weirdoes and a wild-looking dog appearing out of a hedge beside him. He had no problem with us cutting across the land. Unfortunately that land included a cattle yard so deep in dung we had to almost wade through it to reach the lane: we arrived home smelling of cow shit, stung by nettles and bugs, scratched all over by briars and thorns, knackered – and two hours worse off than we would have been without our little adventure.

The two locks connecting Shannon Harbour to the river Shannon are the busiest on the Grand Canal and, with lots of boats attending the rally, never busier than over the midsummer weekend. While impressively competent, Jason wasn't the miracle worker needed to simultaneously put boats through two locks a quarter of a mile apart. So he did the lower lock, and volunteers helped out on the upper. Enjoying the physicality of locking, we weren't long offering to help, and helping gave us an introduction to arriving boaters.

Taking lines, closing gates and winding racks with our shiny new lock key, we lost count of the number of barges and cruisers entering the harbour we'd considered full to bursting several days earlier. I kept wondering where each boat was going to squeeze in, and was constantly amazed at the way it was never any bother. How, after a brief exchange of cheerful greetings, ropes were passed and latecomers stacked outside earlier arrivals. Where boats were once two or three abreast, they were now five or six, with the climb ashore getting ever longer and more complicated. Just when I thought it was so solid nobody would ever move again, a large barge with a wheelchair-bound boater arrived. Where that was going to go so he could get ashore was a mystery, and then the boats on the wall all pushed out, and the barge was roped and eased against the quay.

By the Friday night the rallying boats were disappearing beneath vast amounts of bunting, flags, pennants and lights. Happy children ran wild and loose on the grass, and a general feeling of bonhomie filled the warm still air. Being moored across the canal from the main gathering meant there was a sense of physical distance to our observing; as there was a social distance when, later that evening, we stood on the fringes of the jolly crowd outside the pub. We barely spoke to anyone, and retreated to bed hoping we'd find it easier going in the morning.

Never having been to an official rally, we had no idea what was involved. We'd somehow learnt that we should register in the morning, though quite where and when nobody seemed certain. Being early, we sat in the sun and watched and waited for developments, before being seen as strays and gently guided to the marquee of rally central. Here we were greeted by the Rally Commodore, Pat, with a generous smile, a large Buck's Fizz and a warm croissant. Which was nice. Now officially present, and clutching our first ever brass plaque and a rally programme, we stood chatting to other early risers. We were still in awe of the Grand Canal, so to find many of the people we spoke to had little enthusiasm for it was a surprise that left us suspecting either the Shannon was so amazing people were reluctant to leave it, or that they'd been across those long lengths of bog so often it was no longer the novel shock we'd found so enthralling. On hearing we'd allowed a year to explore and play, everyone we spoke to was full of ideas and enthusiasm about where and how we should go boating, and we listened to tales of fun and adventure and suggestions of places to see and people we had to meet. Our inability to say exactly where in England we came from, and our insistence that we considered the barge by the lock as home irrespective of which town or county, or even country, it was moored in was clearly thought a little odd. Though not too odd to be invited for coffee and cake on one of the barges at the edge of the boating throng.

The same relaxed confusion of registering seemed to affect pretty much every rally event, particularly the timing. With the gap between advertised times and the reality of an event starting seeming to average out at about an hour, our English punctuality was distinctly useless. While tempted to follow the logical route of setting all our timepieces back an hour, we quickly found the answer was to simply listen out for Donna.

We'd first met Donna at registration, and we couldn't help but notice that her being a New Zealander in no way diminished how she was obviously comfortable and welcome. Now we began to see why. For Donna was at the centre of everything: soon discarding the loud hailer she'd been given as the event's crier, she just filled her lungs, threw her head back and hollered out the news. We knew something was about to happen when children cowered and wincing adults covered their ears and, even if we couldn't see that detail, we couldn't not notice the explosion of frightened jackdaws bolting from the shaking masonry of the old hotel. If we missed it the first time, we only had to wait for the echo of Donna's shout to roll back from somewhere across the Shannon. While we didn't go to everything, we did make a point of not hiding away and watching from a distance.

We didn't need to meet many boaters to quickly learn that our notion we'd quietly sneaked in under the radar was complete nonsense: everybody we spoke to seemed to know we'd motored across the Irish Sea, and then taken our time on the canal, though just how this could happen was beyond us as we'd not announced our arrival or seen it mentioned in any public forum, and we'd barely met a soul since leaving Dublin. Being so in the public eye wasn't something we'd anticipated, but *Hawthorn* didn't help as we only had to look at the lines of boats to realise our home was very different to the converted working boats and fibreglass and steel cruisers around us. Later, having studied the way everyone knew each other, and how comfortably people moved around the rally from boat to boat and group to group, I began to wonder if the interest in us was simply down to the novelty of our being new faces. It was an odd feeling, but not one we could do anything about even if we wanted to.

While we were invited onto several boats, and spent some time looking over the sorts of grand cruisers we'd never seen on our English travels, we were the wrong side of the harbour to have many visitors. The owner of one of the ex-working boats shouted across from his mooring directly opposite to ask if I'd mind his coming over to have a look at our wheelhouse. It seemed, and we could see, that he'd not made one for his barge, and apparently he liked the look of ours. 'Of course, come over whenever you fancy.' I shouted back, and then slipped up by adding, 'The kettle's always on', and something about having tea. He didn't quite collapse in fits of giggles but he grinned broadly, and I was sure he was still grinning, mouthing 'T!' and shaking his head as he ducked back into his crowded cabin.

Along with rallies, one of the things that Jill and I would very quickly say we don't normally do is fancy dress. So imagine our delight on discovering the weekend's main event – the Saturday night dinner in the barn-like workshop WI had made available – was pirate themed. Knowing nothing about this, having nothing suitable in our wardrobes, and being reluctant to chop a leg off and unable to search rural County Offaly for a crutch and a parrot, we went as we were. Which was odd, for if there's one thing guaranteed to make the self-conscious stand out at a fancy dress party it's being the only ones dressed in everyday clothes.

Jill had earlier offered to lend a hand serving supper, so I arrived on my own and had to search for her amongst the tables so laden with food, drink and discarded muskets and swords I was impressed by the strength of Irish trestle tables. I couldn't see her, but no matter; having spent the day on the fringes of the crowd there was bound to be a familiar face to head for. There wasn't a chance: all I could see were false beards, huge wigs, make-up and peculiar hats. Finally seeing Jill had finished serving and was now chatting away merrily with a space beside her, I cleared just enough room to further burden the table, and sat down. The food was good, and the company warm and accepting. Of course we had lots of questions to ask about boating in Ireland and the Irish, and then the conversation somehow got onto the canal-side trees we'd been seeing. When I mentioned I'd been struck by how few oaks there seemed to be, the Long John Silver opposite laughed, leant forward, and said 'That's cause your lot took them all!' He then went on to deliver a lesson on how, from as long ago as Tudor ship-building right up to the twentieth century, when they'd been taken for pit props and trench boards in the First World War, the English had helped themselves to pretty much every oak in Ireland.

I sat listening. While it was all very interesting, the two words that really registered were 'your lot'. I hadn't seen that one coming, in fact the last time I'd heard anything similar was in a Glaswegian bar, but I didn't think a fancy dress party in a County Offaly shed was the place to launch into the Marxist diatribe about colonialism and class I'd fired back on that occasion. And there was, and this was one major difference to the much angrier Scottish encounter, no malice in the pirate's statement. I understood our nationality marked us out but that 'your lot' was still rattling round my head long after we'd left the shed and were settled in our usual location at the edge of the crowd outside the pub. I suspect that, but for a peculiar meeting, it would have rattled around for rather longer.

Standing in the cool night air we quietly observed an extraordinary character. While most of the fancy dresses we'd seen were of the type easily picked up in a few minutes in any high street joke shop, the guy we were watching looked unusually comfortable in his outfit. While slightly shorter and lighter than Johnny Depp's movie character, Captain Jack Sparrow, so close was his portrayal that everyone who passed him seemed to comment. And each time someone said something he'd grin and reply with a piratical 'Ahh!' or 'Splice up the mainsails', and we even heard him threaten more than a few with 'Runnin ya thru!' He should have been drinking grog, or at the very least rum, but it seemed his chosen tipple was Coke. It was all very weird, and only got weirder when he clocked us watching him, stuck out his hand and said, 'Hi, I'm Eric.'

Eric! Surely not the self same Eric that the Hazelhatch boater had suggested we look out for, and whose number we'd been given again in Sallins? Of course it was, and yes his boat was the lovely Dutch Tjalk moored just below the lock we were above. We'd walked Hobbes past it several times, and on each occasion noted how the open stern deck always seemed to be  busy with company. He wasn't a drinker, and we'd had enough, so we offered him a cup of tea and a slice of ginger cake back on *Hawthorn*.

After being regaled by Eric with all manner of tales and stories into the early hours of the morning, we rose late on the Sunday. Well, late for us: the rest of the rally seemed to have gone into hibernation mode and it was midday before people started appearing in numbers. The real drinkers were easy to spot: they were the ones who walked about zombie like, wearing sunglasses and peaked caps and keeping their hands over their already bowed heads, desperate to avoid bright sunshine. Clearly anticipating that the Sunday was going to be about recovery for many adults, the day's events seemed to be primarily aimed at the children. With sports, modelling and miniature garden competitions, there was something for every child to be involved with, and even those that didn't compete were rounded up and Donna painted their faces. Seeing a dog show included, Jill went back to *Hawthorn* and knocked up a quick fancy dress outfit for Hobbes. She returned, with Hobbes looking distinctly self-conscious in the scaly dogfish coat she'd made from workshop scraps.

The very last gathering was the prize giving, something we went to out of politeness and interest rather than anticipation. Eric too had wandered up and we stood together at the side of the marquee while Pat announced the winners. Every child seemed to have won a prize, and we weren't paying much interest when we suddenly became aware that the whole marquee was looking at us. Eh? 'We're only chatting with Eric,' was our first thought, but then Pat repeated: 'And the best newcomers award goes to Giles and Jill Byford.'

Bloody hell! We'd won a prize! And somehow gotten married!

Embarrassed of *Hawthorn* sidled up, and took one side of the small silver cup being presented. Pat held the other, and a photo or two was taken. On my way back to Jill I passed Eric on his way up to receive the prize for best fancy dress. Then we were called again as Hobbes had won the dog show!

Our plan of remaining on the margins and trying not to be noticed clearly hadn't worked very well and, given we'd met many generous souls and been the recipients of a lot of encouragement and advice, we were very glad it hadn't. Touched by how welcoming Pat and his family had been, Jill and I made a point of approaching him before leaving the marquee for the last time. Seeing he was in the middle of a large group I gently cut in.

'We'd just like to say thank you to you and your committee, Pat,' I started, though I didn't get far before Pat interrupted me by asking 'Whatever for?'

'Well, we've had a great weekend and you've made us both feel very welcome, yet we're not very certain we deserve the trophy for Best Newcomers. Not that I'm saying we're not grateful, it's just, well, you know…' I tailed off.

'Think nothing of it. It didn't occur to us give it to anyone but you two. In fact, I don't think there's anyone in this room who would say you shouldn't have won it.'

I could sense a few grins breaking out in the listeners around us. And then, with the crowd drawn in and everyone silent, Pat leant forward. Grasping my hand, he looked me straight in the eye, and added 'After all, you are the first newcomers in two years!'

We'd made his day. Everyone burst out laughing, and Pat was still grinning from ear to ear and shaking his head when we left the marquee a minute later.

Our first rally over, we went back to *Hawthorn* and tried to find somewhere to keep our silver cup for the next year. Seeing the missing plate for where the name of the previous year's winner should have been engraved confirmed our suspicions that the reason we were of so much interest to so many was simply because we were fresh faces. We hadn't seen that coming but then neither had we anticipated such a warm welcome, or being the recipients of so much advice and encouragement. And we really hadn't expected to meet Eric. Avoiding the rally would have been much easier than attending it yet, having learnt how socially intimate the Irish waterways were, we'd survived without making some terrible faux pas. Not that we'd have to wait long for that, as I'd be putting my foot well and truly in my mouth soon enough.

EMBARRASSED IN BALLINASLOE

Our cluelessness about the Shannon was a blank space that many of the boaters we'd spoken to over the weekend were keen to fill. Places were recommended, routes suggested and advice offered. We listened to tales of wonderful quiet weekends at anchor in backwaters, the fun of being on huge rallies, the horrors of being battered by the wash of over-powerful boats and the excitement of passages down the flooded river. Lough Derg, just a few miles downstream of us, was described in glowing terms by many, with the phrase *the jewel of the Shannon* being used more than once. It sounded truly magical. Swamped by all this information we sat in the post-rally calm of *Hawthorn* on the Sunday night looking over charts and trying to decide whether to go south to Derg for a few weeks, or to turn north to the miles of interconnected waterways, loughs and canals that would fill our summer and autumn with numerous possibilities. Finally a decision was made. We'd already missed going south down the River Barrow when we passed the branch canal to it while shouting hellos to the guy on *Blackthorn* at Lowtown. So why not leave all the boating south of the Grand Canal for the following spring? From what we'd heard both the Barrow and Lough Derg were spectacularly beautiful, so saving them to last would ensure a scenic conclusion to our Irish experience. With that in mind, and Jason deservedly enjoying a day of rest, we put ourselves through the last two canal locks, and boated onto the Shannon for the first time.

Just being back on deep water and not in any hurry was a treat, and we soon settled down as *Hawthorn* pushed up the Shannon at 3½ knots. The wide and gently meandering river certainly suited our desire to go gently, to indulge in what was for us far too special a day for urgency. Other than the happy faces and waving hands of passing boaters – one of which was a 3' foam hand that had us, and the guy wearing it, in fits of laughter – all we could see of man was the odd small tractor turning hay or cutting silage, and the chimney of a power station on the horizon ahead of us. Well I say ahead: the river's gentle meanders meant it moved from port to starboard with such regularity we couldn't really say if it was ahead or not. So vast was the river's flood plain that we needed our binoculars to see distant fences strung with the debris of winter floods – a seemingly impossible event in the bright sunshine and skylark song of a late June day. Unconstrained by the dredging and straightening suffered by so many of England's rivers, the space felt larger and wilder than we'd ever anticipated, and it may have been its scale that meant we took the first opportunity presented to leave it when we reached where the River Suck joined the Shannon just below Shannonbridge.

For the first few miles the River Suck was as benign a space as the Shannon. That is until we reached Coreen Ford where we made our way round a couple of tight bends praying nobody was rushing to meet us. Upstream of it the river got progressively narrower and shallower, and by the time we were turning off into the cutting below its only lock at Pollboy, the river ahead was skipping and dancing over rocks. We felt for the lockkeeper here, for his lock had been in the most delightful spot with water, meadows and woods, and then a bridge carrying the Dublin to Galway motorway had been built virtually over his head. Half an hour later, after a run that was narrow, twisting and rocky enough to have us on our toes, we were pulling into a newly built and empty harbour in the town of Ballinasloe.

It's an odd thing how, while Jill and I had imagined all sorts of confusions, delights and shocks would come our way in Ireland, neither of us had ever anticipated it would be so rural that shopping without a car would be difficult: that we'd actually be delighted to find a Lidl supermarket within sight of where we stopped. Our huge rucksack was dragged from a corner and we took the short walk over to stuff it with pasta, rice, flour, potatoes, onions, oats, tins of tomatoes, kidney beans, chickpeas and all manner of other essentials. I barely managed to stagger back. And then we wandered round the town for a while, though the only building I wanted to go into was a second-hand bookshop. With Jill and Hobbes waiting outside, I wandered round for a few minutes. Then, unable to find anything in what seemed randomly stacked books, I opened the door and slipped out without seeing anyone.

That evening, while sitting reading in the evening sun on *Hawthorn's* bow, the sound of a foghorn and siren in the distance made us look up. For a while we'd been discreetly clocking the arrival of dignitaries and what looked like press on the far side of the harbour, so we assumed the great collection of flags, pennants and bunting moving slowly across the fields towards us had to be something to do with them. Clearly whatever the foghorn was announcing as coming our way was attached to a boat, yet the river was so low all we could see was a mass of colour seemingly suspended above the green grass. That was until it cleared the final bend, when we made out a Dutch steel cruiser beneath it all. The whole lot flew past us with a final long loud blast of sound, and pulled up beside the jetty nearest the road. The dignitaries lined up against it, a photographer shouted a few commands from the bank, and then the boat started to move away and the dignitaries dispersed. Everything had happened so fast I doubted the boat was even tied in. It was all a bit of a mystery, and would have remained so had the boat not pulled up a little way outside us.

A wild head of hair with a similarly uncontrolled moustache was thrust out of a side window and the man under and behind it all fixed us with his gleaming eyes. 'Hello,' we said, before asking what the palaver was all about, and we learned it was a publicity shoot promoting something called the River and Arts Show being held in the town in July. A leaflet was proffered though, with the cruiser several feet off our side, it needed to be spiked onto a boat hook to get it on board. Jill picked it off, looked at it for a few seconds, and said 'I know this. There was a poster about it in the window of a second-hand bookshop just up the way.'

To which the wild-haired boater exclaimed 'You don't want to give that thieving bastard any money!'

And I said 'Given the crappy state it's in I'm unlikely to.'

Oh, how the world turns on tiny things. If only I'd said 'crazy' rather than 'crappy', or considered the possibility that self-deprecation might be as much a feature of Irish culture as it is of English; if only, as his next comment made abundantly clear, the man on the boat wasn't the shop's owner.

'Ever since I opened it people have been trying to get me to tidy it. But I won't; I like it as it is.'

Coots clattering in the reed beds, the gentle splashing of the cruiser's exhaust, the rumble of traffic – I could almost hear seconds ticking as hours on the distant town hall clock. Oh God! Me and my bloody mouth! I could sense the flush of embarrassment coursing through me, and would have welcomed a vast and lunging pike snatching me from *Hawthorn's* gunwale.

There was only one thing for it: looking him in the eye I gave a sheepish grin and asked 'Have you got a spade?'

At no point had he really taken offence, but I was relieved when his loud laugh eased the tension. A brief conversation followed, and an opportunity to put things right was arranged: I'd go into the shop in the morning and, as long as his daughter – who knew where everything was, it seemed – was at work then books would be found. I should have left it there but no, I had to add to my shame by asking the guy's name.

When he replied I was sure he'd said 'Meehall'.

'Meehall?'

'That's it, Meehall.'

'How do you spell Meehall?'

'M-i-c-h-e-a-l.'

'Ah, Michael.'

'No, Micheál,' says Micheál, spelling it out again, and explaining the fada (acute accent) and how it's the Irish way of saying Michael.

'What time do you open Micheál?'

'About 9.30.'

Clearly thinking he was talking to one prize prat, Micheál put his head back into his boat and left the harbour with as much panache as he'd arrived. My embarrassment churned in his wake. Jill just looked at me, but it was one of those looks.

Allowing for Irish time, and suspecting Micheál wasn't likely to worry about the odd half an hour, I walked into his shop a little after ten the following morning and declared 'I've come to do my penance!' But it wasn't penance, far from it: the first thing Micheál offered me was a huge grin, the second a cup of coffee, and the third an introduction to his daughter Sheena. It was soon clear that when it came to finding things Micheál's relationship with Sheena wasn't unlike mine with Jill: despite being the ones to make the mess, we somehow expected the woman in our lives to know exactly where everything was.

Picking up on my preferences and tastes, Sheena began to dig out a few jewels and, as my small pile of collected literature grew, relations with Micheál took a turn for the better. After giving me stick for a bit he eased any remaining guilt by launching into a long list of tales of his own embarrassing moments. These concluded with one unrepeatable toe-curler of a story that had me doubled up with laughter and wincing on his behalf. He wasn't wrong when he boomed at the end of it 'Last night you wanted a spade – on that occasion I was looking for a fecking digger!' After shaking his hand, I left a few euro lighter, and several paperbacks heavier. We were done with Ballinasloe, and we thought we were done with its River and Arts Show, yet little did we know it was far from done with us.

While putting *Hawthorn* through his lock, the lockkeeper at Pollboy warned us to watch out for a pair of large barges working their way up river. He went on to explain that WI were dredging any shallows to ensure none of the deeper boats coming up the river, on a rally timed to coincide with Micheál's festival, were damaged on shoals or shallows. We'd just had a bit of a close shave with a hire boat full of lads charging up it at full throttle, so going down river with the flow through those tight bends, with a chance of colliding with something much larger, harder and even less manoeuvrable, was not an appealing thought. Tiptoeing down with just enough throttle to keep steerage we were relieved to clear the tight rocky bends and to return to water wide enough to pass the barges when we met them. The only really tight spot left between us and the Shannon was Coreen Ford, and we'd be unlucky to find them there. Typically, just a couple of hundred yards above its first blind bend, a RIB came up the river to meet us, and we were told to pull over: the barges were dredging the ford itself, and we would have to wait for as long as that took.

With nothing to tie to, we motored *Hawthorn*'s bow into the bankside reeds, turned the engine off, and sat eating lunch in the company of the brown-eyed cattle drinking from their watering hole beside us. When the barges did come into view we were glad to be well out of the way for, while one was a rather pretty workboat about the size of *Hawthorn*, the other was a large pontoon with a big digger sat on it. They were strapped side by side in a hellish solid raft we would have very much been the worse for hitting. At least here the river was wide, though why the workers on the barges were waving their arms and yelling at us to slow down when we were stationary in the reeds was a complete mystery. All was explained the moment we looked behind to see the hire boat we'd just missed earlier coming as fast as it could down the middle of the river, pushing a huge bow wave with a mountainous wash rolling down both banks behind it. Seeing we were going to get battered, we hung on and hoped we didn't get driven too far into the field. Fortunately, and this was our first lesson in the damping qualities of reed beds, the greenery we were jammed into took most of the force, but the working boats just downstream of us did a bit of a dance of their own. As did the men on them, and the air filled with a peculiar cacophony of colliding metal, slamming chains and pretty much every swear word and rude gesture imaginable. By now, fearing we might need help to get off the river's edge, *Hawthorn* was in reverse. We moved, and the lads on the dredging kit gave us the thumbs up. We were able to go on our way.

Keeping a little over to leave room for any boat coming upstream, we made our way round the dredged bend. Except it wasn't dredged: with a violent scrape our starboard side suddenly lifted and, while I was still lunging for the drive lever to take *Hawthorn* out of gear, *Hawthorn* then dropped off whatever we'd run over. Somewhere beneath me there was the most enormous bang. I almost went through the roof with the shock of it. What in hell's name was that?

Leaving the engine ticking over and out of gear, we listened. Unfortunately whatever we'd hit was only half way round the bend, and without the engine in gear the flow was now pushing us ever closer to the bank. Fearing we were about to ground in the river's shallow margins, I tried the drive. Everything sounded and felt normal, and we were able to cautiously make our way into deeper water. The bang had been so violent it felt seriously terminal, almost like a shotgun going off. Ah! Got it! That's why it had been so bloody loud, and why nothing seemed to be broken: the boat had slipped off the rock, the prop had hit it and, just as John from our hydraulic suppliers had promised it would, the pressure relief valve had opened with a mighty bang. Now I was truly thankful we'd found out we had the wrong hoses a year earlier: if we hadn't, we'd now be drifting, with oil everywhere and no means of getting ourselves moving again until a hydraulic engineer could get to us. The only downer was a slight leak from our stern tube.

Knowing the dredging crew were going to have to come back through the ford, I rang Pollboy Lock. The dredgers hadn't got that far yet, so the lockkeeper redirected me to the Inspector of Navigation. Within minutes of reaching him we'd been offered the use of a dry dock in Shannon Harbour to fix our leak, a navigation notice had been published about the hazard and the dredging crew had been detailed to return and sort out whatever it was we'd hit. I doubted things would have been nearly as easy if we'd been through something similar in England. Relieved to know the end of our world wasn't imminent, we reversed off the reeds we'd drifted against while on the phone and slowly returned to the Shannon. Joining it, we immediately pulled in at Shannonbridge.

While the hydraulic drive had been one pain in the arse to get right, it had been worth it: we'd no bent shafts, torn-out bearings or engine mounts, cracked drive plates or couplings. Even the propeller had come through a massive impact unscathed and the leaking shaft was starting to reseal as Paul promised it would when I rang him that evening. *Hawthorn* was holding up, and we were soon moving north again.

LOUGH REE

'Oh my, that's mad,' I exclaimed, pulling the engine stop and letting *Hawthorn* drift on Lough Ree. With 60' of water below us, a calm day and the nearest land the islands we'd passed between a few minutes earlier, we weren't going to hit anything. We went and sat on the bow and looked north up the lough to where the water fell over the horizon, and then east to the thin smudge of shore-side green between the water and the sky. We knew from our charts that Lough Ree had to be big, yet the reality of being on it was enough to induce both excitement and fear, with the tiniest dash of smugness thrown in.

Jill and I had been reaping the rewards of our intentional ignorance of Ireland, the Irish, and how fresh and new everything felt since leaving Dublin. We'd been fascinated by the landscape and people we'd seen and met on the canal, relieved by the warm reception in Shannon Harbour, and surprised by the River Shannon itself. Yet, it had been easy to compare each of those experiences: the Grand Canal was superficially similar to many waterways we already knew, the boating folk at the rally harbour weren't that different to many we'd met in England and, while a little broader and wilder than most we'd known, it wasn't hard to compare the Shannon to other rivers we'd spent time on. But we'd never boated anything like Lough Ree, and to have first primed ourselves by looking at images, or even worse taken a sneaky peak with a short diversion when we drove close by in 2007, could only have reduced the impact of first experiencing it.

Taking in Ree's scale also brought a sense of guilt at just how easily I'd thought 'Yeh, yeh! It can't be that big or that bad – it's only a bloody lake', when kindly souls, and there had been more than a few of them, gently suggested we needed to be wary of it. I appreciated their caution and comments now, particularly once I considered how we were experiencing this space in the benevolence of a calm summer's day when the water reflected and refracted the light so much the white cruiser in the far distance appeared to float in a shimmering haze just above the water. How much breeze would be needed before boating became uncomfortable could only be guessed, but seeing the length of potential reaches and the absence of shelter left us thinking it wouldn't be much.

A little spooked by the lough's scale, as we'd felt when first boating the Shannon, we decided we'd bolt from its wildness into the Inner Lakes due east of where we'd rested. Here we hoped to experience a night anchored at a spot we called Ted's Mooring.

We'd briefly met Ted – a boating biking mate of Eric's and the second name on the piece of paper handed to us by Gene in Sallins – at the rally. Yet we only really started getting to know him when he and his girlfriend, Joelle, called on us at Shannonbridge while we were waiting to make sure our stern tube had stopped dripping. While we put the kettle on they peeled their leathers off, and then we all lazed about in the sun discussing the River Suck's vengeful spirits and our plans while in Ireland. Seeing the vast empty spaces of our cautious charts, Ted had asked for a pen and offered to add possibilities.

And that was when he pointed to the corner of Ree, and suggested Coosan Lough as a spot to anchor in for a swim.

'But we can't go in there, there's a no-navigation cross on the entrance.'

Ted laughed, coughed an expletive, and pointed out how hire companies liked to keep their boats on the main system where problems were less likely to occur and easier to deal with if they did. He'd then put a large X roughly where he'd anchored at, and I took the pen and wrote his name beside it while half-jokingly saying we'd know whom to blame if it didn't work out.

Grateful for the confidence our GPS gave us on this vast space, we started the engine and boated due east towards the woods of Hare Island. Drawing nearer, we could then make out the channel into the Inner Lakes, and it wasn't long before we were passing through a narrow pinch point and the water was opening up again in front of us. We found ourselves looking down a straight length of water about a quarter of a mile wide and maybe four times as long. Acres and acres of reed beds made a daunting task of working out where water stopped and land started and of finding the much narrower channel Ted had pointed out. Fortunately a speedboat suddenly appeared beside us, and when it roared down the lake and then turned sharply into what looked like reeds and land, we guessed we were following either a suicidal maniac or someone who knew where to go. Chasing his wake we found the opening, and a couple of minutes later we were leaving the reeds and entering a pool of about twenty acres. After the shock of first seeing Ree, it felt wonderfully sheltered and intimate. Keeping a careful eye on our depth gauge, we motored over to where we guessed X marked the spot, and dropped anchor in ten feet of water.

What little breeze there was slowly blew us round, and the anchor chain came tight. Ted's mooring was perfect: we couldn't see a house, there were no other boats and, other than the splashing and calling of water birds, the distant rumble of Athlone's bypass was the only sound. Finding the sort of magical adventure we had hoped Ireland would deliver, we decided this was the ideal spot to spend our first ever night at anchor. Our third very different mooring in as many days, we were rapidly learning how much variety was possible when it came to staying on the Shannon at night.

Seeing our stern tube resealing, Jill and I had left Shannonbridge for the monastic site of Clonmacnoise. Once again we found ourselves in a broad, flat landscape watching towers on the horizon meander from port to starboard and back again. In this we were no different to visitors using the river for the past millennium for, unlike the modern monstrosity of the power station now astern of us, these stone round towers had been built by monks when Clonmacnoise was a centre of early Irish Christianity. Now an important heritage site with no pub or shop for miles, we'd been told – by Micheál no less – that the only people who stayed there overnight were those wanting a dark and silent night of remote peace. He was right: come the evening there were only a few boats left and, as if to reward those that remained, dusk brought the treat of hundreds of swifts filling the air above the river with a swooping, chirping joy. The uplifting beauty of the night's dark silence was so intense, and so much what we hoped to experience in Ireland, that we got greedy and decided to stay for a second. This was a mistake as a boat full of serious drinkers arrived, fired up a BBQ on the jetty beside us and ran a generator into the early hours while they partied. We left early the following morning with rather more noise and haste than was necessary in the hope we might disturb their lie in, and with people shouting after us that we'd left our dog. 'He's not ours,' we shouted back. 'You can have him!'

When first walking off the jetty after arriving at Clonmacnoise, what we thought was a Golden Labrador appeared to be stuck up to its belly in the soft sand of a little beach. Guessing it was in trouble, we went to see what could be done and realised our mistake: it wasn't stuck; it just had improbably short legs. Not knowing if it was wild or stray, the next mistake we made was rewarding its wagging tail and imploring eyes with a biscuit.

For the next two days the dog we called Clonc was a constant companion, either lying beside *Hawthorn* or wandering round our gunwales looking in our portholes. Which was fine: we didn't feed him and he seemed to take himself off home at night. The problem was that he wanted to come walking with us, and his short legs weren't short enough to stop him chasing cattle, or to prevent him raiding the site's visitor centre. Its staff obviously knew him well, but everybody else assumed the bugger was ours and it seemed we spent all our time trying to explain he wasn't. We were glad to abandon him in the end, though looking back as we left we noticed he wasn't long watching us before moving on and staring in the window of a hire boat, wagging his tail and giving it large with his eyes. He'd lined up his next bunch of suckers, and we were already forgotten.

Arriving in Athlone a couple of hours later we were put through our first Shannon lock, above which we pulled in to meet the Assistant Inspector of Navigation who'd seen us from his office beside it. Knowing we'd smacked the rock on the River Suck he wanted to check all was well with *Hawthorn* while, needing to register our home on the Shannon and wanting to say thank you for all the help we'd got from WI both on the canal and since our grounding, we were happy to see him. The registration couldn't have been less painful: just one A4 sheet of questions and no fee at all and we were, very happily, on our way.

Needing to shop, we moved to the river's other bank, which gradually filled with hire boats. By the evening the only space left was the one reserved for the Viking Trip Boat we'd watched plying its trade from below the town's castle. It was immediately astern of us and, conscious we were in the middle of  a busy town, when it came to moor at the end of the day I took a rope and asked its skipper what sort of night we might expect.

He paused to think a moment, and then said its being a Thursday meant we'd probably be fine, and then he set about propping his boat several feet out from the shore with long steel poles full of embedded nails. I'd never seen anything like that, and it rather undermined all his verbal reassurances. We needn't have worried, for nobody seemed intent on being a pain in the arse, and when we did have visitors aboard they came from the water and were invited to moor beside us. They were off to a restaurant and the high spirits they arrived in were nothing compared to those of their return at midnight: the women had a full glass of wine apiece, and the men a pint of Guinness in each hand. In order to make life safer and to reduce spillage, we opened the wheelhouse as a shortcut for their giggling and laughter. We'd expected our night in town would bring some excitement but this was fun.

After the noise of being in Athlone, our first night spent at anchor, on the hook, with only the distant squawk of a heron and clattering of coots disturbing us, was a joy. The light breeze of the afternoon had dropped to a flat calm by evening, and in the gathering gloom of late dusk I ran Hobbes ashore with the dinghy. We slept with the windows open to hear the sounds of water birds splashing and calling in the reeds about us, and thanking Ted for his chart marking.

Winching the silted and lily-leaved anchor back into its hawse pipe the following morning, we returned to a Lough Ree that was even calmer than the day before. Having been so blessed, we should have been relaxed and at ease, but we were in a state of nervousness fuelled, rather ironically, by the time we spent in a lake boat on Lough Corrib on our holiday two years earlier.

Dog tired from the slog of building *Hawthorn*, we'd chosen the west of Ireland to see what we made of the country. There had once been plans to stop and look at some of the waterways, or to use the rented cottage as a base to explore them from, but all we really wanted was a few quiet days walking and some local boating. Jill and I had been taken down to the shore to be shown how to use the lake boat that was our main reason for choosing this property, when I casually commented to its owner how surprised I was to see so few boats on the lough.

'You won't be once you've been a few hundred yards in that,' he replied, going on to add 'The lough's as much rock as water, and not just random shoals but whole slabs of jagged keel-ripping nastiness you'll need to keep an eye open for.'

And he wasn't lying: we'd only gone a few hundred yards before the water ahead of us changed colour from blue to white, and we'd had to skirt a football pitch sized slab of limestone that lay just under the water's surface. After just a few short trips we were so struck by how dangerous the lough was we were surprised anyone boated it at all.

It had spooked us, and we'd carried that memory with us onto Ree which, at least to my ignorant mind and eye, appeared to be very similar. We could see no reason it wasn't and I soon felt I couldn't trust the GPS chart we'd bought believing it to be the most up-to-date chart of the Shannon. While no expert, I knew enough about maps and charts to suspect the straight lines and regular, evenly spaced contours on the screen weren't true representations of what was beneath us. So we used the electronics to give us position and the binoculars and hire chart for direction, and kept a watchful eye on our FLS in the hope it would warn us of approaching shallows and impending disaster. Above all else, we made absolutely certain we remained inside the water defined as safe by navigation markers. We might have been less nervous if the lough had been busy, but it wasn't: for most of the morning we had it to ourselves, and when we did see another boat it was static off a little island.

Assuming this was a local boater, I envied him the excitement of being able to wander at will, to fish or swim or simply chill, in the almost private space beyond where we less confident and competent boaters ventured. Exploring islands, anchoring in sheltered bays, discovering routes for ourselves: these were all things not really possible on fresh water in England, and one of the motivations for bringing *Hawthorn* over the Irish Sea, yet to see the reality of doing so was daunting. I was optimistic there might come a time when playing in this way might be possible but, for now at least, I vowed to be a good boy and not a wanderer.

Ted and other boaters at the rally had told us that the problem with Ree was the absence of moorings, and we knew from looking at our chart that we had very few options. Although its apparently filter-blocking weedy canal made it out of bounds to hirers, we headed for Lecarrow harbour. The harbour was small and busy and the only gap was between two expensive-looking GRP cruisers. Though I was sure we'd fit in between them, their owners were soon out on the quay offering help, taking ropes and nervously watching. We'd inches to spare, and all was well with the world.

Much later a man on a little white cruiser asked if he could tie alongside. So it was my turn to help someone in, and while doing so I couldn't help but notice his decks were covered in blood.

'What is all that? Are you okay?' I asked him.

'I'm a little cut up.' The boater, a short, bearded fellow I judged to be in early retirement, turned a foot over to show me his sole. It was lacerated, and looked very sore.

'What happened?'

'Well, I thought I'd visit an anchorage I used to go to years ago. Only I got the wrong island.'

'Wrong island? You weren't just off one of those in the middle of the lake?'

'I was. And I went aground and couldn't get off.'

'We saw you and assumed you were at anchor fishing or just enjoying yourself.'

'I know, I had no radio or I would have given you a shout.'

A stranded boater radioing for help! That would have taken our day's excitement into the stratosphere. Would we have gone? Of course, though I'd probably have put the anchor down and taken the dinghy first though, as the boater soon explained, the barge would have been needed to free him. He'd worked as a diver and thought nothing of going over the side to see if he could push his boat clear, but the rocks were covered in Zebra mussels and their sharp shells had cut his feet. He looked reasonably fit but the idea of him floundering around in the water on his own, miles from help, was a scary one. At least there weren't piranhas in the Shannon.

'It must have hurt but you did well to get afloat again,' I suggested.

'No, couldn't shift it. I had to ring for rescue and the buggers wanted €300!'

'€300! That's a lot of money!' My initial thoughts about the excitement of being a rescuer were suddenly tempered by hearing that Ree had no lifeboat and many rescues were made by private enterprises from various locations round the lough.

'We came to an arrangement when getting me back afloat only took a minute. I was lucky to be carrying some cash.'

Early next morning his engine made an effective alarm call. Once awake, there seemed little point in lying in bed. So it was still very early when we had walked the dog, eaten breakfast and slipped our lines to set off back down the canal. Conscious that those who'd helped us moor the day before were probably lying waiting for the crunch of steel against their craft, I was relieved to get away using ropes and bow-thruster and without having to hand over insurance details.

We only boated the short distance across the lough to Barley Harbour, and then only because it seemed silly not to explore the lough while the weather was so gloriously good. Though, at least according to our cautious charts, even Barley Harbour comes with a warning: it's not to be used in winds from the north as there's no breakwater to prevent waves from that direction smashing a boat into the harbour's stone structure. However, on a calm day with the sun beating down, it was hard to imagine a more peaceful or beautiful place anywhere.

Everybody has his or her own idea of what constitutes a great mooring, and Barley Harbour ticked all our boxes as we sat on the grass and indulged in the view of sky, water and islands beyond *Hawthorn*. The absence of roads meant Hobbes could wander about the grass and go in and out of the slipway to paddle and swim. It was heaven, so perfect we felt we should share it, which we did when two couples arrived with a picnic.

One of the women had briefly lived on a boat in London, so she was over in a flash to have a chat with us. As we usually do on such occasions, we invited her in to have a look round. This then brought the equally curious remainder of her party to join us, and we soon learnt that they were not two couples but four old friends who gathered at Barley Harbour once a year. Hampers were opened, wine was uncorked and a vast array of treats was spread about. Unfortunately, with each assuming another would pack them, nobody had brought plates or cutlery. *Hawthorn* was raided, and the invitation to join them we'd earlier refused as politely as we could became a demand. Not only had we already eaten, we didn't want to intrude on their reunion, so we promised to join them later.

We'd already seen numerous examples of why the Irish are famed for their hospitality, and we were to be the beneficiaries of copious amounts of it that evening. Wine, beer, champagne, strawberries, cake, and lots of conversation, flowed freely. I lay in the warm sun wondering how you topped this or who'd believe we'd been so royally spoilt by strangers. The grass was damp with dew and the light failing when they finally called it a day, and we bid goodbye in the car park and returned home laughing in wonderment at such an unexpected treat.

SHANNON MEANDERS

English people used to be renowned for their willingness to wait patiently. It may have been true of a wartime generation clutching ration cards, but I doubt it's true now, and I know for certain that both Jill and I would rather do anything than queue. Which was why we turned and bolted the moment we saw the dozen or so boats waiting to get up the first lock upstream of Lough Ree at Tarmonbarry. Backtracking a few hundred yards, we turned east into the short canal with one lock that connected the Shannon with the River Camlin. After the vastness of Ree, the Shannon had felt much less threatening since we'd returned to it at Lanesborough, and the canal now seemed positively tiny. After years of what's disparagingly called ditch crawling in England, this morning's variety of huge lough, large river, tiny canal and – though we didn't know it yet – the twisting narrow river Camlin, just a few hundred yards further on, was so much more interesting and fun than we'd anticipated. The constantly changing nature of the Shannon and its connecting waterways was still surprising us almost daily, and would continue doing so for a good while yet.

Above the lock we passed within a hundred yards of the entrance to the Royal Canal. The second waterway connecting the Shannon to Dublin, it had been undergoing restoration for decades. As I'm sure he regularly did, when I asked the lockkeeper when it would open he'd smiled and said that 'There were men who'd been asking that since they were mere boys, and they were now dying of old age!' Thinking it might be fun to go back to Dublin along the Royal, and knowing it was the one bit of water Roger wanted to join us for, we were disappointed to hear that we'd need to stay a lot longer to boat it.

Thoughts about canals to Dublin were soon forgotten on finding the Camlin as challenging as anything we'd ever boated, and steering *Hawthorn* round its many tight turns both demanding and exacting. Done correctly it was all a bit of fun, and even getting it wrong wasn't the end of the world: as long as we

missed the many dark and stubby twisted alders growing at the water's edge, all we crashed into was the soft soil of the river bank or the more giving foliage of a young willow tree. Beyond the bankside trees were flat damp fields broken only by barbed wire lining drainage ditches, and beyond them the birch, bracken and gorse of the bogs we'd become so used to seeing on the Grand Canal. There was nobody about, and while there weren't any signs saying mooring was welcome, neither were there any saying it wasn't. Fancying another night in a different space, we pulled into the bank and called it a day.

We'd only missed a couple of miles of the Shannon by boating round Tarmonbarry lock, yet the river we joined the next morning was very different to the one we'd left. It felt as if we were boating a series of reed-bound loughs with short connecting links of more conventional, almost parallel-banked, river between them. And here I assumed was the difference between Irish and English waterways; the rivers we'd known in England must have been like this too before the value of land brought drainage and dykes to curtail their wild spirits. And then we came to Rooskey and met another extraordinary lockkeeper so happy to chat that he kept others waiting. He seemed as excited about our voyage as we were and, like Ted, was soon penning our charts with marks that promised adventure. Amongst the spots he was keen for us to visit was a series of loughs and cuttings along the Grange River that ran west into Lough Boderg a few miles upstream of where we were chatting.

Constantly blurring the juncture of land and water, ringing islands and announcing shallows, reed beds are a feature of the Shannon. A boon to wildlife, they're full of warblers, grebes and clattering coots; and swans, mink and even otters patrol their edges. We were becoming used to seeing them all the time we were travelling, and nothing gave us more delight than stopping where we could hear their breeze-blown rustling through our open windows while we lay in bed at night. We considered this sound the song of the Shannon, and couldn't imagine the river without it. Curiously, maps and charts do not define the reed-filled spaces, and we were often confused at seeing swathes of green where we anticipated water. And nowhere was this truer than the world we joined at the Rooskey lockkeeper's bidding.

The reed beds at the edge of Boderg were as vast any we'd yet seen, and the marked channel through them to the Grange River wound to port and starboard, before straightening as it passed an attractive stone quay and ran through an arched stone bridge. We should, at least according to our charts,

have soon entered the open waters of Black Lough. But we didn't: where our charts were showing acres of blue, all we could see were swaying reeds. We were in a maze of pools and channels so twisting and winding I doubted anyone would find their way without the navigation markers. Eventually entering open water, we passed a tiny island with a shrunken, almost bonsaied, tree and one solitary swan nesting on it, and it was only here that we got our bearings.

We were on the cusp of three loughs – Black, Grange and Kilglass – the latter being accessed by what, given the chart showed parallel banks and a straight course, could only have been a manmade watercourse. Given a choice of controlled or wild we were only going to choose the latter, so we pushed through one final narrow channel, and entered Grange Lough. Almost immediately both the reed beds and the bottom – we were soon boating in nearly fifty feet of water – dropped away. West of us a long, narrow, reed-bound lake stretched for nearly three miles. At the far end of it we pulled into a mooring outside a pub, the Silver Eel, and a family who stepped off a hire boat to offer their help took our ropes.

Our greeting party were Irish dairy farmers, and the fuss they made of Hobbes instantly endeared them to all of us. They'd been hiring boats for more than enough years to have learnt the art of slowing down, of not joining the tearing hordes who want to see and do as much as possible in their limited time afloat. So we stood on the grass while the farmer pointed out how most hirers roar round both Grange and Kilglass in a morning, and then go back out to the Shannon and onto a busier mooring overnight. It baffled him, but then I suppose the natural pace of dairy farming probably doesn't bring the urgent rush of most modern lives. While we were chatting, Hobbes had been pushing his luck as always, and got a result when the farmer's wife put a plate of ham and egg, not just any egg but a duck egg, on the grass. If dogs could smile he'd have been beaming as broadly as I was when I accepted a similar offer.

Hobbes was having a great day for, on top of all the extra eating, he was able to play in the shallow river that runs down the side of the Silver Eel. I'd taken him over with a ball for what we called a splash and he'd done his usual thing of getting the bloody thing well out of my reach and setting about his own game of pushing the ball under water and catching it when it shot up. Knowing he was now content for hours, I wandered up to the road bridge and was surprised to see the river beyond it was not nearly as wild as I'd anticipated: its banks were nearly vertical and made of cut stone rather than loose rock and soil. Finally getting hold of Hobbes a few minutes later, I mentioned what I'd seen to the farmer, and asked if he had any explanation.

He had: in fact it seemed he had an hour-long lecture on how the variation between summer and winter levels had been much greater before the river was re-engineered in the mid nineteenth century. With a wry smile he pointed out the great beneficiaries of the river's taming were landowners like him: how, by controlling the water's level, vast acreages of what was once boggy low-lying land dried out sufficiently for it to be used for pasture. He suggested that it sometimes only took a casual observation of shorelines to see where the levels had once been, and then went on to say the stream Hobbes had been paddling in was once navigable. If we ventured up it by canoe or dinghy, we'd come to a large lough and a series of further loughs and waterways. It seemed the potential for messing about on the water in Ireland just went on and on, and then the local kids came out to play and we witnessed lots more fun.

The gathering of wet-suited, excited children and their chattering parents beside *Hawthorn* that evening didn't really make any sense. None of them went in the water, and there were no canoes, sailboards or water toys to be seen, and then a speedboat roared into the bay and pulled up at the very end of the jetty. A flat board with what looked like foot straps was passed out and, while a child was fastened to it, a rope was taken from a locker and attached to the boat. A minute later the child with the board on her feet was attached to the other end of the rope. And then the boat took off with the child astern standing on the board and dancing gracefully across its rolling wake. The fun went on late into the evening, and we were still hearing distant screams and splashes long after it was too dark to see the swifts that had been swirling all about us.

LOUGH KEY

As we'd hoped, getting to Ireland under our own steam meant we'd finally stopped worrying about our engine. While I still checked its oil and water daily, in the excitement of exploring we rarely gave it any thought. And then, without a hint of a miss to announce what was coming, it stopped.

This was the deadly scenario of not being able to stop or steer that we'd imagined with the drive failing, so we were lucky there were still a hundred yards of reed-lined shore between us and the railway bridge. And then we were luckier still, for the bridge was covered in scaffolding with men working on it. Fortunately, rather than having to quickly drop anchor in the hope it would stop us before we creamed into steel and stone, the line we were on took us straight into a friendly reed bed. Here, just as on the River Suck, the greenery quickly absorbed our impact and only then, not knowing how long we were going to be there, did we drop anchor.

Not immediately descending into the angry despair I usually did at such moments was a positive thing. In fact, not having seen a chandlery or workshop on the water since arriving, that we'd broken down next to a field full of cabins and engineering kit for the workers on the bridge made me feel our good luck was back. I could even see a diesel bowser. Lifting the board over the engine, I dropped into the engine bay to see what I could find. It didn't feel like we'd run out of fuel – I've run out of petrol and diesel enough times over the years to be familiar with the pattern of coughing and hunting that comes with that. I checked anyway and, as expected, we had enough fuel for many more hours. Neither did it feel like a seizure when the engine locks from lack of oil or too much heat; something I confirmed when it turned over happily on the starter motor. Clueless and concerned, I rang Walsh Engineering.

They were as baffled as me. So I spent half an hour scratching my head and wondering how I would go for help, when the phone rang. It was Steve from

Walsh Engineering. He wanted to know if the spring at the back of the pump was still attached.

'What spring? And where?' Shining a torch where Steve guided me, I found the spring. It was broken.

'I'm not surprised it stopped dead; without that you've not a drop of fuel leaving the pump!'

It seemed we'd suffered something so rare even our experts were briefly baffled. Still, the good news was a spring was in the post, and a fiddle with a pair of long-nosed pliers would make a more than adequate repair until it arrived.

The engine started, and we both reflected on just how lucky we'd been for it to fail when it did. Being close to the scaffold was bad enough, but it was going to let go one day and when it did we could easily have been on a flood, approaching moored cruisers or even going into a lock with boats already in it. We didn't want to think about the damage we could do to others, so we didn't: we boated the half mile or so to the next lock. Arriving while it was closed for lunch and with no Camlin-type loop to get round it, we pulled onto the jetty below it to wait.

Becoming accustomed to how often both private and hire-boat skippers made misjudgements, the roar of an engine and the bang of a boat hitting the jetty behind us just a few minutes after we arrived didn't warrant any interest. But the rush of paramedics past us fifteen minutes later did. With the jetty behind us crowded with people, we stayed aboard and watched as a man on a stretcher was carried to a waiting ambulance. Locking the boat's door, a white-faced woman and a teenage lad followed. We were soon to learn they had approached the jetty with the lad on the helm and his dad on the bow, and then it had all gone pear-shaped with a panic on the throttle, slamming the bow into the jetty so hard the father was catapulted over the bow rail. Their boating holiday had finished the moment the man's ribs broke as he landed half on and half off the jetty. Given just how close we'd been to a major disaster with a barge and a scaffolded bridge, we couldn't help but reflect on the fickleness of luck.

While everyone on the south Shannon seemed to suggest the place we had to visit was Lough Derg, north of Lough Ree people's enthusiasm seemed to have shifted to Lough Key. Already extolling its virtues before we asked him about dog walking, the Rooskey lockkeeper had taken his pen and ringed one mooring. 'There,' he'd said, 'is the best mooring for dog walking in the whole of Ireland.' Then, in common with others before him, he'd waxed lyrical about how boating up the Boyle River to Lough Key was in itself a wonderful experience. To get there we had to go through the town of Carrick-on-Shannon which, after the rural nature of our week on the river from Athlone, we were looking forward to visiting.

After nights in the dark and silent wilds, staying in a busy town centre had little appeal. We arrived the morning after our engine had briefly stopped, with the intention of quickly grabbing all that we needed and then heading out again. Promising to catch up with Jill to help hump the shopping back, I took a diversion into a second-hand bookshop. Unlike in Micheál's shop, I didn't need a Sheena to find what I wanted, and I then got lost in lust over an early edition of Mark Twain's *Life on the Mississippi*. Although I already had a modern paperback version, it wasn't the same thing: it lacked the charm of this version's hand-cut pages, wonderful paper and font and its etchings, though it did only cost about a tenth of the €50 being asked for this hardback. I dallied so long Jill was quite fed up by the time I reached the supermarket, though at least I hadn't compounded the sin by being indulgent.

Back at *Hawthorn* we were invited for a look around the large and busy trip boat *Moonriver*, and then fell into conversation with the owner of the barge moored beside us. Irish generosity being what it is, he stopped us when we were untying our ropes and said we were welcome to help ourselves to his mooring and power any time we were on Lough Key. Our intended hour in Carrick had become nearly three; we were still chatting about how kind everyone was when, a little over a mile upstream of the town, Jill put the wheel hard to port and we left the Shannon for the Boyle River.

The Boyle has all the loughs and islands, short river sections and arched stone bridges of the Shannon. It's just they're all smaller and packed into just a few miles. Finding it every bit as beautiful as we'd been promised, we were tempted to indulge in the immediate views of water, meadows and woods; or to look further at the high rolling hills in the distance, and we would have done had not the volume of traffic in the narrow sections made concentrating essential. It was fun: so much fun we were disappointed to reach the lock at its end in only an hour.

We seemed to have a gift for arriving at locks during the hour between 1.00 pm and 2.00 pm when they closed for lunch. Unfortunately the jetty at

Clarendon Lock was short and already full of hire boats. All we could do was put a line ashore from our bow to the jetty's downstream bollard, and let the flow from the weir beside us hold *Hawthorn* against the rocky bank. And then we sat on the bow in the sunshine listening to the tumbling water and looking at all the woods around us. It wasn't exactly a hardship, and if we wanted amusement we weren't long waiting.

The angle of the small cruiser's bow, the rolling wake astern and the way it ignored the queue and headed straight for the lock's opening gates had us convinced we were about to see a gang of young lads out on the tear. It wasn't: to our amazement, when it passed us we were greeted by toothless grins from two men old enough to be long retired. Their laughing and shouting was so good-natured that, despite our being banged against the rocks by their wake, being annoyed by their lack of boating etiquette simply wasn't possible. Somehow managing to hit both lock gates on their way in, they then passed their lines up to the waiting lockkeeper. Though, when I say lines, I really mean two very short lengths of what looked like baler twine. Not long enough to go round the bollard and back, the lockkeeper tied them off ashore. We pulled in behind them.

While the lock filled the men shouted greetings, roared and laughed, and we smiled and watched and wondered at the merriment of it all. When the lock gates slowly opened the guy on the little cruiser's wheel rammed its large outboard's throttle hard open. If they'd untied their ropes they would have launched out like a rocket, except they hadn't: the boat moved as far as the slack in the ropes would let it, and then slammed into the lock wall. Befuddled by the absence of go, the man gave it all the throttle he had. The air filled with steam and smoke, through which we could just make out the lockkeeper gesticulating fiercely while shouting to, or maybe at, the men. The engine died and, with a look of contempt and bewilderment, the lockkeeper untied the cruiser's ropes. This brought a loud cheer from the men, the throttle slammed fully open again and the cruiser took off along the lock wall before bouncing into the now nearly open lock gate. Somehow missing the first of the waiting boats above the lock, it shot round the bend in front of us. Catching the lockkeeper's eye I smiled and shook my head. We didn't speak, but I've no doubt my eyes mirrored the baffled surprise I saw in his.

The great news was that Lough Key was every bit as beautiful as we'd been promised. Water and land met in the solid greenery of long-established deciduous woods with the junction of the two seamed with densely flowered rhododendrons tumbling into the water. It was full of wooded islands, beyond which the higher land ringing the lough rose. It was almost too pretty, too much like a landscape constructed by Capability Brown for an eighteenth-century romantic, to be real. And that was before we turned a corner to see the island with the ruined castle. Opposite and overlooking this, tucked into its own reed-greened shore in the shelter of a bay behind a wooded hill, was the

mooring on Drummans Island we'd been promised would be a happy haven.

Knowing it was small, and fearing the disappointment of finding it crowded, we approached without much optimism. Yet there was space, and better news followed when Hobbes's spontaneous testing raid on the boat next door was greeted with affection and laughter rather than the usual howls of protest. The owners of the boat he'd intruded on had dogs of their own, and stopped our apologies by gently pointing out the name of their cruiser was *Paws*, and saying they doubted Hobbes could do anything they'd find more distressing than seeing his freedom curtailed. Even without the friendly dog-loving company, a jetty surrounded by woods and walks with a view of a castled island and no traffic for miles would be a simple description of heaven.

It seemed inevitable that, however much we were enjoying Ireland, there would be things we'd taken for granted in England that we were going to miss. Yet, with BBC radio on the Internet and with no need (touch wood) of the National Health Service, initially there hadn't been anything. And then we reached the River Shannon and, in the regular nightmare of finding somewhere to walk Hobbes twice a day, the absence of England's maze of public walks and bridleways was really felt. Since leaving the Grand Canal, most of

our walking had been on roads and lanes. We knew from years afloat how boating speeds made the pace of roads quite terrifying, but here the lanes were narrow and we'd press into the hedge while a car would shoot past with the driver waving, despite often having one hand busy with a mobile phone. So it was a huge relief to find Drummans Island was in a forest park with miles of walks both along the water's edge and through wood and meadows.

How odd it was that this, superficially wild, space was the most familiar one we'd been in since leaving England. It looked and felt, and even sounded with all the barking dogs and playing children, like one of the English parks or National Trust estates Jill and I both knew so well. We weren't even really on an island, just a bulbous peninsula with a shallow, darkly silted canal cut across the neck of land. We crossed it on an arched stone bridge, and walked the avenue formed between two rows of huge cedars whose bark had been polished smooth by clambering children. Ignoring the brutal concrete tower we could pay to climb for a view of wood and water, we reached the car park and crowded visitor centre. Jill waited outside with the dog while I went in. I was gone a lot longer than the promised minute, and returned without the ice cream I'd intended (and Hobbes would have got the sticky end of) but holding a book *Rockingham. Memories of a vanished mansion* explaining all that lay about us.

We hadn't been very wrong in sensing something of the National Trust about the place. For, until very recently, the space the public were now playing in had been the King family's demesne of Rockingham. Both it, and countless other thousands of acres of Roscommon, had been granted to their forebear, Sir John, by Elizabeth I in reward for his being 'very influential in the reducing the Irish to due obedience'. I assumed that meant he'd killed a lot of Irish and, reading that the family were given more land by later English royalty, I also assumed his descendants had carried on reducing the Irish. Still, despite their wealth and power, they couldn't have been that happy: there's more than a hint of keeping up with the Joneses in their engaging landscapers and architects in the early nineteenth century to make the already glorious romantically sublime.

As if that wasn't weird enough, I was astonished to read that the castle on the island in the bay below us – The Rock – was a folly which, at least if the book was to believed, had been the source of the poet W B Yeats's 'unique and mystical style of writing'. I knew enough about Yeats to recall the Nobel Prize committee had credited him with giving expression to a whole nation; to read he'd found this while in a folly built by the English family he was staying with seemed strangely ironic.

Deaths, taxes and the Irish Land Commission all having taken their toll on the King family estates, and with the house Yeats had stayed in burning down in 1957, the land at Rockingham had reverted to the Irish people in the early 1960s.

Seeing all the fine oaks on the walk back home reminded me of the comment over supper at the rally back in Shannon Harbour, and I guessed the King family were the 'your lot' the pirate at the fancy dress implied I was one of. If that had been true my family would have been the ones shooting and fishing, or demanding that the police in the local town of Boyle cleared the streets of barefoot children and badly dressed adults; and wanting to see that caps were lifted and heads were bowed as their cavalcade swept by. Your lot! With a grannie terrified of going to hospital because she was old enough and poor enough to remember the word being a euphemism for the workhouse, I knew my lot would have been scurrying round the passages and kitchens the Kings had built underground to keep the servants out of sight, and that meant we Byford's had a lot more in common with Irish workers than we ever had with the landed gentry. By now uncertain if the Kings and their descendants were English, Anglo-Irish, or simply just rich and powerful, I was rapidly losing interest. Happy to leave the past alone, I closed the book, called Hobbes back from his begging beside *Paws*, and went for a stroll in Rockingham's present.

Taptap. Tap. Taptaptaptap. Taptap.

What the? It's dawn and I've been woken by the oddest of sounds.

Taptap. Tap. Taptap.

No. There's definitely something really weird going on. So I get into my shorts and shirt, and go into the wheelhouse.

Taptaptap.

Whatever it is it's in the workshop. Gently easing the door open I look in. I've half a notion the little people are hard at work making shoes or tents or whatever it is that little people make. But it's not fairies, pixies or goblins I've heard hammering, it's the bloody great raven standing on the gunwale banging at the porthole glass with its beak. I've no idea why or what it's after, and it doesn't hang about to explain. I could curse, but I don't, for that raven's done me a huge favour.

In my rush to find out what was going on, I'd come into the workshop without taking in the outside world, yet going back to bed I pause to do so. What I see stops me in my tracks.

All week we'd been watching boats hired from the jetty near the visitor centre being rowed out to The Rock, and their occupants scrambling over it. And every evening photographers walked round from the car park to stand beside us with the light behind them to get the best-lit pictures. They should have come at dawn, and not bothered with the cameras. For there are times when just being in the present is so much more rewarding than trying to capture it. So I leave the camera below, open the doors to the dawn chorus, and sit in the wheelhouse watching the light and mist playing over the water, trees and folly castle. It was a view I'd been seeing without feeling for days, and now feeling it I wonder if I've been a little too hasty in judging Yeats's genius.

This was the day we intended to walk to the Kings' town house in Boyle that, like their estate, was now a public space and included an art gallery. That there was also a farmers' market in its courtyard each Saturday may also have been mentioned. We dragged the big rucksack we use for such expeditions out of its corner, put our boots on, and readied for a long stroll. Except it wasn't: to get off the jetty we had to pass a little cruiser, the owners of which we'd first met down river and were now getting to know rather better. While we dismissed it as just a stroll, they were appalled we would walk that far. They were going to Boyle by boat and we were implored to join them. So we did but, and they'd known Hobbes a day or two by now, only once they'd hidden all their food and sealed all their cupboards. Not used to boats as small as this one the experience was good fun, particularly when we realised how much a cruiser moved and rolled in waves *Hawthorn* would barely notice. And then we were in the shelter of the River Boyle, though only very briefly as we were soon joining the canal that led to a rather grand harbour.

We were already having a magical week, but the display of local cheeses, pâté, meats, fresh vegetables and fruit, a fish stall and all manner of other treats, was something we'd not seen before in Ireland. The market was busy so, with equal reluctance, Hobbes and I backed out and settled in a shady spot while Jill went in for a hunt.

She returned a few minutes later with coffee and cake, though I did wonder why she put a foot on the straps of her little rucksack when she took it off and sat down to join us. The answer arrived on the breeze a few seconds later: she'd bought a cheese so richly pungent she was concerned it would be off and running round the streets of Boyle if it ever glimpsed a chance of freedom. It wouldn't have gotten far, for Hobbes had backed off in alarm and was now standing, one paw over his nose and his hackles raised, ready to kill or be killed. Bloody hell fire, Tony Blair had gone to war on flimsier evidence of chemical weapons than what we were now lumping about! Still, having the beast in the bag did mean we sat and drank our coffee in an uncrowded space, and not a soul stood near us while we wandered round King House looking at its displays of art.

Once out of the town we walked along quiet lanes for half an hour. Reaching Rockingham's woods we took a track and meandered home. Far from being a chore, the walk had proven the perfect way of getting the appetite that the treats in our rucksacks warranted.

LOUGH ALLEN

We left Lough Key and set out for the highest navigable stretch of the Shannon at Lough Allen. A swan going to the same point would have flown just seven miles; for a fish or a boater it was three times that. It was another one of those days that would astound us with its variety of water: we may have started and finished on large loughs, but in between we'd twisting rivers, islanded loughs and even a long canal to climb. By the time we were leaving the Shannon to join the Lough Allen Canal at Battlebridge, the river ahead of us was so shallow children were paddling across it. Except we didn't turn into the lock: as usual, it was lunchtime, so we had to moor below it.

Chatting to a lockkeeper who spends half the year working a seasonal shift for WI, and the other half teaching English as a foreign language in Italy, waiting didn't hurt. Which was fortunate, for even after lunch we had to wait for the boats coming down to clear a section of canal too narrow for boats to pass on. When we did get going it took a little while to adjust to losing the speed we'd become accustomed to in just two weeks on deep wide water. That was my problem; Jill was perfectly happy walking Hobbes up the foxglove-festooned towpath. Drumleague lock at the canal's mid-point was deep, very deep, and with racks in the gates high above us we feared a serious soaking while it filled. Not helping was how the lock had been badly automated, with the controls so far back from its edge the keeper couldn't see the boat in it. It didn't matter: he went gently and we survived. Above the lock our dawdling pace and open doors meant we couldn't miss seeing how thick the banks were with wild raspberries; we knew we would just have to harvest them, though that meant we'd have to come back with the dinghy. In less than an hour we each picked a large bowl of the sweetest, ripest berries we could imagine finding anywhere, and then we finished a disjointed but strangely perfect day with a walk to a shop in the town of Drumshanbo, just beside us, to buy sugar for jam.

That we were about to head into a space even wilder than Lough Ree was made clear by the warning about weather on the hire-boat company's chart. Not being on one of their boats, we ignored the instructions to ring one of their marinas before going onto it, choosing instead to listen to the coastguard's forecast and to stick our heads out the window. Both suggested all should be well, and we rang the lockkeeper we needed to clear the third, and last, lock on the canal.

After all the insistence that Allen was a huge, deep body of open water likely to kill us, we were surprised to find its first mile was shallow and sheltered – though only until the markers ceased, the banks fell back and we found ourselves on the lough proper. It's huge, virtually without any shelter and, seeing the mountains that rise from its shores, we could appreciate both its reputation for suddenly changeable weather and why it's the least boated of all the Shannon's navigable waters. Which is a shame, for it's daunting and frightening – and really quite special.

The other reason we've heard for people avoiding it is because it has only two moorings, and neither of these is near a shop or a pub. With the weather fine and the day quite calm, we avoided running into the cages full of young salmon that are the only obstacle in the middle of the lough, and headed for Spencer Harbour on its western shore. Where, despite the plentiful jetties, the only other boat present was a steel Dutch cruiser.

Nearly everybody we'd met on the water had been interested to know what our plans were, so we'd had a number of conversations about Lough Allen over the past weeks. While some had wondered why we'd venture to such a godforsaken space, other people had been more positive, and a few had suggested we should try to speak to a man called Norbert, who by all accounts virtually lived there. While we'd been given his phone number and email address, we assumed the river would do as it had with Eric and Ted, and that we'd bump into Norbert when the time was right. And so it was, and we'd only been in the harbour a few minutes when the tall, sleight, man on the other boat padded his bare-footed way down to us, stuck out a hand and said 'Hello, I'm Norbert.'

'Norbert? Surely not the Norbert who spends months at a time up here?'

The odds on its being a different Norbert were slim, so why I even asked the question defeats me. Of course it was 'The Norbert' and, of course, we sat in the sun and became willing listeners as he shared a little of his vast knowledge of the lough. He'd been coming here for years, although initially only twice a year on month-long pilgrimage breaks from his busy and pressured retail job in Germany. It seemed there was something about Allen's emptiness that suited him and made it the place for him to relax and wind down. Perhaps he'd excelled at this, for he finally wound down to the point he couldn't wind up again. After packing in work he'd bought the tidy but unpretentious Dutch steel cruiser we'd seen him get off, and never looked back.

Allen's remoteness makes it an obvious choice for the Norberts of the world, and he spent months at a time there. Fishing seemed to be his greatest passion, and he had even taken a good fish from beneath the jetty we were sitting on. He smiled when he told us how he'd dropped a spoon into the water and had been picking it up with a magnet when he felt a series of sharp knocks. Trying again with a rod and lure a few seconds later, he'd promptly landed a three-pound perch. That's the sort of fish I only dream about, and yet here he was catching one while washing up! I suppose you've either got it or you haven't.

Fishing, and a desire to spend time in silent solitude, were the reasons Norbert knew the lough well enough to be able to potter about in all sorts of sheltered and private spaces outside the marked navigations we were so consciously respecting. Though he did stress caution: Lough Allen was the reservoir used to control the Shannon and, even without a change in weather, a man many miles away only had send an electronic command to open sluices and the water level would start dropping. Hearing this explained our surprise at joining Allen through a lock with two sets of breast gates: one to put a boat up onto the lough, and the other down. The difference was potentially many feet and, as Norbert pointed out, sneaking in over and behind a sand bar didn't mean you were going to get back out.

Norbert bore all this in mind when he began to mark our charts with routes and anchorages we might like to have a go at over the next couple of days. The details were wonderful, and he added sandy-bottomed bays good for lying at anchor in, rocky shoals to be avoided, various sheltered inlets and even a route up the River Shannon from where it left the lough's northern shore. The Shannon route came with enough warnings that we thought we'd save it for a dinghy run rather than risk beaching our home miles from help, but many of his markings promised the adventures we'd hoped Ireland would deliver.

Norbert's knowledge wasn't restricted to boating, and he soon set about explaining the history of where we were sitting. Again, as I'd so easily missed how industry had shaped the Bog of Allen, I hadn't realised that the rural tranquillity surrounding us in Spencer Harbour had an industrial past of barges loading coal and iron, or bricks from the works in the field beside us where, as Norbert pointed out, a chimney and buildings could still be seen. There had been a village here, though without a pub. So the men would row the six miles to the town at the top of the canal, Drumshanbo, for a pint or two. Unsurprisingly, as small boats on large lakes are deadly in bad weather even for the sober, the drowning of returning drunks was not uncommon. To give us an idea of just how rough the lough got, Norbert told us there were times when even the sheltered jetty we were on moved so much the only way he could get up it was by crawling. If the jetty was bouncing that much neither Jill nor I could imagine just how rough it must have been in his cruiser, and it was one experience we were determined to avoid if possible.

Knowing we were going for a long walk and he was headed away to solitude, we thanked Norbert and said our goodbyes. After filling a water bottle, we dug out Hobbes's lead and the map we'd bought in Drumshanbo the previous afternoon. Our hope was to walk to the top of the hill beside us on the minor lanes that ran up it, which we might have done if we'd twigged the map's scale was half what we were used to, or if we had left much earlier. Breaking through the treeline, we stopped at a waterfall the weather had left nearly dry, and while Hobbes tried to cool off in ankle-deep water, Jill and I sat and took in the view.

With the exception of the grey water far below us, and the grey-blue sky high above, virtually the only colour visible for miles was green. The lough was framed with a ribbon of dark green deciduous trees; the hillsides above that were a patchwork of light meadows and dark conifer plantations. The bogs and moorland that topped the mountains were mottled greens of numerous tones. Knowing that green was a colour Jill struggled to paint, I couldn't help but tease her that she'd be driven to abstract landscapes or go mad with frustration. We watched Norbert's cruiser, the only boat on miles of water, push east from our mooring and then turn north to head up the lough. Thinking how slight our chances of meeting Norbert would have been if he'd been hiding in one of his secret spaces, we were grateful for our earlier good fortune of catching him while he was briefly somewhere public.

Returning to *Hawthorn* we removed our boots and sat on the jetty with our feet in the water. Bloody hell it was cold, more than cold enough to instantly dismiss the swim I'd been talking myself up for on the trudge back.

To cover all possible boating options in Ireland we'd brought an inflatable kayak with us from England. There we'd occasionally use it to paddle a couple of miles down the canal on a Sunday for a couple of pints in the pub, and we hoped to get a lot more fun and value out of it, gently exploring the margins of the Irish waters. Seeing it might suit the options Norbert had given us to play in, I dragged it out and blew it up.

Unfortunately the following morning the weather had changed, and waves rolling up the lough ruled out many possibilities. Except one island, Inishmagrath, which had shelter behind it. Dropping anchor in 6' of water we clambered into the kayak and, with Hobbes between us, paddled ashore. From a distance we'd thought the island was covered in trees, but it wasn't: there was a ring of them round its edge, but its centre was a large round meadow. It was a bit like a giant tonsured monk's head, except it had a tumbledown cottage for an ear, and an old church on its crown.

The church appeared to have been derelict for some time, but while most of the cottage was in the trees, the modern concrete blocks used to rebuild the gable we could see suggested it may have been used recently. Which brought on a brief conversation about the reality of being able to survive off a few acres and half a dozen sheep, and the mental qualities required to do so. While we didn't doubt it could be done, even in the kind weather of a decent day we knew it wasn't for us. Neither was the lough's second mooring at Cleighran on Allen's eastern shore. It wasn't a happy spot for us though, leaving aside the absence of walks, the close proximity of a road and the mooring's exposure to the north and west, the reason for much of our unhappiness there came from a place and time we were trying hard to forget.

In much the same way we couldn't possibly sell *Hawthorn* knowing she was potentially a deathtrap, once we'd sorted all our issues we then found ourselves having to deal with the moral dilemma of deciding if we should publish what we'd been through. It wasn't something either of us wanted to do, but then we knew the only reason we, and Don who'd now changed his, found out about the steering issues on our homes was because someone had suggested they were dangerous. The thought of having to explain to a Coroner's Court why we'd remained silent made the decision for us. We'd not rushed in, but having been badly burnt in not getting qualified advice when building *Hawthorn*, we'd had the article checked by the legal and technical experts we'd need to call on if we had to defend it, before sending it to the specialist boating magazine keen to publish it. There had been a further delay while they took their own advice, but that it had now been published was clear from the emails friends who'd read it were sending. While supportive and full of kind intentions, these mails only made us feel as if we were picking a barely healed scab we were trying to forget having. While all that misery now seemed a long way from our joyful Irish present it was still close enough to give us both a sleepless night.

While Allen itself was very quiet, a lot of boaters are happy to go only as far as the moorings in Acres Lake beside Drumshanbo. There was only one week when the canal from there to the Shannon was really busy, and that was the week the town filled with musicians attending a major traditional Irish music summer school. Ignorant of this, we'd timed our run down the five miles and two locks between the town and the Shannon for when the school was starting. There might have been a time when spending all day on such a short distance would have driven us both mad, yet falling into the cheerful company of other down-bound boaters, and with the sweetest, ripest wild raspberries we'd ever seen within easy reach, here it seemed a blessing.

Liking Lough Allen and being delighted to have met Norbert, we felt we were only just beginning to get to grips with its potential as a space outside the norm, as somewhere we might hide and be private in. Yet it wasn't so remote that our phone stopped working and emails ceased, and that they did changed our world. We were done heading north and, while we didn't yet know it, our days of solitary work-free wandering were coming to an end.

NOT SO ALONE

It was easy to feel chuffed with how much fun we were having exploring Ireland and meeting the Irish, and how vindicated we felt with our devil-may-care sure-it'll-be-grand attitude. Yet the one, critical, element of our non-plan that hadn't worked out quite as we'd anticipated was finding the cost of living much higher in Ireland than we'd expected. Though it wasn't one we were relishing, the answer was for us to exploit the fact that we'd arrived with a workshop full of materials and tools, and the skills to make a little money. Unfortunately, like our budget, it wasn't nearly as simple as we'd imagined, for it seemed that the majority of Irish boat covers were unlike anything we'd made before.

I'd spent all our boating years looking over every cover we passed: seeing how well it fitted, how it was made and, particularly if something was different and better, how it had been put together. The moment we knew we'd really got the hang of the narrowboat covers our business was built on in England, was when one of our larger competitors started copying something I'd designed (I didn't mind as I'd started by copying them). And then we'd come to Ireland where there were few boats of the type we were familiar with, and many of the cruisers we did see were very grand things with flybridges and acres of cloth stretched over huge and heavy stainless frames. If that wasn't challenging enough, these cloths were held down with a complicated array of buckles and strange fittings, and full of zipped sections the making of which we couldn't imagine. Creating such things seemed improbable, and we weren't long seeing there weren't nearly enough narrowboats in Ireland to keep us going. So the only chance we really had was to make repairs, or to see if we were offered something better suited to our existing skills.

Looking at it when we got to the rally, we were relieved to see that criterion did apply to the small barge that had passed us on the Grand Canal near Robertstown, and that its owners were serious about our designing and pricing a cover. We'd taken photos and made measurements, and then scarpered up river promising we'd be in touch with ideas and prices. While all fine and dandy in the beery joy of that weekend, by the time we'd been offered the work a few weeks later, we were nervous as hell about it. Not because the owners were awkward or for matters of money, but because by then we'd become aware of the intimate nature of Ireland's waterways and knew a lot of people were going to be watching what we did. Which was great if all went well, and grim if it didn't. At least the barge being in Shannonbridge meant we had a few days cruising to enjoy before biting the bullet.

Covers, work and the cost of living were forgotten for the few days we had to run back downriver. Retracing our steps so soon felt odd, though knowing where and when to plan to stop made life even easier. We shopped in Carrick but only for an hour, as we wanted to overnight on the quay at the top of the Albert Canal we'd used when coming upstream. We'd liked this spot not only because it was walled and gated and Hobbes's wanderings were restricted, but also because the stonework beside the water was full of nesting swifts, and we took joy from watching their comings and goings just a foot from our portholes. Less fun was seeing a cat try to exploit our gunwales to get amongst the nests. Opening the door and hissing 'Cat! Go get!' we sent Hobbes out to see him off. Some chance: once faced with all its teeth and claws and hissing, our boy backed down and wandered off.

One thing did change once we started to boat on water we'd already been on. Way back in early 2008, Paul had gifted us a book of aerial photographs of the Irish waterways he thought we might enjoy looking over before we left. While doing so had been very tempting, we feared seeing images of the spaces we'd be boating would diminish the shock of experiencing them, so we buried it beyond temptation. Now we dug it out and, applying the rule that we'd not look at any places we'd not yet visited, went over the pictures of the northern Shannon. We were immediately relieved not to have looked before, for what we saw on its pages was far removed from what we were seeing from the water.

All the photos in the book – Kevin Dwyer's *Ireland, The Inner Island* – were taken between 1997 and 1999. What immediately struck us was how quickly the Celtic Tiger's impact had changed the land beside the water, as spaces that were just fields in the photos were now full of houses and marinas. Which wouldn't have been the end of the world if they were occupied and lively, but they weren't, indeed far from it: everywhere we went on the north Shannon there seemed to be rows of unloved and unfinished buildings.

Just below Rooskey's lock was a development of at least fifty dwellings in different states of completion, and there were more in Carrick-on-Shannon, Leitrim village, Cootehall and Boyle. In fact the only place that didn't seem to have changed at all was, quite appropriately for once, Clonmacnoise. We knew the Celtic Tiger had long stopped roaring, that these abandoned houses were unlikely ever to be finished, yet where they'd been built was so rural and distant from any major town or city we were at a loss to understand who was going to be investing in such unrealistic real estate. The extent of the dreaming, the idealised vision, was clear when we walked the dog past the Rooskey development and stopped to have a look at the promotional poster pasted to its hoardings. A smiling man, a woman and two perfect happy children looked down admiringly on the boat moored in front of their perfect house. Two houses by the drive into the site appeared to have been finished and occupied; yet all there was behind them were overgrown ruins. We were grateful that we'd arrived long after the party was over, for I'm sure we'd have really struggled to cope with its full-blown swing.

We were in Lanesborough when we saw a barge approaching with bodies readying ropes and dropping fenders. It was clearly about to moor behind us, yet we didn't want to rush out and insist on taking ropes as we know not everyone, including us at times, needs or welcomes offers of help. Offering help got potentially trickier when we saw the rope wielders were women, so insisting on taking a line had the added potential of being seen as patronising and sexist. It was all a bit of a minefield, but standing like a lemon waiting to see if a rope was going to be passed was no help either. The approaching boat's long fast bow and huge stern counter suggested speed and power, and its decks were much higher than those on the ex-working barges we were used to seeing. Guessing that was going to make getting ropes ashore harder than would be normal on a low squat beast like *Hawthorn*, we offered help. It was graciously accepted, and introductions were made. They were almost not needed: we'd been told to look out for this barge, *Knocknagow*, as its skipper, Brian, ran a website called Irish Waterways History, and he was much too well connected to be unaware of our wandering presence. Not that this immediately came up as, in a scene reminiscent of the child catcher in *Chitty Chitty Bang Bang* (though without the dancing) Brian set about scattering the quayside with dog biscuits from the deepest pocketed trousers we'd ever seen. His own dogs weren't that bothered, but Hobbes tore into this manna like a half starved beast and, fearing his bursting, Jill and I were soon giggling and scrabbling about on the flagstones collecting as many biscuits as possible while promising he'd get them later. We were invited aboard and stood on the huge open stern deck while Brian suggested a glass of whatever it was he had in the large, translucent plastic container he was proffering. Which, despite looking like Tilley lamp fuel, we were delighted to find was a rather good cider. And so it began.

Brian and his family were on holiday, and their barge appeared to have been ballasted with all manner of good beers, a staggering amount of very fine cheese and, judging by the volume of treats being offered by Brian's wife, Anne, their daughter and her partner, somewhere on their travels they must have cleared a large deli counter. We sat in the evening sun eating and drinking and discussing all manner of things. Then, with ominous black clouds rolling up Ree behind us, Jill and I, and Hobbes of course, were invited for supper below.

It was some night, and while I couldn't recall all that was discussed, I do remember that our being on Lough Allen brought an explanation that the reason the Irish had traditionally preferred burning peat to coal wasn't just because they cut their own turf but because coal needed to be burnt in a grate. And grates were expensive and only lasted a year or two. While an odd thing to remember, in such small details a much larger picture could be glimpsed. Stuffed in every sense, we left at half eleven. Early the following morning, while I lay in sleeping off the night's excess, Jill got up to bake bread. Then, in a small gesture after

such largesse, she popped next door with a still-warm loaf.

Expecting to be in the busy noise of Shannonbridge for the rest of the week, we spent our last wild night on the river back in the entrance to Coosan Lough. Anticipating solitude and dark silence, we were surprised when a boat pulled alongside us. Surprise turned to delight when we recognised Norbert. He'd spotted us through the reeds and bushes, and called in to see how we'd got on. I suggested a glass of whiskey…

Our few days of merriment and relaxation felt a world away when we arrived at Shannonbridge. The boat we were working on was waiting, and we had a few days to complete the work before the customer returned. First things first, I took a cup of tea over to it, removed the existing cover that came down at angle that made ducking under it awkward and standing upright impossible, and sat looking at what we'd committed to. Two cups of tea later we started.

Not having bent stainless tube or worked with fittings and battery drill, let alone the sewing machine, for months, work was a shock. Being in the public space of Shannonbridge's harbour also meant we got the odd interruption, particularly from members of the Heritage Boat Association (HBA), which includes owners of many former working boats. They were gathering to start their summer cruise the following Saturday.

Our customer being an HBA member, we'd promised to have the new cover fitted on the Friday so they could leave with the rest of their gang the following day. In all our years making covers in England we'd never got used to the nervousness that comes when a customer first sees what we've done on their boat. Yet there, we had a long-established reputation and plenty of work; while here in Ireland, where everyone knew everybody and we were newly blown in strangers and possibly chancers, we waited on judgement knowing it might dictate whether we ever worked again. We missed our customer's arrival, but not their single word text 'Yippee!' Relieved of England joined Happy of Ireland on their boat and a pint in Killeens with the gathered HBA gang was suggested and welcomed. They were all headed for a week cruising some of Lough Ree's less boated margins, and we were invited to join them. Curious to see beyond both the buoyed navigations we'd been cautiously respecting, and how Irish bargees spent their holidays, we weren't long accepting. Things were going along nicely until I risked asking what time people were leaving.

'Twenty to or twenty past?' said someone at the bar.

Various answers came back, and it was soon clear that the fleet would be leaving at both times. As I suspect was intended, our confusion at the absence of further detail brought smiles. And then someone explained that twenty to was early and twenty past was late, though it may have been the other way round, and no idea of a more precise time was offered. It didn't matter as nobody seemed in the least bit bothered, and we were going to have to stop in Athlone anyway. Finally hearing the fleet would be gathering in the only part of Ree we knew quite well, Coosan Lough, at least meant we knew where to head for.

Passing where we'd drunk whiskey with Norbert just a few days earlier, we arrived on the lough's open water expecting to see a great raft of boats. They weren't there. 'We've been played! The buggers!' I briefly thought before seeing, against the trees in the distance, blue flags flying. And then the VHF radio we'd previously only really used for weather forecasts cracked into life: '*Hawthorn, Hawthorn, Hawthorn.* Are you receiving?' We were, though the radio was not needed when a RIB full of grinning lads roared to meet us.

So much for our knowing Coosan: we'd no idea that hidden within a few boat lengths of where we'd spent our first ever night at anchor was the most wonderfully secluded and sheltered spot. We followed the RIB in and saw half a dozen barges and a number of cruisers with their bows into the reed bed nearest the open lough, and their sterns pointing towards the treed bank a few yards behind them. People were sat in wheelhouses, on cabin roofs and dozing idly in floating tenders. Our bow joined the others in the foliage, our stern was tied off to the last boat, and we were in. It couldn't have been easier.

There wasn't much going on: a swim was suggested at one point but those who'd been there before remembered how, with the lough being bottom fed through a number of springs, there were patches distinctly colder than comfortable. It seemed the only energy being expended was that by wet-suited youngsters having fun with the RIB, a rope and a wakeboard. As with the kids at the Silver Eel, it looked fun, but not having a wetsuit or the courage to ask for a go we sat in the sun chatting. The HBA's plan seemed to be to have a good time and to let everything else depend on where the weather and peoples' fancies took them. Which left Jill and me thinking that the HBA's week seemed like our year in miniature.

That evening everyone piled into dinghies and tenders, and headed to a patch of scrubby woodland on the lough's southern shore. Here, with trees growing through it and sheep sheltering below it, were the remains of one of the unpowered wooden G Boats built during the Second World War, or Emergency as it's called in Ireland. The wood had long since rotted away, but this one was built with steel bow and stern sections. There was no mistaking their shape, and closer inspection revealed that the steel used must have been of good quality for it was remarkably un-pitted for its age and exposure. Knowing it was possible that the G boat in the trees beside us may once have been towed by one of the barges we spent the evening relaxing on only made the whole experience odder.

Our destination the following day, a little bay with a castle beside it on Ree's west shore, was called Safe Harbour. Before breaking the fleet and heading out, there was a brief discussion about what names to use on the VHF radios. Something that probably seemed a good idea and a bit of fun to those familiar with each other, but one that succeeded in completely confusing us. In recognition of our services to the boating community in finding the rock on the River Suck, we were called *Minesweeper*. The only other name I even briefly remembered was *Rubber Duck*, though I had no idea to which boat it referred.

Being the last boat to arrive we were the first to leave and, having taken a direct route up the lough while some of the others tacked west into the weather before turning north, we were the first to Safe Harbour. We anchored, the next barge – the now familiar
4B – came alongside us and then an M boat joined it. Each arriving boat tied off the one next to it and, by calling boats to join in an order that made mechanical sense, a solid raft was soon built.

While it was likely to have been used by both the Celts and the Vikings, the most obvious historical remains on the Rindoon peninsula are those of an Anglo-Norman castle and defences. Going ashore in dinghies and tenders, we wandered about taking photos and upsetting nesting jackdaws. After we'd returned to the boats some crazy loon suggested a swim before leaving. People disappeared to change, and why some took their time to don wetsuits was obvious the moment I (and it was only I for Jill's somewhat saner) leapt in: it was so cold the first impact ripped the breath out of me. Still, the layer of insulation Jill's cooking has built up over our years together served a purpose, and I was in for longer than first seemed likely.

Where we'd only gone north and south, the HBA now headed due east across the lough's broadest section towards the sheltered security of a bankside mooring on the River Inny. Our being first into Safe Harbour brought the benefit of leaving last, and following those who knew where they were going made it easy for us to take our time to study the landscape and to have a proper look at the poetic-sounding Inchturk and Inchbofin islands as we passed them. Clearing the sandbar where the Inny River flowed into the lough with only a couple of feet to spare, we motored up the rapidly narrowing river in the fading light. The other boaters had seen how Hobbes struggled over some of the boats, and we were grateful to see that a space next to the bank had been left for us. Other than a tiny laneway that appeared to stop the moment it crossed the river on the bridge limiting the barges' navigation, we were in the middle of nowhere.

This laneway proved a godsend the following day when, the heavens having opened in the morning, the presence of a motorcycle on one of the barges made collecting cars possible. Ever since arriving at the rally in Shannon Harbour we'd been watching with interest how the Irish engage with their children and how they were encouraged to play together yet welcomed into any adult group almost as equals. And then there was the adolescent independence of having RIBs and tenders to play with, and as much water as anyone could want to learn to sail on. While our experience was limited to the kids we'd met while boating we'd been struck by how confident and happy those children subsequently seemed. This theory might have been stress tested when two days of cold wet weather promised the potential of explosive cabin fever amongst the cruise's younger members, but this was denied when it turned out the ever caring adults had only gone and collected the cars to take children to the nearest cinema.

Jill and I used the cold wet weather to take a good look over the ex-working barges moored around us. Most of these were the M boats that had worked up and down the Grand Canal and the rivers Barrow and Shannon. These were identified by a number – the older the boat the lower the number – with the oldest dating from the early 1920s, and the newest the late 1930s. Many had been laid up as trading dwindled and then ceased altogether in 1960. At a little over 60' long by 13' beam they were big hulls, and once idle they became attractive prospects for conversion by those with a little money and good hands.

In addition to the Ms there were a number of even older barges, including *4B*, and a few tugs and private launches in the Heritage Boat Association's fleet.

An untrained eye at a gathering of English ex-working narrowboats would see only virtually identical vessels, lovingly kept as close to their original working state as possible. In contrast, the Irish owners of ex-working boats had kept their hulls and numbers, and then built the superstructures needed to make boating enjoyable in the country's inclement weather. After the restricted space of ours, we envied them their massive wheelhouses, which were more than capable of seating over a dozen people in comfort, and it wasn't surprising that they were the centres of social gatherings. Some of these boats hadn't changed hands since being restored, but they all seemed much loved, and the staggering number of rally plaques they boasted was evidence of just how long they'd been valued.

Despite its having a saloon more than big enough for the twenty plus people who'd played Trivial Pursuit in it the night before, the following morning I was to get a lesson in how fast *4B* was through the water. Leaving the Inny River just behind us, it gradually drew alongside when we reached the open lough. Seeing its skipper, Cliff, beaming broadly, I guessed we were being gently challenged. So I nudged our throttle a little bit further, and Cliff nudged his. Now committed to playing silly buggers, I gave the throttle all we had, and watched our speed go past 6 knots. We'd nothing left, but *4B* had: Cliff waved, bowed and opened his throttle further (I've no idea if it was flat out) and we could only smile and wave at his grinning, laughing family, and turn across its wake as its skipper eased *4B* further on.

Their stern was the last we would see of them, or of any of the folk we'd spent the past few days with, until the autumn. We'd had great fun, and didn't doubt more was there to be had if we stayed, but our once empty diary was getting crowded: we were going north to Enniskillen with Eric and Ted.

MISFITTING

While we'd travelled the Grand Canal alone, and had needed and welcomed the peace, we were more than ready to see what being amongst the Irish boating public would bring when we arrived in Shannon Harbour. It had been great, and even after that event we'd been relieved to find the Shannon a much more sociable space than the canal had been.

The way the river brought boaters together in and around its locks while travelling, and its harbours when at rest, felt like the perfect balance to us. As had been beautifully illustrated by the ride to Boyle, the surprises of meeting Norbert on Lough Allen and *Knocknagow's* crew at Lanesborough, trying to guess what was coming socially on an unplanned day was a fool's game. If we'd been allowed to design the perfect mixture of solitude, sociability and surprise we wouldn't have been able to come up with something that suited us better. So, particularly given how content we were, we'd thought long and hard before signing up for heaven knows what with Ted and Eric.

Many of the great friendships we'd made boating in England started when we shared a double lock with another narrowboat. Finding the two crews got on and travelled well together we, or they, might adjust our plans in order to keep the bonhomie coming. Sometimes we'd stay in touch, and even for the years we were static working and fitting out Hawthorn, we'd have the joy of friends calling in for a few days. Then there were those people we couldn't drop fast enough: those boaters who expected us to do all the work, made comments about how the country had gone downhill since Maggie's demise or even said we shouldn't stop where we'd suggested because it smelt of curry. It was surprisingly easy to invent reasons to stop, to turn in another direction, or to invent work that needed to be doing. I'm not naïve enough to think this didn't work both ways: people desperate to lose the leftie-leaning *Guardian* readers with the ever-hungry dog did exactly the same to us. But that was in England and, even before Ted rang to say he and Eric were headed north and to ask if we wanted to join them, we were quickly learning that boating in Ireland was very different.

Though I don't like the word unbelievable, I couldn't help think it when I put the phone down after Ted made his suggestion. I hadn't said yes, that was a decision I could only make with Jill, but taped to the noticeboard inside the door I was leaning on was the note from Gene in Sallins with Ted's and Eric's names and numbers on. Where we'd once laughed about the chances of meeting either of them, we now worried that the intimacy of Irish waterways meant we'd not be able to drop them by saying 'We're just stopping for water' or 'We've a job to look at…' While this did bring pressure, we only had to look at how every suggestion we welcomed brought only good things, and there was something about Ted and Eric that promised adventure. So it was decided: we'd join them on the wall in Lanesborough and move upstream from there.

Meeting where we did answered a question we'd been asking ourselves the past few weeks: where did Irish boaters get their diesel? The complete absence of any options for refuelling other than hire companies' expensive pumps (which we never saw private boats use) had been troubling us for a while now. So to arrive at Lanesborough to find Eric and Ted digging fuel cans out from lockers was interesting. The interest didn't last: even with tiny tanks to fill when compared with *Hawthorn's*, Ted and Eric seemed to spend all day walking to and from the petrol station a few hundred yards up the hill from where we were moored by the bridge. Clearly we were going to have to give some thought to refuelling or, as Eric appeared to have wisely done, bring a mate to do the heavy work.

Given we were guests and the destinations were unknown to us, falling in with the HBA's timekeeping had been a simple thing to do. Not nearly as simple was finding that departing Lanesborough to begin our run north crept ever later the following morning. Eric's declaring 'I don't do mornings' the night before had boded badly enough, and Jill and I were pacing up and down in eagerness to get gone long before there was any sign of life on board *Nieuwe Zorgen*. Our frustration at the delay was only compounded when a hire boat tied outside us, and its crew disappeared into the village.

The problem with leaving Lanesborough late in the morning was that Tarmonbarry lock was closed for lunch when we got there, the holding jetty below it was already full of boats and more were waiting in the pool beside them. This gave us a chance to find out how well Hawthorn's anchor would hold three barges – something that might prove handy later – while we had our own lunch.

Though, as we did on our first run up river, we should have headed for the Camlin. Instead we lost three hours, and then found we couldn't all get into the lock together. Ted and Eric went on, while we spent half an hour discussing the frustration of leaving late and wondering how long we'd last if today turned out to be normal. And then things just got worse when, instead of going on to Dromod as agreed, we found Ted and Eric above the lock at Rooskey. With Jill having to catch a train from Dromod station first thing in the morning we had no choice other than to go on alone.

Fortunately, Eric's barge can be sailed, and there's nothing like sailing as a bonding exercise. With Jill in England, Ted away for a couple of days, and Eric's mate recovered by his wife, Eric suggested there was no better way of killing time than taking *Nieuwe Zorgen* for a blast round Lough Bofin. I agreed, though not knowing the first thing about sailing I was swamped by just how much I had to learn to help set the mast and unfurl the sails. There were luffs, halyards, lifts and leeches, and by the time we got to foot and head all I knew was mine was fried. Clearly enjoying himself, Eric seemed to delight in my confusion, as I did his when what we'd rigged didn't function as he'd intended. When correct only a mechanical heathen would have failed to appreciate the simplicity of how it all went together, and the way the counterbalances on the mast's base made lifting its great weight a simple operation. And then we pulled it back down, put the ropes running up it where they should have been, and pulled it back up again.

Clearly I wasn't the only one fascinated by the transition of *Nieuwe Zorgen* from a state of compromised grace to one of considerable beauty; we seemed to have gathered quite a crowd of onlookers. Now getting close to where we needed to be, we sorted and tidied a heap of ropes, pulled the heavy canvas jib sail out from its locker and, apparently, hanked it onto the rope called a forestay, and then readied the mainsail. There'd been a fair bit of head scratching but, finally, we were able to stand back and declare Eric's home ready for action. Chuffed at our success, we put the dogs on board and the kettle on the hob, and motored out of the harbour.

I can't deny my excitement at the thought of sailing, and I was looking forward to the rush of wind filling the slack canvas and the groaning and whistling of all the rigging. None of that happened: the sails flapped a bit, and the only whistling was the boiling kettle.

Our lack of pace didn't matter. The silence and peace of sailing is so utterly different to the steady throbbing of a diesel engine that only a soulless philistine or someone with a deadline would want the latter. Being able to hear birds chattering in the reeds and the laughter of children playing ashore made a welcome change to my normal boating, and with people unaware of how their voices carried over the water, we laughed at passing boaters commenting on the unusual sight of a Dutch barge sailing. Finally, about an hour after we started, a gentle rippling along the hull suggested we might be gaining some momentum.

As Sod's Law would have it, this happened when we were approaching the narrow neck of water separating Lough Bofin from Lough Boderg. Though only slight, the breeze was behind us, and the mainsail and massive boom were sticking way out over the port side. I could see no reason not to sail straight through, and neither could Eric. The crews on the two hire boats coming towards us may have thought differently, yet they managed cheerful waves as they scraped along the reed bed. And then we were in the shelter of the trees, and drifting idly again. Ah well, it wasn't like we had an agenda or a need to prove something. Easing back into the wooden bench running round *Nieuwe Zorgen's* stern deck we idled in the evening sun.

Anybody wanting to study tension would have been more than interested by the reaction we got when we returned to Dromod harbour under diesel power. The half-full harbour we'd left was now jammed solid, and the downside to a sailing barge was now very evident: sticking several feet forward of Eric's bow was a long steel shaft – I believe it's called a bowsprit – that could have been designed for punching holes in the sides of fibreglass cruisers. Even if the harbour had been nearly empty I'd have been nervous, but with it packed this bowsprit had disaster written all over it. And I wasn't the only one to notice: every boat we could possibly spear had crew readying fenders and poles to keep us at bay with. Even worse was that the way the harbour had filled meant we had to turn

Nieuwe Zorgen to get alongside Ted's *Heron*. It was a nightmare I looked forward to seeing Eric deal with.

Hats off to Eric's brilliant answer: he buggered off up to the bow and left me on the tiller! Agh! The throttle couldn't be reached from the tiller! Double agh! Nightmare! Bloody hell, Eric you bollocks! Why me? More by luck than by good helmsmanship, I got the thing where we wanted without hitting anyone, Eric threw a line from the bow and I caught one at the stern. I sighed with relief, Eric laughed his delight and, probably thinking what we'd just done was practised and planned, our onlookers all lost interest.

That Eric and I dined poorly that evening was entirely my fault. You'd think that living with a top notch chef would have seen me subconsciously absorbing a little of Jill's culinary magic, but the meal I produced would prove that theory wrong. I called it 'Woeful Sad Spaghetti', and hope never to eat it again. Fortunately with Jill back on board and Ted having returned with Joelle for crew and company, the next meal was closer to the quality to be expected of a celebration. What we were celebrating nobody seemed quite sure, but there was certainly a bit of a buzz in the air. And then Ted raised his glass and said 'To Misfit Mariners!'

We'd heard both Ted and Eric use the term before, and there had been one occasion when Eric referred to our coming travels as 'The Misfit Mariners Northern Tour'.

'What's with the misfits?' I asked.

'Coz we're Misfits,' replied Eric with a smile.

I smiled back. 'I can see you're a misfit Eric, in fact you're so bloody odd there's never been a box made a shape you could be put in. But what about you Ted?'

It was Ted's turn to laugh. 'I'm a misfit too.'

And then they both smiled, and chorused 'We're the Misfit Mariners!'

When Eric went on everything became clear: 'We're the only two live-aboards who don't stay put at Sallins or Hazelhatch and choose to move and wander. We got called misfits one night on Gene's barge, thought it apt and funny and have used it ever since.'

'And it's better than lots of other things we're called!' chimed in Ted with another laugh.

The reason really didn't matter: 'Misfit Mariners' was both easier to say than Ted and Eric, and sounded nicer. From here on we'd be travelling with the Misfits.

SHANNON ERNE
WATERWAY

It was 2.00 am, and we had uninvited visitors on the roof. So I pulled on shorts and went up to the wheelhouse to stand and watch three pissed lads wobbling and laughing while they threw shards of doner kebabs about. The moment they saw me they scarpered down the quay to a little hire boat moored a hundred yards upstream. And then the penny dropped: these were the same shits that took Hobbes's tennis balls off our roof and threw them in the water every time they walked past *Hawthorn* while we were in Dromod. Bastards.

The dancers' identities were the only surprise, for Jill and I expected a disturbed night when we put ourselves alongside Carrick-on-Shannon's quay wall that afternoon. Next to a car park and as close to town as it was possible to get, it wasn't a spot we'd normally have chosen. But then we wouldn't normally have arrived so late in the day that all the choice moorings were full, or too late to be able to shop and then push on to a quieter spot. No matter; we'd no choice and, while Eric moored on the wall in front of us, Ted came alongside. And then Eric had walked back to us. He was still laughing about something that happened a few minutes earlier.

We'd been motoring along quite happily enjoying the sunshine and views, when the large hire boat coming towards us suddenly veered and, without appearing to slow, buried itself in the reeds. It was full of Japanese girls of student age. Being first there, we'd chucked them a line and gently dragged them afloat.

'I wish you'd let me tow them out,' he said. 'They were gorgeous!'

'I did you a favour! Ask Jill, she'll tell you that at least four of them were looking at you and cooing, and given how messy that could have got we thought it best to protect you from exhaustion and depravity!'

Eric smiled, and we took the dogs for a walk.

He wasn't smiling first thing the following morning when, at the godforsaken hour of eight, a glowering Ted was banging on his door. We'd only just explained the reason we were sweeping salad off *Hawthorn's* roof was the idiots on the hire boat by the bridge. There'd been a brief pause, during which he rapidly reddened, and then he'd gone straight on to *Nieuwe Zorgen's* stern and raised Eric from the dead. Now Ted's a proper biker complete with goatee beard, shaved head, earrings and, when riled, the maddest of crazy angry mad eyes. I knew and liked Ted, and he was scaring me. So I had to feel for sleep-dazed Eric as he tried to grasp the reason for the monster at his door. He soon did, and seconds later the pair of them were ashore and purposefully striding down the quay. It seemed we were about to find out if vengeance really is sweet.

'Whoa! Hang on!' I shouted, quickly following them. The child in me was screaming 'Go on! Get the three of you to jump onto the hire boat's gunwale together! It'll roll so much the idiots will think they're going over. And imagine waking to a full-blown blast of Red Ted! They'll need counselling!' While my inner child was grinning and giggling and dancing in expectation of revenge, my boring adult consciousness started nagging away about *Hawthorn* being too big and obvious, and Ireland too small for this sort of thing: that somehow making enemies, even if they deserved to be scared witless, wasn't a good idea. I was torn, but it didn't take long to angrily walk a hundred yards, so I had to decide quickly. The adult won an uncertain victory. 'Let it go, lads,' I pleaded.

'Nah! They're getting it!'

'Honestly, let it go,' I urged, sensing the awful cliché 'they're not worth it' and keen to avoid it.

'What? Are you sure?' Ted and Eric chorused.

'I'm sure. Honestly, they're only idiots and Ted's scaring the beejeezus out of me as it is. They'll need care for months!'

They paused and turned, and then Ted said something I hadn't expected: 'But they can't do that to a Misfit Mariner and get away with it!'

Well that threw me: we may have been travelling with them for the past few days, but I'd never considered myself, or Jill, or *Hawthorn* as ever likely to be official Misfits. I had to admit that their willingness to go to battle on our behalf was a shock, but it was a nice one. While we slowly walked back to our moored homes, I rolled what had just happened round my head. 'We've been in Ireland eight weeks, and now we're in a gang! How mad is that?'

Revenge, of sorts, was ours a few hours later when, having left the Shannon and just started up the Shannon Erne Waterway (SEW), we saw a little hire boat coming our way the far side of the bridge we were approaching. It was them; hooray! While upstream gives way to downstream is the navigation rule on a river, we were now on a canal, and just who had right of way was a bit of a grey area. It wasn't grey for the lad on the hire boat's helm who simply assumed it was his. Oh how I smiled about not getting involved in fisticuffs earlier, for the coming moment of revenge was so sweet we could have been boating on nectar. Suddenly, aware that I was not going to stop and conscious of how high and hard our bow was, the helmsman started shouting and swearing. Then, wisely deciding that a hedgerow was softer than stone or steel, he bottled it. With Jill taking our wheel, I stepped outside the wheelhouse to see if any of the lads would meet my eye as we glided by. No? I thought not. Of course they couldn't move until Ted had passed. We couldn't hear what was said, but we enjoyed his obvious joy at their discomfort. And finally Eric on the tail of our little parade had his turn. Touché, job done!

Ten minutes later we were moored at the first of the eight locks and three miles that would take us to the SEW's summit. While there were a few boats ahead of us, we thought nothing of it as the locks were all automated and we assumed we'd get along easily enough to make the summit in a couple of hours.

Our optimism was soon shattered. For, while working the locks was simple enough – you put a credit type card in and pushed a few buttons – the locks themselves were smaller than we were used to and took a lot longer to work than their manual equivalents. We were going to have to put the boats through one at a time. This would have slowed us right down even without our being at the back of a queue of several hire boats. Given the social nature of working locks, it was only a few minutes before we'd learnt that the hire boats were crewed by Norwegian fishermen and their families. Ah well, the weather was kind and if you're in a hurry on a boat you've chosen the wrong transport.

The second lock was in a deep rock cutting. A great cascade of water spilling down a rocky chute beside it made it as tricky a lock to get into as any we'd ever seen. We'd caught up with the last two Norwegian-crewed boats so we got a chance to see how they managed. They were good, bloody good, and even we got in without too much grinding. Recalling how dry it had been, I couldn't help wonder at the struggle we'd have after a wet week or two. That would be a challenge and, while I couldn't yet imagine I'd ever get homesick for the safe predictability of the English waterways, I could see a time when the wildness of the Irish ones might be really frustrating. The first lock had been very shallow, but this was dramatically deeper, so I'd plenty of time to think about these things while in the lock's dark and dripping shade once the gates astern had slowly growled shut. Looking up I waited for the sun to frame Jill's head.

'OK?' she shouted.

'OK!'

We had no ropes ashore and, while there was not enough free space for anything but the smallest boat to be in with us, there was enough for *Hawthorn* to gather serious momentum if the flow was nasty. It was not too bad; in fact the lock was well designed and *Hawthorn* was barely moving. Which was good, for we'd already seen the major problem, even danger, with the SEW's automated locks: the control box was so far from the lock's edge that the operator couldn't see the boat in the empty lock. We'd been worried about this in Drumleague lock on the Lough Allan Canal, but that was operated by a WI employee familiar with all the quirks of that one lock, whereas here we'd be doing the lock, and taking responsibility, ourselves. I guessed the designers of the lock's automation must have known this, for they'd fitted countless alarms to make certain anyone within a hundred yards knew the gates were closing or the boat was too close to the lock cill. These alarms, the lock's depth and not being able to see Jill all combined to leave me feeling more vulnerable than I was used to. I was not a fan, and I wasn't surprised to hear that Jill wasn't either once she and Hobbes were back aboard.

Knowing we'd have to wait at the next lock, there was no point in rushing. At just over tick-over we were making 2 knots, which both made steering easy and meant the engine's noise didn't drown out the summery sound of skylarks. We idled along looking at the boggy meadows beside us and the sheep-strewn heights  above them. After about half an hour, with the next lock visible only a few minutes distant and Jill busy below, *Hawthorn* very gently hit something. It wasn't much, just a bump not unlike hitting a floating wheelie bin or a waterlogged branch. While odd, it wasn't totally unexpected in the middle of a shallow canal. Thirty seconds later I felt exactly the same sensation again, which was odd as bumps are usually isolated. By the third bump I was off the stool we sit to steer on and, unable to see because the dinghy on the cabin roof behind me blocked the view, at the door and looking astern.

What the…? Right behind us, and I mean within inches, was a small white cruiser with its canvas hood folded back. My gaze was met by two broad toothless grins. Ach no, surely it couldn't be? I looked again: one man was in his mid sixties, and the other looked considerably older. And then the penny fully dropped: we were being rammed by the same two old boys we'd seen being a little mad going onto Lough Key. Where the hell had they come from? We hadn't passed a moored boat, seen a side cutting where one could be kept or passed a slipway where they might have launched. One thing was clear though: they wanted past. I put the wheel down to port, shifted *Hawthorn* over a few feet and watched as their bow rose and their stern dropped. By the time they were alongside their engine was digging a great hole in the water that I was trying to stop *Hawthorn* falling into, and their wash was really starting to roll. The two old boys were waving and laughing and shouting something about our boat being as big as an oil tanker. Then their stern lifted and they came on to the plane. And they were gone, flying across the remaining few hundred yards of canal towards the open lock gates at a speed that made a mockery of the 5 km/h speed limit. There was a boat already in it, but room for a second it seemed. I struggled helming in their wake, though laughing so much I could hardly stand didn't help.

When the rest of the gang caught up a few minutes later we learnt the old boys had roared up to the second lock while Joelle was opening it for Ted and, leaving Eric bouncing in their wake, gone straight in. When full, the moment the gates were open they'd launched away with the same mad abandon we'd witnessed a month earlier.

Still, they were enjoying themselves, unlike the English couple we met coming the other way in the fourth lock, That was just embarrassing, though not for Ted and Eric.

'Ah, the happy Englishman!' Eric whispered, while nudging Jill, nodding in my direction, and adding 'Is that how he talks to you when we're not about?'

'Show us your knuckles Giles,' chimed in Ted, taking my hand and turning it palm down and pretending to look for evidence of punching. The pair of them were most amused, and well on their way to a happy few minutes joshing. When the boat left the lock the mood changed as the Norwegians arrived in. Their merriment had been obvious earlier, yet that was only a warm up. For some reason they were now wearing their underpants over the top of their clothes, and that included women with skirts on. And they were singing opera so loudly the lock chamber echoed with their joy. The contrast of their happy presence with the misery that had just departed was striking.

Fortunately the fourth lock seemed to be the pinch point, and the going became less frustrating as we neared the top. By now there weren't any boats heading down, though this didn't speed things up as, being automated, the lock took just as long to drain without a boat in it. Tiring now, we ground on, taking it in turns to lead and follow and to help Eric along, with the sole intent of getting the bloody hill over and done with. We arrived on the summit in the early evening, and immediately looked for somewhere to stop.

It seemed we had two choices: either pull in where we were above the lock, or boat on for an hour or so to the village of Keshcarrigan. We looked at the lack of room above the lock, listened to the busy road a few feet away, and decided to go on. Poor Eric groaned: for the rest of us there was someone to share the load, to make tea, steer or chat with, but he was on his own and weary. We made him a cup of tea and I joked that if he started moaning I'd get tired and ratty myself; and he'd seen what tired and ratty Englishmen were like.

An hour later, having boated through a couple of small loughs connected by long rock cuttings, we were pushing out onto the much larger Lough Scur and what we considered the summit proper. After a day of so many stops and starts and narrow rocky passages, its size was both a relief and the first real opportunity we'd had to pull the boats together for a chat. Concerned that the lateness of our stopping might mean we struggled to get a mooring, Jill and I suggested a wild mooring or a night at anchor. With nobody disagreeing, the only issue was deciding where.

Seeing nothing obvious, we pushed on and passed through a narrow channel between two islands. For some reason, possibly because it could be argued that this spot is where the Shannon's drainage basin meets the River Erne's, the channel markers changed from the Shannon's individual red and black markers to the combined red and white markers of the northern Erne system. In some ways the new markers were easier to use as, unlike the red and black where the correct side depended on our direction, all we had to do was make sure we didn't pass these new markers on their red side.

Just through this narrow channel the lough opened up again. The navigation turned to starboard, so we turned to port, ran a big circle to check we had plenty of water to swing in if the wind changed, and dropped anchor. After tying Ted to starboard and Eric to port, Misfit Island was declared fit for purpose.

Fit for purpose was an understatement. The wildness and social remoteness of the spot we'd chosen was the perfect antidote to the busy town centre and the larks of the previous night. We made tea and sat on Eric's stern looking out across the water to fields rising on the short steep hills south and east of us. The wind would gently turn us, so a few minutes later we'd be looking west over the wooded islands we'd just passed, and north to the high drama of Slieve Anierin – the mountain on the eastern shore of Lough Allen – forming a dramatic backdrop to the wooded shore. Other than our chatting and the occasional lowing of cattle in the distance, it was blissfully silent.

Being photographers, Ted and Joelle were itching to make the most of the situation and light. So we hauled the outboard out from storage and dropped the dinghy in the water, and they pottered off. With things to do, Jill and I went below leaving Eric to do what Erics do. It seemed Erics put on music at times like these; at least that's what we assumed on hearing the melancholic tones of what sound like a single flute. We'd been around him for long enough to know his stereo was rarely off and his music tastes were rich and varied, but this was both a new sound and one that perfectly suited this space and moment. The music stopped, and then started again at a different pace. It was not a recording: it was someone playing a flute. It had been an odd day but surely not so odd that we'd moored next to an island with a musical leprechaun on it?

Of course it wasn't; it was only Eric playing a low whistle, something he'd never mentioned he was able to do. Hearing he did, and rather well it seemed, we left what we were doing to enjoy the moment and the view, and to wonder at how lucky we seemed to have been in falling into this company.

Later, after we'd all eaten the supper Jill had prepared on *Hawthorn*, Eric and I piled into the dinghy with the two dogs. Hoping we'd be able to land on the meadow that ran down to the water's edge we'd eyed for this moment in the light, we pottered southwest into the darkness. As always there were reeds to crush before we grounded the bow and Eric stepped out to drag the dinghy ashore, and we both set out to walk up the hill through the dew-soaked grass. Then, out of the blackness, we heard Norwegian voices singing, and we turned to look back to where the anchor light we'd left to guide us home glimmered in a pool of darkness that reached right back and up to where the great black bulk of Slieve Anierin met the star-filled sky.

※

It had been such a long time since Jill and I had boated with anyone we'd forgotten how much fun it is, how the sharing of an experience somehow makes it more significant than it might otherwise be. It probably helped that none of us had been this way before meant we were equally ignorant of what might be coming, and equally delighted when the river or landscape served a sudden treat. *Hawthorn* became the mothership and led the way, though not because Jill and I particularly wanted to: simply because we were the only boat with a wheelhouse, two constant crew, a GPS and a flat surface to lie a chart out on where it wouldn't get wet or blown away. It's not that Ted and Eric didn't have charts – we'd given each of them a set of the ones we were gifted in Tullamore – it was just a lot easier for them to follow us than it was for them to lead. We had another VHF radio – the hand-held bought for the grab bag on the Irish Sea crossing – which we dug out and lent to Eric, and we shared the walkie-talkies we'd had for years with Ted. While we could now talk to either of them, they couldn't communicate directly with each other but had to come through us. This gave us the power we frequently enjoyed of winding-up both of them by passing on fabricated messages whenever we thought it might be fun. Possibly the greatest benefit of these shared communications to us was that Ted seemed to have extraordinary eyesight, and with his view unimpeded by a wheelhouse he saw things we'd never see, and having seen them his first reaction was to share them. He had a thing for birds, and we seemed to be forever stepping outside to look where he was pointing just after our walkie-talkie had crackled into life. By now we'd been boating long enough for Eric's body clock to start slowly coming round to something nearer to ours and Ted's, though Ted was not the best of sleepers and it was not unusual for us to start our day looking over photos he had taken in the dawn light. It seemed all was well with our world, and everybody was happy.

Though I can't imagine how any boater wouldn't be on the long descent from the SEW's summit to Upper Lough Erne and Northern Ireland. The flat lands of the Irish midlands were long forgotten in the rolling hills around us, and after Lough Scur we were on an infant river that wound through the land connecting countless shallow reedy loughs. Following the logic that the navigation had to run down the centre of each lough would soon lead to disaster, as there were some we barely brushed, and others we never seemed to enter. And then we approached Ballinamore through a steep and overgrown rock cutting that ended in a generous mooring above a weir.

We headed into town to shop, and came across the weirdest Tesco supermarket buried deep in the rubble of a building site with a long-idle crane swinging above it. As with Rooskey, there were posters on the site's hoardings full of images of smiling happy people living in the apartments that would now not be built and shopping in arcades that would never open. Still, the upshot was that the Tesco was so quiet we were welcomed in and almost guided round the shelves by its conscientious staff. Normally averse to supermarkets, we mentioned our surprise to the barman of the pub we called into when returning home. He listened, and then explained that few locals shopped there, choosing instead to drive the twenty miles to Enniskillen over the border where everything was much cheaper.

Now stocked and watered, we pushed on and made what was to prove a rather good decision. Nobody boating the SEW in 2009 could realistically claim they'd not heard about Swan Island Animal Farm on Lough Garadice, for there were boards advertising it on bridges, trees and even on poles in the fields beside us, for miles before we reached it. According to these it was the experience of a lifetime, a must-do event without which our holiday would forever be imperfect. Now, Jill and I, and probably Ted and Eric, would normally bolt from anything so presented, and we were going to, right up to the moment we arrived on Lough Garadice. And then we'd looked at our charts and saw that Swan Island was the only mooring that would let us enjoy this stunning space of water and islands surrounded by rolling hills, full of woods and meadows set against a distant backdrop of high mountains. It was so perfect it didn't matter what Swan Island was about, we just wanted to sit and look at it. So we chanced our luck and pulled onto its floating wooden jetties.

It has to be said that the jetties had a certain home-made look about them, and we'd only been there for a couple of minutes before the owner, Pat, came down to greet us. He was happy to see us, but he did point out that his jetties weren't ever intended for full-grown barges, and that if the wind got up from the wrong direction we'd drag them about and do no end of damage. Promising we'd be gone if such a thing looked likely, we asked the obvious question 'How much do you charge for mooring?'

'A tenner a night, though if you come up and use the bar or restaurant you get them for nothing.' And then he was off through the paddocks full of llamas, donkeys, alpacas and goats, back to the bar and restaurant in the traditional low white cottage a short distance up the hill.

'A tenner a night unless we go drinking! Did he just say what I thought he said?' I asked Jill and Eric.

'He did!'

Instantly calculating that meant I could effectively drink three pints for nothing every day we were there, the warmth I was already feeling after Pat's welcome rapidly spread to a smug glow. A glow that continued to grow while we took in the view, and only got brighter when the owner of one of the other moored boats came over to ask if we might do some cover work. Once again Ireland's towpath telegraph was way ahead of us: having heard about us from a friend of a friend, he knew we were heading north and had been waiting for us to arrive.

Even the job was reasonably straightforward: some sheets with windows and zipped doorways off a barge's hard-topped wheelhouse. So we spent the following two days working, and wandered up to the bar in the evenings to pay our mooring fee. A small space full of comfortable furniture, with very fine Guinness served by Pat's wife, son or daughter, it felt more like their front room than a conventional pub. There was usually live music on, though this could be anything from a guy with a keyboard to a group of accomplished traditional Irish musicians. By a kind coincidence, we finished the work the day the kitchen was closed and a BBQ was fired up outside. So Jill celebrated a night off, and we ate steak on the restaurant's terrace while looking west over our moored home across a lake burnished orange by the setting sun to distant gold-rimmed mountains. It was ridiculously perfect.

We'd put into Swan Island for one night and then spent a week there. Jill and I were briefly on our own while Eric, his father having driven over to collect him, returned to Dublin. We knew he'd be back as he'd left his dog, Oíche, with us. In the middle of the week Ted reappeared, though sadly without Joelle. We'd enjoyed her witty and intelligent company and insightful perspective as a fellow non-Irish outsider, and we knew she wasn't full of enthusiasm for her normal life back in Liverpool. Everyone looked forward to her return. And then a narrowboat turned up. Ted and Eric both knew the people on it, and noises were made about their joining us on our northern adventures. Our little gang having settled down nicely, Jill and I watched with caution. Yet we knew that was how the river worked, and that we'd either roll with it or take a different direction.

For some reason, it may have been a nephew's or niece's birthday, that evening Pat's extended family were all in the bar. A gifted bunch, they'd come with instruments and fine voices and, seeing a good evening building, Eric collected his whistles and settled down amongst them. Jill and I left at two, and Eric sometime nearer six. Pat arrived down in the morning about half ten and announced that he'd been up all night, had just collected a bull and now really ought to go to bed. Our week at Swan Island had been one hell of a treat but there was no way we were going to top that night. So we thanked him for everything and promised to return when heading south. It was time for us to slip away.

To our surprise the guy on the narrowboat declared he had to go first as barges were too slow and he didn't want to be held up. This raised a few eyebrows, particularly mine and Jill's as we knew the type of boat he was on well enough to be sure it was a plodder. Still, the next few minutes might well bring a laugh, so we let him off and followed along a minute or so later with Ted and Eric just behind us.

Steadily increasing our pace as we closed in, by the time we'd reached where the river left the lough we were right behind the narrowboat and barrelling down a short straight towards what we knew from our charts was a right-angled bend just before a harbour. Missing the turn completely, the narrowboat surged straight on and then, panicked by only seeing concrete walls, disappeared in a cloud of black smoke as the engine was revved flat out in reverse to try and get it to stop. We turned to port with our walkie-talkie and VHF busy with Ted and Eric's laughter. Given the ribbing he got when we moored together a little later, we'd thought the guy on the narrowboat would realise there was little point in tearing off, yet the next morning he did exactly the same thing: charging ahead of us all and then going straight on instead of heading for Belturbet. We all made the turn and, fascinated to see if he was going to boat off into the distance still unaware of his solitude, we watched to see if he looked back. Eventually he did and more black smoke and curses followed.

It had taken us twenty-two hours and a serious battering on the Irish Sea to get to Ireland from the UK, so we found boating down a narrow river with the republic of Ireland on one side and the UK on the other more than a little odd. Passing through the un-spanned arches of a border bridge blown up in the Troubles did feel weird, and we weren't surprised that our companions suggested we remain in the republic for as long as possible by hugging the border all the way to Belturbet. The Misfits weren't for staying in the town for long, so we left the folk on the narrowboat to it and headed back down the River Erne past the incongruous development of huge chalet-type buildings a whole hillside had been cleared to build. We were studying their empty unloved forms when a speedboat roared round the corner just in front of us, which only mattered because the space beside us was already full with an overtaking cruiser. The speedboat just got through, though the look of shocked horror on the face of the guy on the wakeboard behind it was priceless!

UPPER LOUGH ERNE

'We've got to bring Eric in here, Jill! He'll love it!' I said looking at the vast array of shotguns, air and BB guns, crossbows, bows, slingshots, catapults, camouflage and knives stocked in Enniskillen's big boys' toy shop Home, Field & Stream. We were only in there because we hoped they'd have the leather rain hats we were needing now the summer seemed to have given way to one long, cold, grey monsoon. Fortunately there were plenty in stock, and fortunately Jill's being with me meant I successfully suppressed my own childish desire to indulge in tools of death. Still, I was coming back with Eric, and we both knew what that would mean.

Truth be told, arriving in Enniskillen was a bit like Christmas for all of us. It's a lovely town with lots of water, gently sloping streets full of shops and alleys much easier to walk than drive. We'd moored close to its centre, equidistant from the old town, the new shopping mall and the huge Tesco and Asda supermarkets we headed straight for on arriving. Once in the stores, it was easy to spot the owners of all the cars from the republic that jammed the car park, as they were the ones with trolleys, and it was often plural, piled high. Yet we were no different: it had been months since Jill and I had been in any shop of a similar size, and the opportunity to stock up on treats and essential items, at a lower price than we were used to, was not one to be missed. The only restriction was we were going to have to carry our purchases home, so we limited ourselves to about a hundredweight of groceries – tinned tomatoes, chickpeas, pasta, flour, rice etc – and then staggered back to the dinghy, which we'd left on the jetty nearest the shop to save several hundred yards of trudging. Unburdened, and refreshed after a brew, I returned alone.

High on my own very short list of things I missed from England was good beer. Not that I'm knocking Guinness; it was just that the absence of anything other than lagers or gassed beer in pubs left little other choice. The problem with Guinness is that its quality varies hugely, and you can never be sure what you're going to get when you order a pint. We'd had some very fine Guinness in the pub in Dublin, at McIntyres' in Shannon Harbour and in Pat's front room at Swan Island, yet we'd also had some flat and nasty muck even I could barely finish. And then I'd come under Ted's tutelage and learnt to look about the bar to see if Guinness was being drunk, and if it was by how many, and then to check for the regular white rings left where the head should have settled after each swallow. The only problem for me was, not being a fan of commercial lager, sweet cider or cold, gassed beer; a pub with bad Guinness was a disaster. What I did like, and *Hawthorn* had crossed the Irish Sea partially ballasted with, were the English bottled ales that visitors and happy evenings had seen us out of weeks ago. So, seeing shelves of Black Sheep, London Pride, Green King IPA, Adnams bitter and many others, I filled a trolley and rattled to the checkout.

'Euros or sterling?' asked the lad on the till. It said much about the volume of cross-border trade to Enniskillen that we'd been asked this question in every shop we'd been in. I paid in sterling, cleared the aisle and humped the rucksack onto my back. I'd gone mad: the bloody thing weighed far more than the massive shop I'd just done with Jill. I'd been concerned my trolley full of booze might give the impression I had a drink problem, so my bent-kneed wobbling through the car park could only have confirmed an onlooker's suspicions. It wasn't graceful, but I made it. And then I bent down to untie the dinghy, and the rucksack pulled me over onto my back. I lay there like a stranded turtle giggling and assuring passers-by that all was normal.

Being in Enniskillen also gave me a chance to get on the Internet, something I hadn't been able to do since last using Pat's at Swan Island and, were it not for our blog, something I wouldn't have bothered doing. The blog was now much more of a problem than I'd ever thought possible as, not only did it demand constant updating, but we'd learnt it wasn't just friends and family who were reading it: the Irish boating public did too. There had been times when complete strangers had approached us to say they liked it. And then I'd made the foolish mistake of finding out how to check its hit count, and been astonished to see it was a vast multiple of what I'd expected. That had completely thrown me; so much so that I didn't post anything for a fortnight. My posts that day filled in the gap between Swan Island and Belturbet, and from Belturbet to the present.

The extraordinary, land-locked archipelago of Upper Lough Erne leaps out of any map of Ireland. All islands, inlets, bays and meandering twists of river, it was the space we were always drawn to looking at on our Irish road atlas, and our keenness to start exploring and playing on it was the main reason we didn't hang about in Belturbet. Not that we'd even really started into it when we moored for the night at Galloon at the lough's eastern end.

We'd have been hard pushed to find a more remote spot: there wasn't a house to be seen and the band of grass running along the middle of the lane beside us suggested we were unlikely to be disturbed by traffic. The dogs were delighted to find freedom and space – and Oíche was beginning to look like she needed exercise to run off her now distinctly rounded belly. Ted, who had been off wandering with his camera since we arrived, soon returned and suggested we should all come and have a look at the graveyard he'd just found.

His interest was not surprising. Many of the headstones were old and weatherworn, and making out any writing was difficult. However, what did remain clearly visible on some of them were skulls and crossbones. We'd learnt over the past few weeks that Eric was a qualified archaeologist; so having him along at moments like this could be hugely advantageous and interesting. We waited for his pronouncement.

'Pirate graves!'

'What? They're miles from the sea!' chorused the rest of us.

Never willing to let a fantasy slide back to the grim truth of reality, Eric soon came back: 'They must have retired here after abandoning their boat near Belleek.'

'Hang on!' We're supposed to believe they rowed up here one misty morning in tenders awash with treasure? And then settled down in new-built bungalows for a life of rural bliss, mead-making and death from old age? Get a grip!'

Everybody was laughing now, though with a certain caution. For we'd all felt an odd and uncomfortable air about the graveyard. It was a place neither Eric nor I wanted to pass later that night when we took the dogs for their evening stroll in the pitch-black silence of rural County Fermanagh.

Much later, while I was posting blogs in Enniskillen, my curiosity got the better of me and I typed 'skull and crossbones on gravestone' into Google. This quickly confirmed our suspicions that Eric was only joshing, and ruled out Knights Templar and Freemasons as other possibilities. It seemed the most likely explanation was something much more down to earth: the symbol was used as a *memento mori* – as a reminder that you have to die – and was likely to date from the eighteenth century. What was interesting about that was their age, for the graveyard had been a long way from the water and we suspected it was once hard against its shore. Since our meeting with the dairy farmer at Grange Lough, we'd been seeing signs of dry shorelines on all our travels and were curious about this further evidence.

At some point between Belturbet and Galloon, the Misfit fleet had crossed the border. It wasn't marked, and there was nothing that made our transition obvious. We had to wait to arrive amongst the familiarity of National Trust signs and symbols at Crom Castle to be absolutely certain we were in the United Kingdom. Given not one of the Misfits had any interest in the house's contents, which we suspected would be the usual velvet drapes, polished silver and period furniture befitting the vast Victorian-styled building, we went for a walk around the castle's huge estate. Crossing parkland studded with grand trees, we arrived amongst the ruins of an older castle on the lough's shore. Well, it would have once been on the shore but, as with the Galloon graveyard, the shore had retreated since the castle was built.

Eric's interest in weaponry, castles, battles and all that sort of stuff meant he was in his element, and we left him wandering about the ruins and taking sight lines across the lough towards imaginary invaders, to go in search of the yew trees Jill, Ted and I were really interested in. They're said to be the oldest trees, or living things for that matter, in the whole of Ireland.

From the outside the yews appeared to be one huge low tree, and then we walked the path into them to stand looking up at incredibly twisted branches forming platforms just asking to be sat on. Judging by the polished nature of the trees' lower limbs we were far from the first to have this

idea, but we scrambled up as high as was comfortable. And then we called Eric over, and tried to hide when he appeared below. Given away by our giggling and Hobbes's and Oíche's barking, he soon looked up.

It hadn't been that long since the owner of *Blackthorn* had informed us there was another *Hawthorn* on the Irish waterways system that we should greet when meeting. We'd only just arrived and were as green as the countryside back then and, while noting the name, I'd not thought much about it then or since. Yet here came the other *Hawthorn* , briefly pulling alongside so its owner, Eamon, could say hello. Which he did, while looking over our home with the skilled eye many years working on boats brings. I'd enough skills of my own to appreciate the time and attention to detail that had gone into building his *Hawthorn,* though I was astonished to hear this pristinely beautiful all-white steel river boat had once been used as a dredger. A heritage boat quite different to the barges we'd been with on Ree, its original purpose was servicing flying boats working out of Lough Neagh during the Second World War. I was hugely impressed; so much so I suspected we'd have called our own boat something different if we'd built it in Ireland.

With Eamon heading off to home and work on Lough Derg on the south Shannon, we too moved on. Though not far: passing the folly of Crichton Tower on the island in front of the yews and old castle, we headed into one of the numerous long fingers of water we had to choose from. Finding the jetty we hoped to moor on was packed with boats, we went to anchor and *Nieuwe Zorgen* and *Heron* strapped on to us. Then madness descended, and we went swimming. Well, the lads did: Jill wisely opted to stay warm and dry while we gasped and shivered in shock at the Baltic temperature of Trial Bay's water, which only the wet-suited Ted could handle for long. At least we were well away from ears too delicate for our language, and I was able to stay in long enough to swim round the boats' sterns and check all the props. Afterwards, while trying not to shake all the tea out of the mugs Jill served it in, a strange buzz crept into our slowly warming limbs. It was nice, but not so nice I was keen to repeat it.

Just where Mr Narrowboat had ended up we had no idea. Then, late in the evening, he appeared in the distance. Ted gave him a ring, and we learned that a nicotine crisis meant he and his crew were not going to stop until they got to Enniskillen, still well over three hours away. We looked at the light, considered they had only a road map to navigate with, and wished them luck: there was a maze of channels between them and the town, and in an hour it would be dark. They had Ted's phone number, and we hoped they didn't need it.

A lazy day followed that saw us just move the boats to the now-free jetty, and take a long walk to Crom Castle's private church, on a peninsula across the water from the big house. It was locked, and we were wandering round the graveyard working out the family's history from what was written on the headstones, when we saw a grave marked by a sculpture of a bronze hand holding a sword with a dragon wound round it. It was about three feet tall, and would be striking anywhere, but set against a backdrop of lough and trees it really was most impressive.

Eric rushed over to have a proper look. And then declared the predictable: 'Pirate!'

That afternoon a mate of Eric's arrived by car to the small lane beside our mooring. He loaded his two guitars and small pack of dogs onto *Nieuwe Zorgen* and we all headed off up the lough for half an hour in search of somewhere new to visit. Spending an evening listening to two fine musicians enjoying themselves while moored on a little island miles from anybody, was another experience Jill and I had not seen coming. But then I don't think Darren had anticipated a long ride, in a dinghy comically crowded with instruments and dogs, back to where he'd parked his car against a hedge.

Taking a week to cover the water the narrowboat had in an evening, we drifted west with nights on islands and shore-side jetties. When the Upper Lough ended and we were back on a river, Ted had to leave again. We all pulled into a jetty where he could get his bike off, and promised to wait until he came back in a few days' time. The only notable event while we waited was a nutter in a passing speedboat waving and shouting hello as if he knew us. Then, needing food and stimulation, Jill and I took *Hawthorn* the few miles upriver to Enniskillen for the day. We shopped and walked around, and then dawdled back with me steering while I read the first newspaper we'd bought in months. The only mistake was I paid it more attention than I did the river and, lazily assuming that the deep water would be in the middle of a straight section, I missed a navigation marker and we clipped the bottom. It was only a kiss, a minor bump, but it sent Jill scampering up the steps wielding the bloody great knife she uses for chopping vegetables – including, she promised, the one on the wheel if he did it again.

We'd also bought a map – the Ordnance Survey of Northern Ireland (OSNI) Activity Map of Upper and Lower Lough Erne – that brought astonishing detail to the area we were playing in. Leaving aside the things we'd passed since leaving the SEW (all of which we could visit if we wanted when returning), just seeing all the water, islands and possibilities west of where we were made both us and Eric keen for Ted's return.

So the moment Ted was back we were rolling his bike onto *Heron's* stern and setting off up the river while he was still grooming dead insects from his beard. Enniskillen's moorings being restricted to just 48 hours wasn't a problem, as there were so many temptations on the water beyond the town we were never going to stay longer. Soon sated, we followed the river past the castle and under the high arched bridge full of the slow-moving traffic the town's narrow streets and one-way system caused. We had another treat in mind, one that meant we had to first navigate round the odd little boat at anchor just above the flow-control barrier, and squeeze through the narrow channel of Portora Lock. Only used in the winter when the water levels of the upper and lower loughs can be at different heights, we were all glad to get through its open gates without adding more paint to its well scraped walls.

After a week's solid rain, the river was starting to rise significantly. We were headed for Devenish Island, a monastic site just a mile or so below the town.

LOWER LOUGH ERNE

Our only regret on visiting Devenish Island was that we arrived years after the do-gooding Health and Safety mob had put an end to visitors climbing its round tower to get a proper view down the lough north of it. Instead we stood at its base watching the little ferry take the last of the day trippers to the shore-side car park half a mile distant, and the warden locking the small, plain visitors' centre. He asked if we were staying. We said we were, and he replied 'We've a party coming in just before midnight, so you may be a little disturbed.'

Someone was going to have to make the obvious comment, and it was Ted who said 'We're more than a little disturbed already!'

The warden barely smiled, but he did say the visiting party were druids there for a ceremony. That was a surprise, and Eric was instantly torn between his formal archaeological training and his informal love of Hammer House of Horror movies. Unsurprisingly, he plumped for the dramatic option of fire and dancing virgins.

'Will there be lots of naked women?'

'I doubt it, but you never know.' The warden smiled a little more broadly, shook his head, climbed into his boat and left us to the silence of the old stones.

We weren't alone long before another barge arrived. It was a big one, so we went out, took its ropes and tied it alongside *Hawthorn*. The river's rumours had worked ahead of us and its skipper, Jimmy, had come to see the fleet of barges now collected on one of his favourite spots. Accepting our invitation to supper, he spent the evening telling tales of excitement and adventure collected over a lifetime on and around the water, both here and in other places. And then, leaving an invitation for us to join him on his yacht club mooring, he followed the last of the light over the horizon. When the druids came and went with little fuss and no flames or dancing, Eric suggested we should get up early and look for sacrificial blood. Knowing what Eric was like first thing in the morning, we feared the only spilt blood would be ours if we disturbed him. And yet he did get up early, and for the strangest reason.

What woke Jill and me was a loud bang of steel on steel beside our heads. It was 6.00 am and we were moored on a calm day in the middle of nowhere, so what could have rammed us was a mystery. And then again, bang! Only this time it was followed by a loud, long scrape that had me almost feeling our paint being ripped asunder. Once again I was dressing and muttering and grumping my way into the wheelhouse; looking out, I saw the little boat we'd passed while it was at anchor just above the lock the previous afternoon. Its skipper was struggling to get his line over our bollard. Lost for words at such an odd invasion, I went out to take it and pass it back without speaking.

'God bless you. Good morning. I hope you don't mind me tying outside you. God bless you,' bawled an elderly American man with such volume I looked behind me to see if the waking dead were erupting through the graveyard's grass.

Ugh? I thought, though I did at least manage to be civil. 'Forgive me, but I was asleep and that's some awakening.'

'God bless you. Really? I've been enjoying God's wonderful day for hours! It's such a fine one and a blessing to see the Lord's work at its mightiest! God bless you!'

Getting rammed by a holy man while on a mooring on a holy island? It had to be a wind-up, and I was looking about for a camera crew and smug presenter to clobber. But it wasn't, and I stood half dressed outside our wheelhouse for ten minutes while I was brought up to date with this extraordinary gentleman's travels. And he had woken the dead: Eric appeared, rubbing his eyes and more than a little narked at all the incoming. He grunted, eased the ever-fatter bellied Oíche onto the jetty, grunted again and went to put the kettle on.

Jill and I thought our own experience in Ireland a little unusual. Yet what we were about was as nothing in comparison to this guy's south-north transition of the Irish navigations. Using only the power of the wind in his sails and his own sweat and tears on the oars when it was calm, he had spent months getting here from Ardnacrusha at the bottom of the navigable Shannon. His determination to succeed was both impressive and a little scary: he was still distressed at just how close he'd come to having his achievement wrecked by a newspaper reporter unthinkingly pulling a rope while he was in one of the Shannon's locks – something he'd just managed to stop by bawling at her. We'd only passed him the day before because he went to anchor as the wind was blowing upstream harder than he could row down. Clearly a deeply religious man, his stock phrase was 'Praise the Lord!', and every sentence started and finished with a reference to God's work, or love, or blessings. With our own recent voyage of faith fresh in our own minds we had some context for his enthusiasm, but I wasn't surprised both Jill and I were keen to go on the dog walk that Eric promptly suggested. When we did we found Ted at the top of the island. He was taking close-up shots of dew-dropped spiders' webs in the morning light.

Being up early wasn't the end of the world. We made mugs of tea and then sat with the OSNI map open and a hundred square miles of exciting opportunities spread across our galley table. The great thing about this map was it included all the information a navigator wanted – depths, shoals and markers – as well as all the details we'd expect of any OS publication. We easily lost an hour dreaming of routes, anchorages and all manner of excitement, with Eric the Archaeologist constantly butting in.

'Look! Bunnahone Lough has three crannógs on it,' he'd say. And we'd ask him to show us, and find ourselves staring at a small isolated patch of blue the far side of the high ground to our south. It was miles away, and we'd need a crane and lorry to boat it, and Jill and I didn't even know what a crannóg was, so another ten minutes passed while Eric talked about small man-made islands just big enough for a family to live on.

'And look at all these raths'.

Of course we had to look, and there were indeed dozens of them dotted round the lough's perimeter, and then we'd ask what a rath was, and by the time we'd had a lesson about hill forts and Celtic peoples another half an hour had passed. It was all informative fun, and something else we never expected.

Devenish Island has two hills and, after failing to cross the wet and reedy valley between the second hill and us, Eric and I took the dogs and the dinghy across the bay and beached it on the firmer ground we couldn't walk to. Minutes later, having made a couple of circumnavigations of the shallow ditches that were the only evidence of its existence, we were at the centre of both rath and hill. For the first time we could now see miles down the lough, and the view of wooded islands, meandering shorelines and reed-filled bays rewarded our effort and fuelled our desire to be away exploring.

Ted needed to get ashore and back to Dublin for a couple of days, so we headed for the moorings at the yacht club Jimmy had offered. The wind had picked up, and the water was rough enough for us to plan our route to take advantage of as much shelter as we could find behind the islands and, as he'd learnt to do in choppy times, Ted pulled *Heron* into the calmer water in *Hawthorn's* lee. When  we arrived at the club the jetties were bouncing. There was room for Ted in the shelter of Jimmy's big barge, so we left him at it and scarpered across the lough to the shelter of the jetty at Carrickreagh beneath the trees and hills of the lough's south-western shore. We were only just a mile across the water from the turbulent violence from which we'd bolted, yet it was so calm and peaceful we could have been in a different world.

The wind was unrelenting and it brought so much rain the warm dry summer we'd been so surprised by was forgotten. Fortunately the forests on the hills behind us are public spaces, and we damply strolled about them trying to find the caves and raths our map promised. Yet the past is so easily lost beneath the ugly uniformity of parallel-planted spruces that we struggled, and the only real winners were the well-walked dogs. Finally the sun came out, and Eric decided a swim was in order. Using a rope from the top of his mast as a swing, he launched himself in a long lazy arc with a full Tarzan holler. And then he plunged down. I'd swear he was in the air longer than the water, for he was out so fast it was hard to believe he'd ever been in, and he was off down his gunwales to warmth and shelter shivering something about nuts in his neck.

Ted's call to say he was returning was the signal we were waiting for, though we didn't go directly to the yacht club but headed down the shore to another monastic site on the island of Inishmacsaint. Here the ruins are much less picturesque than those on Devenish, though there is a stone cross purporting to be the oldest in Ireland that's meant to rotate three times every Easter. Disappointed that we were not going to be witnessing this miracle, we stood in the rain in front of it for all of a minute.

It wasn't just Ted waiting for us at the yacht club. Eric's dad, Mick, had also arrived, as had my brother, Austen. This at least explained the weather, for Austen had been motorcycling round Ireland for a week or two for each of the past few summers, and claimed never to have seen the sun. He was cold, wet and thoroughly fed up with biking and camping. I didn't know whether it was best to give him a hug or wring him out, though I suspected he was relieved when I did neither. The thought of a warm dry bed and as much of Jill's cooking as he could get down himself brought some cheer and, by the time he'd had half a dozen brews, half a cake and about a dozen roll-ups, he was more than ready for a wander.

There are fairys on Lough Erne: not the mushroom-dancing sprites of popular folklore but the most wonderful Edwardian racing yachts. In the water they looked elegant and slight, though it wasn't until we studied one standing on the shore that we really appreciated the full extent of their beautiful lines, and the deep keel and sweeping curves that, according to those who know these things, make them a joy to sail. All the weight below the water means they carry a lot of canvas and go like stink, while leaning at angles that would have a bargeman like myself more than a little panicked. The one we were looking at was in a bloody great hangar: a relic from the Second World War when the site had been a base for Sunderland and Catalina flying boats supporting convoys and searching for submarines in the Atlantic. This history also explained the staggering width of the slipway just north of the club's jetties.

With Austen leaving and no sign of improvement in the weather, we hung around and chewed the cud, with both Jimmy and other local boaters. Many of these were serious sailors, as happy at sea as they were on the lough, so it's not surprising they headed straight for *Nieuwe Zorgen* and requested a sail on her. Fascinated both to see how she handled in such experienced hands, and how Eric would cope with his home tearing along as hard as they could push her, I waited for news of imminent sailings. We were made welcome in the bar, as was the American we met at Devenish who had also arrived. His goals were shifting and he was now talking about going on through Belleek and somehow bypassing the hydroelectric dams across the River Erne. He then hoped to sail down the Atlantic coast. Not having seen or heard from the folk on the narrowboat we joked that it was already well ahead of him. Though superficially just a bit of fun, there was genuine concern behind our laughter.

Lower Lough Erne is huge, and while we had already been forced to change our plans because of the wind, we were still several miles east of a dotted red line drawn on all our charts and maps. It marks the change from the sheltered, island-filled southern end of the lough to the wide-open spaces of what's known as the Broad Lough, and along it are written warnings about how rough the open water gets in the wrong weather. We didn't need to read them, for we couldn't forget that the Broad Lough was the only piece of boating Roger went to the trouble of warning us about while we were still in England. Our concern was that we knew this line wouldn't be on the road map the narrowboat's skipper was navigating with. With luck his boat was tucked into one of Enniskillen's backwaters, or safely in some calm corner we didn't know about. If not? Then heaven only knows where he'd got to.

Finally, the wind dropped and the rain eased. Despite having been made very welcome, we were beginning to get a little harbour-crazy and we were all keen to press on. So we did, crossing both the lough and the chart's red line. Risking going only as far as the sheltered bay below Tully Castle, we joined a hire boat on the public mooring. This being Ireland, Eric's dad and the folk on the hire boat turned out to be friends from thirty years ago. So cue long pause for reminiscing. The castle is a fortified house, though not nearly fortified enough to stop the locals driving out the Scottish planters who'd built it, just two decades after it was established in the early seventeenth century. We read about the massacre that followed and then wandered back to our boats with gloomy hearts.

Conscious that the breeze is often lightest first thing in the morning, we were boating out of Tully Bay earlier than normal for a Misfit cruise. Keeping close into the shore and not bothering to hurry, we eased our way along beneath the high drama of the Cliffs of Magho. In reality very steep hills with only their upmost edges sheer, the

slopes beside us were full of deciduous woodland that made quite some backdrop. Though I could see why Roger had warned us of this place, as the long exposed shore beside us offered no shelter and would be a dreadful spot for a solitary boat to suffer a breakdown in the wrong wind. What made this shore even worse is that few boats come with the sort of tackle needed to anchor securely in the very deep water of the Lower Lough, and then to hold on the hook in the sort of seas it was capable of throwing up. Courtesy of our salt work Hawthorn has rope and chain aplenty, but Eric had a different answer: as if to prove his independence not just from us but from all engine power, he raised his jib sail and grabbed what little

breeze there was. Taking to the dinghy, I ran out into the lough to photograph the three boats together against the landscape's drama. Which was fine until the camera batteries died. So I went and borrowed Ted's, which was fine until the batteries died, then I went and borrowed Eric's… And yes they did.

Within two hours we were passing between the markers keeping us out of the eel nets stretched across the shallows just above the channel we needed to follow to take the river to Belleek. As had been the case for many weeks now, being mothership meant *Hawthorn* was in the lead.

Even while still on the lough we'd become aware of the pace of the water being dragged down the River Erne ahead of us, and once on the river its speed and power had me questioning the wisdom of going down it. Jill grabbed the chart and pointed out a mooring in a backwater just approaching on our starboard side, so I put the wheel hard down and, with a long slide sideways, was able to drive into the promised shelter. Ted and Eric followed us in and pulled alongside. Ted was the only one of us with any idea what Belleek was like, so we asked him if it was worth a battle visiting.

'It's okay. I used to drive through on my way to work in Donegal, but I haven't been for years. The last time I went I remember getting stopped by squaddies on the bridge there who gave me money and asked me buy them lottery tickets from the republic. So I did, and an ice-cream each just for luck!'

It's weird how a simple question about the wisdom of boating a flooded river could dig up such an odd memory but, unfortunately, it left us none the wiser about going on or not. So I added 'I know it's only a few miles and we'd be there in minutes, but getting back is going to be a nightmare slog. Neither Jill nor I are saying no; we just want everyone to agree about what we're getting into.'

Ted, Eric and Mick pondered. It was a strange moment for, while Jill and I couldn't care less, we know lots of boaters for whom getting to the absolute end of a navigation matters enough to risk life and limb. We were not sure which camp Eric and Ted fell into, though the sounds of a kettle clinking and a water pump running on Eric's boat suggested he had more pressing concerns than ticking boxes. There was no rush: the kettle boiled, the dogs were put on the bank, charts were consulted, a cake tin popped open, two men came out of a farm house to stand watching us and a decision to give Belleek a miss was made. Our northing was over, and that was a significant moment.

Now relaxed, we sat for an hour considering what we'd achieved and just how much fun we'd had achieving it. For Jill and me there was still the thrill of the River Barrow and Lough Derg to come the following spring, yet until then we'd be backtracking, reacquainting ourselves with people we'd met and returning to now familiar spaces. Or so we thought, which goes to prove just how little we knew.

Truth told, we'd only barely begun to see the potential of some of the water we'd already boated. While the HBA had opened doors to some of Ree, much of it still waited if we wanted, and we'd only just touched on the potential of Norbert's gifts on Lough Allen. We'd not been to Kilglass, and were guessing we'd need lifetimes to explore all the other possibilities we'd glimpsed in the past few months. As if to prove a point, the first thing we did on returning to the Broad Lough was head for a mooring in its north-west corner some miles from our route that morning. Where, now on his way back from Donegal, Austen joined us.

We'd barely seen another boat all week, so we weren't surprised to find an empty jetty with room aplenty and the silence broken only by the steady dripping of waterlogged trees long after the rain had ceased. I suggested, and Eric and Austen were up for, taking the dinghy fishing. None of us actually expected to catch anything, and it was really just a couple of hours out with the lads messing. And then Austen, who had the lightest tackle, hooked a pike so large it dragged the dinghy where it wanted for several minutes. The beast just fitted our landing net and, terrified of the panic its flapping, biting presence promised if loose amongst us, there it stayed while we unhooked it. If only we'd had a camera with batteries, we could have taken a picture. Our Belleek decision was vindicated when it poured all night, though this did leave us feeling sorry for Austen, who'd departed at a time to suit catching an early morning ferry in Dublin. Then, and just why is still beyond me, we did something rather silly. We decided to go to Kesh.

'Bloody hell fire! This is madness, Jill!' I said, grimly hanging onto the wheel and edging the throttle up as the dark brown surge of rushing floodwater hammered against our bow. 'And look at those overhanging trees; Eric's going to be in massive trouble if he leaves his mast up. You'd better radio him.'

'Me radio him?'

'Well I can't! I've got my hands full dealing with this lot! Unless you want to steer, that is!'

Jill had never used the VHF, and she wished she didn't have to now, yet the state of the river gave her little choice.

'*Zorgen, Zorgen, Zorgen*. This is *Hawthorn*. Are you receiving? Over.'

The ever informal Eric was. 'Yep; is that you Jill? Wow! Go ahead. Oh, over.'

Jill quickly told him the river we were leading our little fleet into had a bit of flow on it, and that the tree canopy would have him in all sorts of trouble unless he took his mast down.

'OK. There's a little jetty here I can pull onto to take it down.' There was a long pause, and then he giggled 'Over.'

'Bit of flow on it?' Who was I kidding? A couple of gentle bends up from its junction with the lough the River Kesh had pinched in, and was now running at a good 4 knots. It was one hell of a struggle just to make ground, the river was too narrow for us to turn and, even if we were willing to risk something so foolish as drifting back, we couldn't because *Heron* was hard behind us. As long as we didn't break down this wouldn't matter, but Jill was quickly back on the radio to Eric suggesting he opt for somewhere safer.

Hawthorn's length was a real problem when we reached a right-angled bend and the flow just grabbed the bow and slammed it into the bushes on the outside bank. Unable to do anything, we let the flow ease the rest of *Hawthorn* against the bank. Thanking the heavens we'd gone for overkill when choosing it, we used our bow-thruster to drive the bow out and then drove the stern round once we had room forward of it. Our wheelhouse was full of tension, which only eased slightly when we were pointing upstream again. Ted, who had been balancing the much shorter *Heron* on the flow behind us, followed. He couldn't pass, and if something on our drive let go, or one of the bloody great lumps of wood flying past fouled our prop, he would be in a difficult spot. There was also an outside chance we might meet a craft surfing downstream: a disturbing thought neither of us wanted to think about until it happened, and wouldn't have time to if it did.

We were both hellish tense. We had no idea how far we'd come, or how much further we would have to go or even if there would be anywhere safe to moor upstream. I was kicking myself at missing just what the dirty stain in the bay below the river's mouth had meant, and then for my blasé confidence in overriding Jill's suggested caution. With the bow-thruster needed to get round several bends, we slowly ground our way on, up against the foam-flecked water rushing through the tree-lined avenue we were trapped in. Release came as the trees thinned above a last tight bend and we saw an empty jetty a hundred yards ahead. It had taken us an hour to boat just over half a mile.

The mooring was on the outside of a wide bend, and we couldn't see the back eddy running up it. The moment *Hawthorn's* bow was alongside it we suddenly surged forward. Aagh! Full ahead to full astern in a split second – thank heavens for hydraulic drives! Jill dropped a line over a cleat, and we stopped with our bow just short of the river bank. Ted had a similar dance as he came alongside us. We grabbed his ropes and lashed him in. And then we were all laughing and Hobbes was barking. That was completely mental, and brilliant, and the sort of adventure we were unlikely to forget.

A little later a local man came down with a camera. He had not seen the river so flooded in years, and was amazed we'd got the barges up it. He brought the worrying news that there was a large hire boat on the jetty in the village upstream. It was late in the afternoon so we doubted they'd be a problem that evening but, if they moved in the morning on a river this flooded, our being on the outside of the bend meant *Heron* was going to get clobbered. So we walked into the village and crossed the arched stone bridge that was vibrating with the power of the river surging through it. The hire boat was moored a hundred yards downstream, and its windows were seriously steamed up. Hoping the steam didn't have an amorous source, I knocked on its door. Phew: there was no hint of honeymoon in the half dozen burly men sat around a table playing cards. I struggled to express my concern and, with their English being as good as my non-existent German, it took a while for us to agree that they really would be leaving – quite literally come hell or high water – at 8.30 am.

'If river same, or higher?' I swept my arm across the water and then made hand signs I hoped would indicate a rise in the water.

'Ja! 8.30. We go 8.30!'

We'd see, and the rain had stopped so the river might settle a little.

We'd only been back at the barges for an hour when the next exciting instalment of our day began with the steady roar of a diesel engine struggling up the river towards us. It took ages to come into sight, and when it did we wished it hadn't. What filled us with horror wasn't the hire boat struggling towards us: it was the four men on its decks, two of whom were using poles to try to keep onrushing debris away from the hull, who hadn't a life jacket on between them. They were probably as stressed as we were and they were clearly intending to join us. Knowing what the back eddy was about to do to them as they pulled in behind us, I quickly scrambled onto *Hawthorn's* stern ready for impact. I was not concerned about their ramming us as I knew there would only be one winner, but the man kneeling behind the pulpit rail on the boat's bow was likely to be in serious trouble if what I feared might happen did happen. Ted had also clocked what was going on, and he was primed to grab and tie a line as fast as possible.

The second the boat was in the back eddy its speed shot up. It slammed into *Hawthorn* with enough velocity to launch the guy on the bow forward and almost onto our stern. I grabbed his collar with one hand and, with the other, hung on for grim death to our handrail. The hire boat was now going backwards, and the man I was hanging onto started to stretch horizontally over the ever-growing space between the two boats. Knowing if I let go he'd be in the flooded river, with a propeller spinning just downstream of him, was terrifying. Jill later told me of the lightning speed with which Ted had tied them in, and the colour of the face of the chap I was holding. It took one of his colleagues to haul him back aboard. Then, just as we had done earlier, the guys on the hire boat collapsed in relieved laughter. The only difference was theirs was Spanish.

With timing appropriate to a film, while hands were being shaken and backs slapped, Eric and Mick appeared. This was good news on two fronts: Mick had bought us all fish and chips and, courtesy of the year he spent in Central America, Eric spoke Spanish. With not a word of English between the hire boat's crew, he set about translating their thanks; thanks that were manifestly real when a bottle of the strangest liqueur was presented to us. We tried it over supper, though without much pleasure, while listening to the tale of Eric and Mick's own adventures after we left them. Their fun included nearly taking the rickety jetty at the bottom of the river with them when a rope fouled it as they were swept downstream by the flow when leaving, and then getting screamed at for mooring on what they took to be a public jetty just round the corner. Stressed enough already, Eric had lost the plot and screamed back that nobody in his or her right mind would insist on putting a boat out onto the choppy lough. They'd ended up on the public jetty just along the shore. This was two miles of dark lanes away, so we weren't surprised when they got a taxi back. As a leaving present Oíche, who was now so rounded we were joking about her having been a very naughty girl, peed on our floor; an appropriately strange end to what had been a very strange day.

The sound of an approaching boat at 8.33 the following morning took me to the wheelhouse to watch the hire boat shoot past. It missed both Ted and the Spaniards, bounced off the bank just downstream of them, and shot round the next corner. We'd been lucky, though mainly because the river was two feet lower than it had been the previous evening. It continued to fall, the Spaniards left, and we followed them at noon. Other than the colour of the river water, the only evidence of the flood was debris suspended in waterside bushes and drifts of fine silt on meadow edges.

We were shortly to see, quite literally, that we weren't the only ones having a lucky day. We'd reassembled our little fleet out on the lough and were headed east for Castle Archdale where Eric was going to trade Mick in for a younger, fitter, female crewmate. Nearly there, we saw the familiar shape of a narrowboat in the distance. A closer inspection with the binoculars revealed it was the boat we'd come to the Ernes with, and that both the RNLI lifeboat and the WI warden's powerful RIB were with it. Clearly it was in trouble, but seeing who was attending and knowing our getting involved would be neither needed nor welcomed, we kept our distance.

The guy on the narrowboat had been lucky that help arrived so quickly after he'd missed a marker, run aground and then been pinned on the shoal by the weather rolling up Broad Lough. The two helpers set about dragging him clear and he was soon able to continue as if nothing had happened. We all knew how fortunate he'd been, and we weren't surprised that both he and his crew were shaken.

RETURNING SOUTH

By now it was late August, and I'd like to write that the summer was slowly fading into autumn, except it wasn't: each day seemed wetter and windier than the one just past. Like migrating birds, Ted and Eric's instincts were to push back south before the rising rivers pinned them miles from their wintering grounds on the eastern end of the Grand Canal. While they could have gone, our being committed to meeting my mother in Enniskillen in a few days' time meant we'd have had to follow on our own. We'd no idea if they'd leave or not, but the subject was never discussed and it seemed a given we'd remain a pack of Misfits for a good while longer. This suited us, for we felt our time with them had been a gift and, while we'd always known this voyage together could only happen once, we weren't yet keen to end it.

So we spent the time waiting for mum in the relative comfort and shelter of the southern end of the lower lough. We wandered about exploring islands and even managed to get quite lost on one, though not as lost as the softly rounded coils of the unmapped hill fort Eric was the first to find in the regimented order of one dark spruce forest. These spaces were spooky enough by day, but late-night dog walks amongst those woods were full of fear.

'Turn the torch off, Eric. Your eyes will soon adjust,' I urged while we were out one night.

'You've got to be bloody joking! It's pitch black and I want to see what's coming.'

Our contrary thoughts – I was convinced that all the nasty things were drawn to the only light, while Eric thought they would flee from it – were probably best left to psychologists to sort. Meanwhile, somehow, Eric was again in

front of me. That he kept leapfrogging past with a little jog whenever I got ahead was down to his theory that 'it's always the guy at the back that gets it first'. I had no idea whether it was well founded, but then I've never been a fan of horror movies, and I didn't really mind as being behind him made it easy for me to drop back a little or tap him on the shoulder. It didn't matter which, for either made him jump enough to get us both screaming.

And then Oíche stopped, bristled, and barked wildly into the blackness. Probably just for the hell of it Hobbes joined in. Eric's plan about being safer in front now suited me and, dashing past him with my torch blazing wildly, I was off down the slope as fast as I dared along the narrow track. Behind me Eric's, at least I assumed they were Eric's, big boots thumped hard and fast. Thinking it was all some mad game, the dogs tore past our giggling flight: at least if the bogey man got us we'd all die laughing.

Once again we were made welcome at the yacht club, where Ted left us for a couple of days and Eric's latest crew departed. There was no sign of the American. We assumed he'd had an armchair ride of an easy time down the flow for the last few miles of his trip to Belleek. We knew he had an anchor, and feared he might have had to use it.

In Ted's absence we took Eric, Oíche and *Hawthorn* up to Enniskillen for a day. The river above Devenish Island was now a very different beast to the one we left three weeks earlier. The flow was substantial: we were soon crawling little faster than we did to Kesh and we were happy to put ourselves on the first mooring we come to. Walking into town we paused on the bridge we knew we were going to have to get through in the next few days. The river here would once have been wide and shallow, but human intervention meant that all the rain caught in the Erne's vast catchment area was now pinched and pushed and forced through this one narrow channel. As we feared would be the case, the water below us was going like stink and we doubted we'd get up it. Back at the yacht club we mentioned our concern to Jimmy, and he suggested we were better off struggling up against the flow than tearing down with it: he was just back from looking at a brand new cruiser that had its upper deck torn off on the bridge's curved structure. It wasn't news to fill us with confidence.

Ted returned with Joelle, and they brought the sun with them. Our leaving now imminent, we had a swansong when we got a tour of some of the lough on Jimmy's barge. He had other mates along and, while we now knew some of the places he took us, their time on the water and connections with its landscape and people changed how we Misfits saw it. There were stories and laughter and a glass of wine or two before a last late night in the club bar. Knowing how spoilt we'd been here, my only regret on leaving was that Eric had somehow dodged having his home thrashed by the club's racing sailors. That would have been something.

There are boaters who argue, and it's a theory of momentum I'm not sure about, that the only way to take on a flooded river is to charge up it as fast as possible. My take has always been that, as long as you're moving faster than the water, then you're winning. I was not sure that was true when we were still a hundred yards short of Enniskillen's pinch-point bridge and barely moving, as I'd been nudging the throttle open for the last ten minutes, and now we were flat out. If something let go, *Hawthorn* was going to cream both *Nieuwe Zorgen* and *Heron* who were staying close behind to try to grab our slipstream. The last thing we needed was a mechanical moment, or for a boat to appear ahead of us on the wrong side of the rive... 'Oh bollocks! Hang on Jill!' A hire boat had flown out from inside the island just above the bridge, and it had to cross the river or hit us. Thankfully its skipper had the sense to give it full throttle, and that meant it was doing about 12 knots when it shot past us. Jill told me it just missed Ted and Eric. I couldn't look: I was too concerned that the boat was in company and fully focused on the thought that more excitement might be imminent. Thankfully it wasn't, and a few minutes later we very slightly started to pick up speed. We'd made it, but only just.

Mum was always going to come to see us while we were in Ireland. She'd have been mad not to and having her with us to share our pleasure was fun. Her presence changed our dynamic and Jill and I became more orthodox tourists for a while. Though not immediately, for the first thing we wanted to do was to share the run back to the special space of Swan Island.

Knockninny, on Upper Lough Erne's southern shore, is a mooring at the foot of a very high hill that we were all, including mum, keen to climb. We were lucky, for not only did we have a map but, by some peculiar stroke of luck, moored in the private marina beside the public jetties was an old boating friend, Alphy, from England. It seems this was the second time he'd seen us as he once roared past us waving and shouting furiously in a speedboat while we were moored a few miles away. Ah, so he was that nutter. We fell in and chatted, and he said that while it was a long way it was perfectly possible to walk to the

hill's summit. And he was right; it is a long way, but the view of the Upper Lough's vast, confused web of green and grey stretching into the distance made it worth it. To the south, Slieve Anierin was clearly visible. It was a steep walk, so I was not surprised when mum found a boulder to rest on. Indeed, far from it: I couldn't help but be impressed and hope I'd be able to manage such exertion in my eighth decade. She did something even more impressive when she climbed into the yew trees at Crom Castle the following day.

On the way there we passed the island, Inish Rath, owned and used by the Hare Krishna community as a centre for their teachings. While we boat gently past our walkie-talkie crackles into life, and it's soon clear that the monks beside us are also using them to communicate in a conversation with several different handsets merrily chatting away. Unfortunately, in the noise and wind of his open stern deck, Ted can't hear them, but he's in high spirits and just for a laugh picks up his walkie-talkie and starts to sing the Hare Krishna song to us. But it's not just us, and while he's roaring and giggling and dancing his happy dance, we're waving our arms at him and laughing while making gestures we hope he'll see as implorations for silence. Finally getting the message, he puts down his handset. Well he's cleared the air, for the silence that follows is profound, and we can only imagine the confusion Ted's just caused on the island he's now passing.

While it had finally stopped raining, we'd no idea how fast the Woodford River would be running when we got there. So we were relieved to find our timing was good and, though high, the river was just boatable. We weren't the only ones glad to be moving: the now falling flood had made the low bridge in Ballyconnell impassable to many of the larger hire boats, and they were now starting to travel again. This was fine, but the flow meant they came onto us quickly and on the narrow, fast-running river it wasn't always possible to keep the large barges of the Misfit fleet in the perfect place to miss them. While we had no collisions, there were more than a few moments of extra tension. We stopped in Ballyconnell ourselves, and went for a walk and a pint in the town, though we wished we'd gone on when some idiots made the mistake of boarding *Heron* in the early hours that night. Unsurprisingly, faced with an onslaught of biker Dub expletives and all manner of personal threats from Red Ted, the trouble moved on and didn't return.

While I took *Hawthorn* on to Swan Island, Jill got a bus from Ballyconnell to collect a hire car in Enniskillen; that turned us into proper tourists. Unable to remember when we'd last been away from the water, we were due a change ourselves, and we were spoilt for choice once Ted and Eric set to with guidance. Just driving on Ireland's comparatively empty roads is a joy, so it didn't matter that Newgrange was several hours away. A prehistoric structure even older than Stonehenge, it was impressive not only in its own right but also in how well getting to it was managed: its visitor centre was miles away, and the only access was in small buses that had to be booked and whose departure was timed so that the site never felt crowded. This meant we all got the time and space not only to see the outside of the huge earthen structure but to go into the tiny chamber in its centre. We weren't surprised to read that English Heritage kept coming and taking notes. Newgrange was Eric's suggestion; Ted's was the Hill of Tara, which was a bit like Glastonbury's with far fewer hippies and none of the King Arthur myths.

One day away from water and boats being more than enough, we planned a bit of a busman's holiday the next morning. The Cuilcagh Mountains, visible in the distance from Lough Garadice, are one vast mass of limestone and, as limestone is rather prone to being, are riddled with caves and subterranean watercourses. Mum likes potholing, and we like boating, so a boat trip through the Marble Arch Caves seemed a perfect destination. Stepping out of a car halfway up a mountain expecting to go afloat was a first, but sadly one that would have to wait as the caverns were flooded. So we walked the dog along the river bounding north down the hill towards the River Erne and Enniskillen, before getting into the car and driving just a few miles to stand beside water starting a much longer journey down the Shannon to Limerick.

What the rivers Thames, Severn and Trent all have in common is unremarkable sources. They start as damp patches in fields or tiny trickles down overgrown and unremarkable ditches. As we now knew, the Shannon does things rather differently: it rises from a seemingly bottomless sheer-sided and darkly brooding pool called a pot about fifty feet across, with a power and purpose that left me doubting it could ever dry out. The water spilled out of the pot to run down the hill as a decent-sized stream that I could just about leap across and Hobbes went straight into for a paddle. When, as he always does, he barked to demand that sticks were thrown, I stood wondering just how long it would take the water absorbing his sound to carry its echo all the way to the distant estuary.

Mum was a little unlucky, for had she stayed another week she'd have enjoyed the most glorious Indian Summer and the best spell of weather since we'd joined the Misfits back on Ree. As we knew when leaving Swan Island on our way north a few weeks earlier, we returned to a few small jobs, and while we cracked on Eric, Ted and Joelle drifted round the lough in a borrowed Mirror dinghy and Eric's canoe. We'd walk the dogs down the lanes and pick the blackberries Jill needed to make the fruit leather Eric promptly christened Pirate Jelly. And then, in one of the daftest decisions I'd made in years, I asked Pat to give me some wake-boarding lessons. Always up for something new, Joelle signed up as well.

Before we even got near the water there was a video explaining the mechanics of what the novice wake-boarder has to do to transit from wallowing in the water to upright and gracefully sliding on it. It was a training video, so of course it looked easy. Perhaps they should also make a training video of how to get an overweight middle-aged man into a wetsuit, for that turned into quite some struggle. My ten-minute battle with rubber was followed by a few minutes on the grass pretending that it was water, and that a 250 hp speedboat rather than a grinning Pat was attached to the rope I was hauling on. Unsurprisingly, given we'd been doing it for well over forty years, neither Joelle nor I had a problem standing up on grass. So, with Jill and Ted along for the ride, we all piled aboard Pat's rocket ship, and set off to have some fun.

Joelle was first to go overboard and, while she bobbed about behind us, the speedboat slowly pulled away and the towrope gradually drew taut. Pat gunned the boat, Joelle surged forward and the rope went slack. The pressure on her hands being too much for her to hang on, she'd let go. Not that it mattered: watching in a rear-view mirror, Pat had put the wheel hard down and, barely a minute later, the towrope was back in her grasp and another attempt to get Joelle upright and boarding was attempted. This had the same outcome, so we went again, and again, until Joelle's hands and arms were in agony and continuing was pointless. It wasn't the most promising of starts: her frustration was palpable and, as I was about to appreciate myself, perfectly understandable.

After half a dozen failed attempts to get out of the water, the only thing I was certain of was that being dragged along face down behind a speedboat was the most physical thing I'd done in years. At each failing I'd bob in the water while Pat circled back with a big grin on his face and encouraging words to offer:

'You bloody lummox! You're pushing four hundred acres of lake! And let go when you're going to crash!'

On one occasion I did get a 'nearly' with a thumbs up, but it was brutal and tiring, and a damn site harder than I'd ever thought while watching kids playing at the Silver Eel and several places since. Fortunately another wakeboarding boat arrived and Dean, a young friend of Pat's, joined us. Into the water went Dean, up came the revs, up came Dean and, with a casual one handed grasp of the tow, Dean straightened his shorts. 'Oh, we've got one here all right,' I thought, as he effortlessly shot out wide of the boat and then soared back in a great graceful arc of power which saw him airborne and twisting for a few seconds. He'd crossed the wake without touching it, and then came back the other way with a somersault thrown in for good measure. I was able to take in some of the extraordinary athleticism and grace of his actions, but they were so far removed from my clumsy efforts they were of little relevance. Watching him, I knew I'd settle for getting up and moving, and to be able to use just one hand while I fiddled with my shorts would be unimaginably rewarding. Dean could keep the stunts: just that would do for me.

Joelle's hands being too sore for her to make another attempt for a couple of days, I got launched in for another try. And this time, with lots of coaching from Dean, I was successful: my knees and back might both be bent and the board pushing through the water rather than gliding over it, but I was up, and I stayed up. Well, for at least a couple of hundred yards until, with my best crash to date, I slammed face first into the water. Pat circled, Dean advised; the wake-board was ripped from my feet in the crash and I bobbed about for a few minutes putting it back on and then we went again. I could get up, but the idea of steering the bloody thing was a foreign land I was unlikely to visit, so I just hung on grimly. Pat had been waiting for that moment: he turned the boat's sound system on and Tina Turner's *Simply the Best* ripped into the afternoon air as, with a huge grin on my face, I ploughed a graceless furrow across Lough Garadice's once-calm reflective beauty.

Any idea that my brief foray over the water had granted me membership of some trendy youthful tribe was instantly dismissed when I went for my 'free beer' that evening. Pat's son, himself a rather fine wake-boarder, greeted me with the news he had heard I was one of the most spectacular crashers his dad had ever seen. I was not sure that this was a title to be proud of but I was certain of one thing: there was an aching soreness about my limbs that took me back to my rugby-playing days. Yet, as I was soon made aware by Pat, I seemed to have gotten away reasonably lightly.

'Shake your head,' he said, sitting down on the coffee table in front of me. 'Eh?'

'Go on, give it a good shake and try blowing through your nose while you're doing it.' Which I did, though nothing happened, certainly not what Pat expected and hoped would. For it seemed it's not only Irish mountains that fill with water: wake-boarders' heads do too. Pat went on to tell me how, completely out of the blue one evening after a long day wake-boarding, he'd bent down to put a plate of food in front of one of his diners and a full pint of water suddenly exploded from his nose! He'd no idea it was there or what was happening and, with his hands full of food, no way of stopping it. The quality and violence of my crashing had given him high hopes that I would prove to be similarly flushed, though why he'd want me to leak all over his own bar was anyone's guess. I didn't get long to rest on my laurels though, for Pat was soon suggesting the next thing I needed to do was to move across the speedboat's wake. 'Next time? You mean I'm still in credit?' 'Indeed you are,' he said.

And indeed I was. Much to Pat's surprise given all the hammering I'd already taken, I was actually up for another bash the following day. Though, while I managed not to crash as often, crossing the wash was never going to happen. A day of rest followed, and then a third and final lesson. Still hurting from her first attempts, Joelle wasn't keen to inflict more damage to either her wrists or her wallet, but a friend of Eric's who'd heard what we were up to was driving up to join us for a play. The moment he arrived I had to smile: the friend was Andrew, the lad who'd canoed across to chat with us in Hazelhatch. We shook hands and laughed, and Jill and I joked that we had indeed met Eric, and Andrew went and changed into a wetsuit that somehow made him seem even more athletic.

Far too weird for words was his instant mastering of the wakeboard! The bastard was up and flying on only his second attempt at launching and then stayed up with ease. Which was enough to have Pat, who had been teaching wake-boarding for a while, saying he'd never seen anyone take to it so effortlessly.

While it was tempting to throw the speedboat's seats at him to force a crash, I sat admiring Andrew's smooth transition from side to side, while listening to Pat's astonishment at seeing such natural prowess. Eventually, and fortunately before the boat ran out of fuel, Andrew tired and fell. So I got to have a final go.

With muscles aching a little less for a full day's rest, I did manage to get across the wake, though not back again. So I continued to pursue the title of 'Best Crasher Ever' currently held by a South African mate of Pat's who, while able to swerve and accelerate with enough speed to launch himself from one side of the wake, could never master the art of landing on the other. He'd get himself well into the air and then let go of the rope and just let gravity do what gravity does. While I lacked the guy's pace, my grim determination to hang on, long after any sensible soul would have let go, meant I was violently, and quite unnecessarily, slammed into the water. I didn't win the award, but it's nice to be good at something. Even Andrew, now wrapped in a towel and – lacking the essential blubbery deposits of a natural water beast – shivering, had to admit it was one area he couldn't touch me on.

There was something about Swan Island that made it special and us reluctant to leave. Yet we couldn't stay, not only because the moorings were exposed and the bar about to shut for the winter, but also because there's a natural time for things to end and we all sensed it coming. So we returned the Mirror dinghy and tidied up, and declared that night in the bar would be our last. It was always going to be a weird one, but just how weird we'd never have guessed.

We, that is Ted, Joelle, Jill and myself, were all up in the bar having a merry time laughing about wake-boarders. I was shaking my head and blowing my nose to try to deliver the flood Pat, now convinced my head was hollow, was determined I had in me, when Eric dashed in breathlessly saying 'Something weird is going on with Oíche. I think she's going to give birth!'

Pat was calmness personified. 'Leave her to it,' he said. Which we did, though Eric was a lot less certain and shuffled between bar and boat for most of the evening. Come midnight, when we hadn't seen him for about an hour, he burst in and announced he was a dad! Oíche had just given birth to one puppy, and more were on their way. Which was nice, so nice we all drank the puppies' health, and continued to do so for another hour, before calling in on Eric's growing brood on our way to bed. By now there were three of them.

By nine the following morning Oíche had had three more. Eric declared them Swan Island Terriers in honour of the location of their birth, and named the largest, the first born, Pat, after our host. Host Pat came down for a look. He was impressed both by their pedigree and by having the biggest bugger named after him, and also because Oíche hadn't lost a pup: something he'd gently suggested would almost certainly be the case when the excitement started the previous evening.

We wondered whether we should go, yet we knew there was no real need to stay: Oíche was used to her home moving, and with the weather ever more autumnal we needed to press on before the Shannon started flooding.

AUTUMN

For some reason, perhaps Roger had once said something or I'd picked it up on the Internet forum, we'd always anticipated spending our winter in Ireland at Shannon Harbour. And then we'd arrived there in mid June, and seen the reality that spending several static months in such a remote spot simply wasn't going to happen. It didn't matter at the time – we were having far too much fun to worry about where we'd be in November – and everything else seemed to be falling effortlessly into place. Confident that the right location was out there just waiting for us to find it, we got on with our indulgent summer. Yet the right location hadn't shown up and, with autumn now fast approaching, for the first time since arriving our lack of a plan became a little worrying.

With no car, we had to winter somewhere we could walk to shops, which, at least on the Shannon, really left only Carrick and Athlone. We'd visited both several times and not seen the sort of mooring we'd be comfortable on, let alone anything that promised decent walks with Hobbes. Even if we had seen somewhere suitable, the evidence of the Shannon's winter floods, hanging from trees and fences far distant from the river, left us nervous about wintering on it. Which left the canal, and the only place we could imagine wintering without a car was Tullamore, and that harbour was very public and noisy with traffic. When we mentioned our dilemma to the Misfits over supper one evening, they looked surprised. And Eric said 'We assumed you were coming with us to Sallins.' And then Ted added 'The Lidl store beside the canal's now open, and you can borrow my car if you want to go further.'

More gifts; problem solved.

As sure as the nights were drawing in and the swifts were leaving, we knew our summer of adventure was ending. A determined push downriver would see us on the Grand Canal in days, yet a collective reluctance to end our playing slowed us down. Wanting to see Lough Key in autumn, we headed for Drummans Island. It was as beautiful as we'd hoped, and without the screams and shouts of holidaying visitors we loved the way the woods were damply silent. While Hobbes revelled in leadless walks, Oíche was too occupied with her writhing brood to join us.

The most extraordinary thing happened at Carrick when, finally conceding to my bibliophilic lust, I set out to buy the early copy of *Life on the Mississippi* I knew had my name on it since late June. It seemed it hadn't, for I couldn't find it. I couldn't have hidden my disappointment well as the bookshop owner quickly offered help, and I told him what I was after. He replied that I'd been most unlucky: he'd just, and by just he was talking minutes, sold it. And he had: to Eric, Ted and Joelle, who'd bought it for me. It was a wonderful gift, made more wondrous as they all struggled for money.

Joining Lough Ree at Lanesborough, we headed for Barley Harbour, and on our way had a few of the tensest minutes we'd had in months. There were two canoeists on the water, though it seemed a little odd that they'd chosen to boat along the buoyed handrails of the navigation channel when they could be in the sheltered shallows. It didn't matter to us as we'd seen them and the Misfit barges weren't fast enough to make a wake, but the charging Twin Screw Diesel Yacht (TSDY) catching us was a different matter.

We'd heard a lot about TSDYs. They were the flash new toys, able to do 15 to 20 knots, that when pushed left huge rolling wakes capable of inflicting serious damage. The ready cash of the economic miracle of the Celtic Tiger had seen a lot of them imported but, now that the Tiger was mortally wounded (Pat had banned all discussions of the economy from the Swan Island bar!), those we had been passed by had only ever been pottering. The one now coming down Lough Ree behind us was the first we'd seen really cracking on: through the binoculars Jill and I watched its skyward pointing bow and the rolling mess behind it, and gently warned Ted and Eric of what we feared descending. Eric should be fine but, with his beloved motorbike strapped across his deck, Ted had good reason to be concerned. Now our concern turned to the canoeists, which we feared the steerer on the TSDY's helm might not see over his raised bow. So we put our fleet behind them and backed right down to stay there. There was no answer when I tried to call the rapidly approaching boat on the VHF radio to express concern for those around us, and the violence of its passing just a few yards away was considerable. All hell broke loose: we'd all turned our bows into the rolling surging water of its wake, and we watched as Ted hung on to bike and boat for grim death. Caught unawares, the canoeists ended up surfing wildly. We could hear stuff flying about below decks on *Hawthorn* and Eric firing expletives at the TSDY on the hand-held VHF he was holding. While not strictly orthodox, at least other listening boaters on the lough would know something nasty might be coming.

That afternoon brought sadness when, strangely for he'd been the firstborn, and largest, and he'd been taxied to a vet the day before when he started weakening, the puppy Pat died while we were in Barley Harbour. A melancholy moment, in stark contrast to the fun of the July picnic we'd experienced just yards from his tiny grave, which Eric built as a dolmen. It was odd to have such a downer at the end of what had been an extraordinary rich and fun experience, for we were finally saying goodbye to Ted, Joelle and Eric in the middle of the lough the following day. They were going on down the Shannon while we were headed back into the Inner Lakes to have a look at a job we might or might not get and weren't sure we wanted. With the lough rougher than expected, *Nieuwe Zorgen* and *Heron* were strapped together and the further we got from them the more they merged as one. It was an appropriate image to carry with us as the gap between us grew.

We'd loved Misfitting. The companionship of others made the past couple of months so much richer than they would have been if we'd ploughed a solitary furrow. We knew there would be times when we'd miss their company, yet we also felt a need to be alone again. It was as if the water somehow knew this too as, when we arrived at the marina to look at the job, we were told *Hawthorn* was too big and heavy for its jetties. We were very gently asked if we'd mind mooring on the island opposite. Mind? We couldn't think of anything we'd welcome more at that moment. Once there, we strolled about exploring, and found the

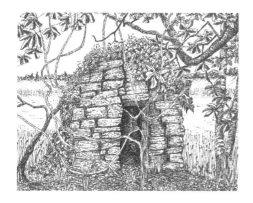

crumpled ruins of a dwelling and, by the shore, an old icehouse that Jill was keen to draw. Later we took the dinghy back over the water to meet the man who wanted to show us his boat. The job was not for us, so we scarpered back to solitude in the reed-lined cutting where *Hawthorn* was moored. Now dying and drying, the once-rustling reeds had developed a rattle.

Despite our delay, when we finally got to Shannon Harbour we found the Misfits waiting and the harbour as solid with boats as it had been for the rally. Apparently they were wintering there, which made us relieved we didn't intend to as they were rafted up together three abreast, and there was nowhere we could put *Hawthorn* so Hobbes could get ashore. Already tired after a long day on the water, we'd been looking forward to a few pints of good Guinness in McIntyres' pub, yet we couldn't get out fast enough. Seeing there was a long, and in places very angry, thread about all the boats in Shannon Harbour on the IWAI Internet forum, I expressed my own frustration. Back came a reply from Conor, one of our new friends in the HBA and the man whose boat had been the first we clothed, that was so wonderfully apt and clever I'm happy to repeat it.

'Ah Giles, think of it as a secret sauce recipe. Your overall experience has been delicious, but even the nicest sauce will have something in it, like chilli pepper, that on its own is distasteful. The challenge is finding the right balance.'

Perhaps I had been a little ungracious, but there was no arguing he'd neatly nailed me. What could I say? Only that the dish was delicious.

Our speed on the canal was much slower than Ted and Eric easily managed in their lighter, leaner, faster boats. Not wanting the stress of playing catch up we urged them on. Besides we wanted to dally at Rahan to chat about our wonderful summer with Alan, the lockkeeper, and taken gently the canal was just as charming in the autumn as it had been in the summer.

Just how wrong we'd been about our boating excitement being over was clear when we heard there was to be a late October rally on the Naas line of the canal just by Sallins. A joint venture between the local IWAI branch and the HBA, it promised a bit of fun we'd not expected. We were looking forward to reacquainting ourselves with some of the boaters we'd last seen when we were racing *4B* on Lough Ree. It seemed the HBA had intended to gather in Dublin but, having said that wasn't possible, WI compromised on Naas instead. It may have been the HBA's intention all along, for the Naas line's locks were so little used they were thick with limescale: while smaller boats might just get through, they were impassable to big barges. Even after three weeks cleaning and the removal of lorry loads of debris, it was touch and go as both barges and locks varied in width. Not having such a vessel ourselves, we watched them play with idle fascination: a barge would start into a lock, get stuck, be dragged out and then go again with a lot more revs and violence and advice and abuse flowing in equal measure from the gathered crowd of onlookers. While possibly only narrowest by an inch or so, the fourth lock proved such a challenge a four-wheel-drive (4WD) with a towrope was used to get the tightest-fitting barges through. It was brutal and compelling, and we took our hats off to the determined way the barge-owners forced the canal to continue to accept boats built for it.

Fortunately, for we'd have been there until Christmas otherwise, only about a third of the thirty odd boats attending were ex-working barges; the rest were an assortment of cruisers and the local live-aboard community. The line was so rarely used that the full harbour became a tourist attraction and townsfolk wandered the towpath chatting to the crews now decorating their craft with lights and bunting.

While a lot smaller and more intimate than our first rally, knowing a few folk made this gathering rather easier. Once again everybody seemed to know everybody else, and the waterside building at the centre of the event seemed full of life and humour. Of course there was fancy dress, and of course everybody went to the pub quite a bit. Once again the rally finished at a prize presentation, though, and we weren't surprised for it had been very different, we were spared the embarrassment of winning. The oddest moment was seeing the first awarding of a trophy given in memory of *Blackthorn's* skipper, Mick Clinton. The more we heard about this man the more I regretted our not stopping five months earlier.

With the rally truly the last event of the year for many, when it ended a length of the canal below the town became winter moorings. We went on to Sallins and moored opposite a mill. It wasn't a bad spot, it was next to the now opened Lidl and there were Misfits and other friendly boaters all around, yet we'd not expected to spend the winter listening to oats being rolled, or to have our world constantly smelling of porridge.

The tarmacked towpath beside us was mainly used by the odd car on its way to and from a couple of canal-side cottages just west of us. At least once a day we walked Hobbes down it and stood in the rain watching the River Liffey surge under the stone aqueduct. And it never seemed to stop raining, and the river never seemed to stop rising. We'd been doing this for nearly a month when, one Sunday morning while we were lying in bed, we heard the beeping of a lorry reversing in beside us, and looked out to see a tanker pulling up. The driver jumped down, crowbarred a manhole open and then dumped several thousand gallons of dirty water into the storm drain below it. When he left another tanker pulled up, and then another: a seemingly endless chain. Bored and curious, I went out to ask what was going on. The tanker driver looked surprised, and then asked if I'd seen or heard the news.

I hadn't, so he told me that the Liffey had burst its banks, and he and his colleagues had been engaged to pump water out of a flooded basement in the town of Clane. While not an expert on Irish geography, I did know Clane was downstream of Sallins, so why they were dumping the water upstream of where they were pumping was a little baffling. Saying nothing, I went back in and put the television on and quickly learned that we were in the middle of Ireland's worst floods in living memory. Seeing all the problems the people of Carrick and Athlone were dealing with – there were countless flooded houses and the only things moving on some streets were boats – made us relieved we followed our instincts and got off the river. And then, amongst the news round-ups from each county, we saw an event in Sallins was gaining momentum.

It seemed the houses on a newly built estate called The Waterways (you couldn't make that up) were filling with water, with some now submerged as far as their first floors. It was only a few hundred yards away, so we wandered up the lane on the embankment between it and the canal, where we joined a small gathering of boaters and locals who'd come to watch the drama. It was a boater who pointed out that the only drain for the flooded area below us was a two-foot pipe that passed through the embankment and discharged straight into the canal. He reckoned it was either blocked, or far too small. It didn't really matter, for the water was still rising and watching people's mortgaged futures drowning wasn't fun. We soon left, and paid little attention to the large digger that rumbled up as we were leaving.

Once home, we put the television on and saw the digger tearing up the road we'd just been standing on. It dug on down, deeper and deeper and across the whole width of the embankment, until the structure breached and the flood surged through. Moments later our home was picked up by the same water we'd just been watching on our screen. Looking out and up through Sallins bridge, we saw moored boats banging and jostling as the canal went up nearly a foot in seconds. Within a couple of hours the news crews were showing the devastation of wrecked homes and cars and lives that the water had left behind just up the lane. That was another experience we'd never anticipated, though not one we'd consider a gift.

With Oíche's puppies now more independent, she and Eric joined us when we strolled that way the following morning. Ignoring the crude barrier blocking the towpath, we went on to stand beside the raw and ragged scar of the breach. Carried by the surging water, much of the embankment was now a beach blocking the canal. We'd been lucky: we'd nearly boated on to Hazelhatch a few days earlier, and had we done so we'd now be trapped.

WINTER

Using Ted's car to extend our exploring as far as the Wicklow Mountains and Glendalough, and with offers of work from local boaters, the winter started with more promise than we'd anticipated. While grateful that work brought in a little money, the other major benefit was that it kept us busy, and being busy kept us sane. Fortunately we were not too busy for a day off with the Misfits in Dublin. Being a Dub, Ted was keen to show off his city, and we were delighted to be indulged. Dublin is the perfect size to stroll around and much more like Manchester or Liverpool, the northern cities we love, than London. Were it not for lonely dogs we'd have happily stayed much longer.

We were still in Sallins at Christmas, as was Joelle, visiting Ted. We invited them and Eric in for supper one evening and presented them with gifts of Misfit Mariner

burgees and T-shirts that Jill had made. And then, with work complete and tired of the relentless traffic in the village centre, the constant smell of porridge and the rattling rolling of oats beside us, we went down with our first bad dose of cabin fever. The cure was simple: we needed to move, to get away to somewhere quieter, before we cracked completely. With the canal ahead closed by the breached embankment, we turned back west across the Liffey and put ourselves up the 16th lock at Digby Bridge. It was the perfect spot: quiet and with the bonus of the best view on the entire Grand Canal across the lock and bridge to the distant backdrop of the Wicklow Mountains just south of Dublin. We stayed there, with Ted or Eric and occasionally both for company, for the remaining winter months, only returning to Sallins once a week to shop and indulge in what we called our Sunday treat.

It doesn't seem to be possible to write about visiting Ireland without describing the mighty craic of a traditional music session. The standard cliché would be how we'd wandered into a pub to find a corner being cleared and instruments appearing from behind the bar. We'd then be treated to the most amazing night of jigs and reels, and end up staying, drinking and singing, and even dancing, into the early hours before stumbling home through damp air sweetened by the smoke of peat-fuelled fires. Our nights in Sallins were a bit like that, only different.

Ted and Eric had been enthusing about these very informal music sessions ever since we'd met them so, keen to see if reality matched their evocative descriptions, we went along the moment we arrived in the village. Involving local boaters, friends from around the area and anyone who turned up and wanted to join in, the number of musicians varied from as few as half a dozen to four times that; people came and went as their fancy took them and nobody minded in the least when they did. Playing ability ranged from the ridiculously talented whistler who was more than able to hold her own with anyone, right down to raw beginners, and the range of instruments was as varied as the skills of those holding them: guitars, mandolins, whistles, flutes, bodhráns, banjos and squeeze-boxes were there in numbers, with the occasional fiddle thrown in.

Given such a mixed bunch of instruments and skill sets, the fact that the music always seemed to be excellent is either because it was, because I've no ear, or because I usually drank too much. It's more than possible it was all three, but then it wasn't as if it mattered, for everybody just had fun. Over a few visits it became clear that the evening's apparently random order was actually far from that: that the music would begin with the first musicians present getting stuck into tunes they, and everyone then joining, knew well. It also became evident, even to my untrained ear, that the less able just stuck to basics while the more gifted embellished freely. Someone, quite possibly Eric, must have told me that timing is far more important than being note perfect, so it wasn't surprising to hear the rhythm being controlled by the more experienced. While there seemed to be a set of tunes, there was also room for individuals to lead with their personal favourites. Watching how nobody was excluded, belittled or mocked, and how even the most out-of-tune-and-time attempt to lead was encouraged, made me conscious of just what a wonderful thing playing music in a group is. Though it could go awry: very occasionally there'd be the painful loneliness of a musician leading off and playing so badly nobody could dig them out. They'd try, but with each withdrawing player the slow death of any hope for the tune or its timing always felt personal.

At some point mid-evening an older man would come through from the other bar and sing *McAlpine's Fusiliers*. A ballad with a softly spoken opening stanza, he'd start in with just one or two guitars behind him, and then it would build and build. By the time the song was halfway through, everybody who wanted to had joined in, and not just instruments but the stomping feet and clapping hands of gathered listeners like us. The song now belonged to anyone in the pub who wanted to sing it, and by the final lines the whole pub was shouting and musicians were getting all the noise they possibly could from their instruments.

It only needed one player to put their instrument down to go to the toilet or bar or out for a fag, and a new game began: a loose banjo might be nabbed by a guitarist, which meant there was a surplus guitar for a mandolin player to have a go with. The mandolin would then be picked up by the bodhrán player, the bodhrán by a whistler, and then the banjo player would return, glance round to see what was going on, shrug and pick up a whistle. As I've already declared, I'm no expert so I couldn't hear a lot of difference, though by that stage I'd have had a few pints and be far too content to care. It was wonderful fun, and there were times when I was moved to tears.

I wish I could say that it was the sheer beauty of Eric's haunting whistling, Darren's guitar playing (neither he nor his instruments had suffered for their dinghy ride) or the extraordinary duets that two of the women sometimes sang that caused my wet cheeks. But it wasn't: it was songs like *Bobby the Dog*, *Syphilis* and *Eggs* that were sung by the comic genius of one occasional attender, Tom Tuohy, that had me rolling on the floor. And I wasn't alone: people seemed to know when Tom was going to appear and there would be a little extra buzz about the place. Just how it was possible for a single-chord song like *Eggs* – a tale of what happens to two young men who find themselves abroad and so skint that eggs are all they can afford to eat – could have the whole pub laughing is one of those mysteries I'll never know the answer to. But it did, as did *Syphilis*, which was sung to the tune of *It started with a kiss* (and ended up with syphilis…). Being the decent soul he is, Tom didn't just arrive and launch into his own stuff: he'd be in there with his guitar playing along with everyone else, and there'd be a few minutes of mock reluctance before he cut loose.

It was Tom's *My Little Honda 50*, for which he'd written both music and lyrics, that gave us a little insight into how things in Ireland sometimes work. It goes:

> *My little Honda 50 she's rapid and she's nifty*
> *She'll do a hundred and fifty on a windy day.*
> *My little Honda 50, hit the nitro and she'll shift me.*
> *Get me away from the Garda anyway.*
>
> *I got her in the Buy and Sell back in '82*
> *A travellin' man in a caravan said "This is the bike for you".*
> *He was lookin' for a hundred, I gave him thirty two.*
> *Took her for a spin out the Kinnegad Road and begod she feckin' flew*

A local song for local people, most of Tom's listeners would have known the Garda (Irish for Guard: police officer) named and the roads raced. It's just a lot of fun and, in comparison with some of Tom's more scurrilous songs, pretty innocent: certainly innocent enough for Tom to play on the workshop stereo while he was working in a petrol station.

And here's the twist that makes this story so Irish. A man filling his car with petrol listens along, and when he goes to pay asks about the song and is directed to Tom. He asks if Tom would mind his brother singing the song, which, particularly given the brother is one of the giants of the Irish music scene, Christy Moore, unsurprisingly Tom doesn't. Months later, Moore appeared on *The Late Late Show* to perform it with Tom in the audience. While there was nothing wrong with Moore's *Honda 50*, it didn't run quite as well as Tom's. It may have had a little muck in the carburettor and I suspected it would probably only do about a hundred and forty. But then Christy Moore confessed he was still learning the song, it was through the cold medium of television, and I was sober.

Tom's tracks can be found on youtube, something unlikely to happen to the noises I started making when the gift of having Eric willing to teach me, and time to practise, saw me buy a low whistle of my own.

Basically a tube with nine holes in it that you blow down, the low whistle looked a simple enough instrument to learn. I suppose for some it might be as easy as it looks, but all I seemed to manage when I blew it – I can't say played as that would suggest some competency – was to inflict pain on those around me. Jill would slowly sink to the floor with her hands over her ears and tears in her eyes, while Hobbes just clawed at the door and whimpered (though not in time). Before long a compromise was reached that I only played it in our living quarters when Jill and the dog were out together. This meant I had to go to the unheated workshop at the back, which was fine while the weather was just wet but not when the coldest spell since 1963 set in.

Leaving *Hawthorn* in the Misfits' care, we borrowed Ted's car and returned to England to catch up with friends and family over the New Year. We were in York when the snow started and, fearing we'd be trapped before reaching Holyhead, we took off early to make sure we caught the ferry. We did, and then got home at midnight to find the canal frozen and snow falling. At times like this – as we remembered well from *Camberwell Beauty* – the cold dampness on unheated boats takes hours to drive out. Knowing that, we'd designed *Hawthorn's* heating to run without power or any attention for a fortnight; opening the door to warmth was the best welcome we could imagine. We awoke the following morning to find Sallins thick with snow and great queues of cars struggling to get over the icy bridge.

A few days later we were standing beside the Liffey aqueduct with Ted and Eric, staring at the most enormous icicles hanging beneath its arches. Ted should take the credit for our finding them, for he'd suggested that its stonework might well be leaky and that the consequences might be worth clambering down to see. They were, but he only got snowballed for his smartness.

The canal's brief thawing a few days later meant we returned to Digby Bridge with Eric for company. Once there, Jill worked on her art while I helped Eric build and install a new bathroom. This was something *Nieuwe Zorgen's* soft round lines made dramatically tricky, particularly so in a space better suited to Eric's slightness than my width and height. We drank a lot of tea, and blew a lot of whistles, and a couple of evenings a week Darren and other musicians would call, and proper music would be made into the early hours of the morning. I'd go, but being still a long way short of competent I made more cups of tea than sounds. And, despite the word being out that I was learning, I still ducked out of the Sunday Sessions.

'Brought your whistle with you Giles?' I'd be asked on arriving.

'Not this week. I don't think I'm quite ready to play with you big boys yet.'

'Eh! Eric? What's going on with Giles and this bloody whistle?'

'Err, I'm just popping out for a fag…'

'Well he can play yours then.'

'Err, I don't think so, I'm going to nick a fag off Eric.'

'No, don't be like that. Sit in here, and if you don't want to whistle then just bang away on this bodhrán.'

No! Not the bodhrán! Recalling what a very fine bodhrán player I'd been to college with had said about most of the people who play them, even without Darren gently smiling and shaking his head in the background, there was no way I'd pick one up in company.

The winter dragged on, and Ted kept saying how amazed he was every time he looked up and saw the Wicklow Mountains still covered in snow, as he'd never known them white for more than a week. Come the start of March we started to make plans for our run down the River Barrow, which would only be possible once winter maintenance works on a lifting bridge at Monastarevin were completed for St Patrick's Day on the seventeenth. We were about to leave when news came that the works were running late. Now fed up at being static, we leapt at the invitation to an Easter Rally over the first weekend of April.

Ten months had passed since we first visited Edenderry; then we'd been on our own with scrambled heads, and a need to hide on the bog and slowly ease our way into an alien landscape and culture. Now, having spent the winter living, working and playing in the boating community, we came down the canal with a gang of mates and entered the town's harbour exchanging greetings and feeling as if we knew everyone. Hardly a soul had come to *Hawthorn* at Shannon

Harbour's rally, yet here the kettle seemed ever on as people constantly visited. Always willing to cook, Jill made a vast vat of vegetable curry for the evening's communal supper, though there was no one there to eat it when it was ready at the allotted hour. Ah, rally time! The curry sat happily on our Rayburn for another sixty minutes. It was a good thing the curry was hot, for when we did eat it was al fresco and bloody freezing! Then it was down the pub for music and a table quiz, and then back home to a sulking dog in the early hours.

Fortunately Hobbes was still fast asleep when the Easter Bunny called by in the morning and left us, and every boat in the harbour, a chocolate egg.

The rally over, we set about departing for the Barrow, something made dramatically harder by gale-force winds. There's no shelter on the Bog of Allen, and the only way to avoid getting driven onto the bank was to crab almost sideways across the canal. If someone were to be shown a still photograph of our line of boats and barges, they'd think we were all involved in some peculiar dance, or that we were all intent on running aground at equidistant intervals. We spent what was to be our last night in company for some time above the lock at Ticknevin before, finally, waving everybody goodbye when we left both our friends and the Grand Canal's Main Line the following morning and headed south towards the River Barrow. Where, particularly after all we'd heard of both its beauty and how challenging it could be to boat, we hoped we'd find the adventures we'd been promised.

THE BUMPY BARROW

After a winter spent on the calm confines of a canal and a frustratingly delayed journey on the Barrow line from Lowtown to Athy, leaving the last canal lock and returning to flowing water brought a welcome sense of exultation. It didn't last long: we only went straight across the river to join the still water of the lateral cut we needed to follow to the Barrow's first lock, Ardreigh, and skiving schoolboys chucked rocks at us while we were doing that. The cut we joined was as narrow and shallow and as hard to get along as the canal we'd just left, so we were delighted to see the WI maintenance gang waiting to put us through the lock at its downstream end when we eventually got there twenty minutes later. Perhaps now we were about to join the river again, we'd finally get going. Shouting our thanks to the smiling crew of WI workers, I put the boat in gear and, as we eased out onto the flow, got ready for the challenge ahead. And then we heard our baseplate running onto sand and gravel, and we stopped a boat's length from the lock gate.

Despite trying everything we knew to get *Hawthorn* shifted, after half an hour of driving back and forward, bow-thrusting and poling, we accepted we were going nowhere. The maintenance crew thought their 4WD pick-up might pull us back to the lock but, apparently for legal reasons, they needed me to request help rather than to offer it. It was a bit of dance, but of course I did, and they took a rope and skidded and slid about a bit and then we slowly, oh so slowly, slid back to where we started.

Once back in the lock we were laughing and joking and putting the kettle on. And while it boiled we stood listening to the disturbing news that there had never been a sandbank below the lock before. The lads were blaming it on November's record floods, and no one had a clue what other surprises those floods might have left on the navigable river's twenty-three locks and forty-one miles to where it reached the sea at the tidal lock in St Mullins.

Then Jim, WI's foreman on the river, arrived. The kettle went back on, and we sat around discussing our options. He'd already started chasing the machine and manpower needed to get us under way, and he was keen we continue on. For not only were we the very first boat of the season, we were also very much larger than the average visitor, and if we could make it anyone could. Basically, he wanted a survey ship, and *Hawthorn* was perfect. What did we think?

To be honest, from the moment it was suggested we knew we'd be going on. It might be the maddest thing we'd done since crossing the Irish Sea, but we'd wanted and welcomed adventure and to turn this one down would be pure hypocrisy. And we didn't have any choice: if we went on to Derg and then came back, the River Barrow could have dropped to the summer levels when the maximum draft allowed would be some 6" less than our 3': we'd neither have a chance of getting down it nor be welcomed for trying. Knowing this, Jill and I looked at each other, and then we sort of smiled and agreed we'd have a go, though only as long as Jim promised he wouldn't leave us stranded in the middle of nowhere.

Our usual lucky selves, with friends from the HBA in a riverside cottage a hundred yards upstream, we were in a perfect spot to pause, and it almost goes without saying we tied outside *4B* on its 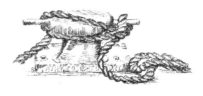 winter mooring – 4B seemed to be everywhere, we were now convinced we'd pass it in the middle of the Irish Sea when we boated back to England!

WI were soon at work with a long-reach digger and dumper; what was unexpected was the man we watched raking out the spoil and occasionally putting something in a bucket. Being curious and having time to kill, it was not long before I went over to see what he was doing. The bucket was half full of water and on its bottom, and barely moving, were lampreys. A bit like eels with one end a god-ugly multi-toothed and otherworldly mouth, they're a protected species that has to be returned to the river. I couldn't imagine eating one, let alone gorging to death on them as King Henry I apparently did.

Unlike on the much wider Shannon, to boat on the Barrow you follow a channel, or boatstream, dragged clear of rocks and debris for horse-drawn barges in the late eighteenth and early nineteenth centuries. Jim stressed that we'd have to keep about 12' of water between our hull and the trackway – as the towpath on the Barrow's called – to be sure of being in the right place. We promised we would, and then came up with a plan that if we hit anything (though it was more likely to be *when* than *if*) we'd push the Man Overboard Button (MOB) on the GPS. The MOB records the position when the button's pushed which, while it wouldn't give an exact location of whatever we'd struck, would be a damn site better than the notes and sketches we'd otherwise be limited to.

It took a couple of days to clear the way ahead of us, and when we did go we were warned there was likely to be another sandbank waiting just round the corner. If there was we missed it, though it can't have been by much as the river was so shallow that even at tick-over the water going through *Hawthorn's* prop – our draw in boating speak – was dragging the river off the bank beside us and dropping its level at least six inches. Not that we were going to get stuck for long as two WI 4WDs kept us company on the trackway; it felt a bit like we were on safari. They left us when, having nervously eyed the long and unprotected weir the river spilled over, we entered the next canal cutting.

We hoped being in the cutting would offer us respite after the stress and tension of worrying about grounding and keeping in the boatstream. It didn't; in fact it was a nightmare: the first hundred yards were so badly silted it took us fifteen minutes of hard blasting to get over, and even then we only just floated. The cutting was narrow, shallow and overhung by bushes and trees for much of its length. It took us two hours to cover the two miles to the lifting bridge and the lock beside the huge derelict mill at its downstream end. Jim and his lads were patiently waiting, and lent a hand to sweep the leaves and branches from our cabin roof. Then they put us through the lock and suggested how best to leave the lock cut without hitting the spit of sand they knew was waiting where it joined the river.

We could see them watching as we approached Maganey Bridge a couple of miles downstream. I feared they might be anticipating our wheelhouse being destroyed on the bridge's curved arches, but we dodged the rocks and managed to keep our line on the suddenly accelerating water. A few miles later the 4WDs stopped because the lads were convinced we were going to need help getting through the long, silted cutting to Bestfield Lock. We didn't, but seeing the wrecked hull of a boat hanging in the trees gave us some idea of how high the river had been in the winter floods.

While in this lock we removed our wheelhouse in readiness for the bridge in Carlow town, now just a couple of miles downstream. Having been told by everyone how low and tightly arched this bridge was, we stopped on the wall just above it and walked down the bank to have a look. It was low and tight, and being on the inside of a bend made getting into it awkward. We were not surprised the HBA had all sorts of tricks for getting through here when they came down a few years earlier. Unlike their high steel structures, our wheelhouse folded so we had lots of room to play with, though we were thankful that the river wasn't really rushing, especially as we had to cross the river along the top of a huge and unprotected weir immediately below the bridge. I thought of the time our fuel pump spring failed on the Shannon and prayed that nothing similar would happen here.

If only Austen hadn't been back in Ireland biking we'd have stopped sooner, but he was and we'd promised bed and board that night. We doubted he'd find the next lock, and then it didn't matter, as there was nowhere to moor. Leaving it, we ran aground mid-river.

After all the stress of anticipating impacts, and the exactness needed on the steering to keep *Hawthorn* where she was meant to be, we were tired, too tired to want to deal with this. Fortunately we were lying at an angle, which meant there was deep water one side of us. We got ourselves going again with a few minutes on the bow-thruster. We really didn't need the final struggle to get into and along the lock cutting at Milford. Thankfully it was worth it: we stopped above the lock in a jewel of a spot with lots of trees and hills around us. Below us the water foamed white after its rush through the oldest hydro-electric station in Ireland.

We'd managed fourteen miles and, including Ardreigh's which barely counts, six locks. We were exhausted, and thankful when Jim rang to suggest we didn't rush on in the morning: the river below Bagenalstown, downstream of us, was full of gravel he was only just starting to clear. So Austen, who arrived in shock that it hadn't rained all day, got a lie in before helping us down the lock and heading away the following morning.

Below Milford the banks were rockier, and the water lapped around and surged over large boulders. What was it with this river? Every other one we'd ever boated got easier the further we got down it; as the land levelled out from the high ground nearest the source, locks usually got further apart, and both bends and banks got softer. But not the Barrow: with nine locks in the next fourteen miles it did the exact opposite. Which meant the river ahead of us was nearly twice as steep as that we'd already boated, and we only had to glance around to see its increasingly rocky nature.

We were about to leave the next lock at Rathvindon when the lockkeeper, John, leant down to suggest we take the next mile or so gently. We soon knew why: the river here should really be only about 2' deep, so the boatstream had been cut into the bedrock. The water was clear, shallow and fast flowing, and we felt our pace increase as we were swept along between the jagged, rough rock faces, in places just inches from our hull. I couldn't imagine how working boats ever managed in this water. It was cruel and savage boating and even downstream on a sunny day the thought of slogging up here against a flooded, silt-filled river seemed improbably insane. While we never hit the sides, we did run over a couple of bumps I hurriedly marked. Though neither of us said anything until we'd cleared it, both Jill and I went down this stretch worrying we might never get back up it. And then we reached the top of a long island that reduced the river to half its width – and we picked up yet more speed. Shooting through the arch of the river's oldest bridge, built in 1320, we passed the castle and village of Leighlinbridge. It looked a promising place to put in to, but we'd started late and John was already waiting at the next lock. Then, as if to make a point to Austen, it started to rain.

After our travels with the Misfits, we thought the Barrow was going to be a bit of a solitary adventure. Yet, with Jim and his men looking after us so well, nothing could have been further from the truth. Now seeing John still willing to put us through the lock in a downpour, we called him on board and sat chatting until it cleared. This may have stood me in good stead when, after he had gone ahead to Bagenalstown to help us by taking a rope, I misjudged the flow and flew past where he was waiting. John was a fellow barge-owner, so there was no getting out of the error. Fortunately, other than adding a bit to our walk to the Aldi supermarket, it didn't matter.

Below the lock we soon approached the digger Jim rang to warn was working. It was still scraping and clawing at the channel and, unsure whether it had seen us, I sounded the horn several times. It stopped moving and the driver, Gavin, got out to shake his fist and laugh, and then Darren left his bucket full of lampreys to grin and wave. The river was running fast again now, and we were soon under the concrete road bridge and descending on the narrow brick opening of a railway viaduct. There were boulders and rocks and little islands, and then John was beside an open lock gate and we could rest again.

Although we'd only done about eight miles and five locks, we were already looking to stop. 'Why here?' asked John, looking at the busy road and adding that going on for a few more minutes would reward the effort. He was a local so we would be daft to ignore him. And he was right, it was worth it: Slyguff Lock was so remote and peaceful we were amazed no one had restored the semi-derelict lock house standing under the mature beech trees  beside it. We sat on *Hawthorn's* bow, listening to the weir and birdsong, and had the conversation we'd been putting off.

Before we'd bounced down it with our hearts in our mouths and our fingers constantly poised to push the MOB, we'd thought the Barrow might be the perfect run for my father and his wife to join us on when they arrived on their mid-May holiday. Now that we had some idea of what boating it involved, we were much less sure. And we were only about two-thirds of the way down it; we'd no idea what the next day might bring, and we'd been boating long enough to know that driving back upstream was going to be much harder than drifting down. Crucially, we also knew we were going to be tired and stressed, and unlikely to be good company while doing it. And that was the best-case scenario: if the next fortnight was dry the river level was going to make returning impossible, as would the floods that would surely follow a few days' rain. So a decision was made: we'd go to the bottom of the river, have one day's rest and then get back to the canal at Athy as quickly as possible. If all went well we'd be in Shannon Harbour when Dad arrived, and Lough Derg had to be easier to boat than this beautiful mountain stream.

Despite our need to press on, Slyguff was such a beguiling spot that we were happy to linger for a cup of tea and a chat with John the following morning. It turned out John's uncle and aunt had been the last people to live in the cottage here, and why it hadn't been restored was obvious when John recalled how winter floods ran through it: one occasion when he stayed there as a young child ended with his father carrying him from the bottom of the stairs and, with the doors all sandbagged shut, putting him out of a ground floor window straight into a rowing boat. Shaking the drips from his cup, John then suggested a short stroll down the track to see the remains of the barges sunk to reinforce the island.

He also brought the worrying news that he thought we might struggle on the river below the next lock. It was shallow and the floods seemed to have changed its shape a little. He was right: the sound of scraping stones here wasn't brief; it stretched on and on for at least a hundred yards. Being shallow meant the flow was strong enough to pin us to the bank if we stopped, so we kept the power on. As we did a few minutes later when, just as we lined up to pass through Goresbridge, *Hawthorn* drove over a sandbank. And then we came to a complete halt in the soft silt at the entrance to the next lock cutting. It was bloody hard work, yet neither Jill nor I suggested turning: determined to make Graiguenamanagh that evening, we let the boat settle for a few minutes and then drove ourselves out.

We were now in a valley so narrow that in places the trackway beside the river rose straight out of it on what looked like a dry-stone wall. My great hope was that all the rock used for the wall might mean there was less for us to clatter, but we still kissed steel on stone occasionally. We'd barely seen another boat moored, but the floods had dumped a large modern barge – it looked to be at least 50' by 10' – a hundred yards from the river near Ballingrane. The rising ground around us filled with woods, and we passed odd boulders that looked like half-drowned stone Volkswagen Beetles.

Our longest pause came when we were leaving Borris Lock. Here we were caught on a sandbar made where the river had breached the narrow peninsular of land between it and the lock cut. We were only fifty yards from open water, but the river was tumbling through the gap so hard it pinned us where we were. The cut we were in was too deep for bankside help, and every time we drove the bow out the flow shoved us straight back. Eventually, by using ropes, our bow-thruster and our keb, we found a way of creeping on, and when we did a cheer came up from the watching crowd of walkers who'd paused to take in our struggle. No longer sure if going on was either fun or wise, we smiled and waved and let the river sweep us out of sight and down the hill towards St Mullins.

The next lock, Ballingrane, was one of the spots WI anticipated we'd get stuck. Fortunately, while there was just two feet of water over it, the sand was very soft and we got through it without help from the waiting truck. While in the lock we had time to take in the landscape round us, and the only comparison we could make with England was with the River Wye. Jill and I, with Hobbes between us, had once canoed down some of it, so we knew it well enough to think barging it would be silly. Yet here we were, somewhere similar. It was all very exhilarating, and exhausting.

The locks, and the long and unsettling open weirs that still made us nervous, were coming thick and fast now. Below Clashganna lock there's a pool used for swimming. Though only just dredged, we scraped across it between playing children standing knee deep in the water. The day's last lock, the double-chambered Ballykennan, was easy enough and, apart from striking a gravel bank inside a bend a few hundred yards downstream of it, our troubles were behind us: the high ground retreated slightly and the river got wider and deeper. Turning hard to starboard beneath the granite face of a low cliff the river had spent years eroding, we found ourselves looking down long lines of boats, two and even three abreast, that stretched all the way to a bridge and buildings in the  distance. We'd reached Graiguenamanagh. Now deadbeat, we ignored the signs telling us we mustn't and moored against the car park. We were only yards downstream from a set of diving boards, so at least we knew we must be in deep water.

AGAINST THE FLOW

Getting stuck on the River Barrow didn't seem nearly such a bad idea once we'd seen Graiguenamanagh. Indeed far from it: with its views of wooded hillsides and distant mountains we were soon beginning to consider the town a sort of southern Swan Island. And then we'd taken a short walk up its main street and found all the shops and pubs needed to live contentedly. For some strange reason, on our way home we fell into conversation about the beauty all around us with an older man I presumed to be local.

'God's own land!' he'd called it and, while slightly concerned this condemned everyone living elsewhere to godless lives, I'd not disagreed with him. Once back on *Hawthorn* Jill and I spread out the map we'd just bought on our cabin roof, as we tried to see where the river ran through the rolling wooded hills downstream of us. We couldn't: all we could be certain of was that it lay

somewhere between the looming heights of Brandon Hill immediately south of us and the Blackstairs Mountains to our east.

'Well, that's that!' I said, looking out over rocks exposed by the falling tide now drying in the little sunlight penetrating the thickly wooded valley of St Mullins. The river down from Graiguenamanagh hadn't failed the drama of its surroundings. There had been two more locks, and the sections of the fast-flowing boulder-filled and  challenging water we'd anticipated. Only really calming once backed up in a long wide pool behind its final weir, the river more than matched any upstream lengths for beauty, and was as difficult to boat as any. Though that last sentence should have a *probably* in it for, exhausted and needing a rest from the relentless tension of expecting to ground at any moment, we'd walked the four miles down. We were all delighted with the decision, not least Hobbes, who was damp from frequent swims and the happiest he'd been in days.

Walking on, we reached the returning tide a few hundred yards downstream, and here we watched wader-booted fishermen spin lures in search of shad – a seasonal visitor as rare as English boaters. Buying tea and cake at the waterside café, we sat beneath the flowering cherry tree and looked to where the towpath stopped and the tide-stained lower boughs of bankside trees marked the start of the river's next adventure. If we wanted to return to England via Bristol and the Thames, that adventure would be ours too.

'You sound so posh you're just like the guy who reads out the GAA results! No you do, you really do, doesn't he?' said the excited young man in the bar, turning to his two companions.

'He does, you're right, he really does!' confirmed the second young man, while the older – an uncle, we were assured – got in the next round of drinks. And then I was handed a mobile phone, and commanded to state 'Kilkenny 4-

15 Wexford 1-6' when it was answered. It was, and I did, and not a syllable more. The three of them fell about giggling, and someone said 'Get Dara. That'll really mess his head!' This time it was Kerry getting beaten, and the roars of laughter from our company gave away their little game while they played it. And then it was our turn at the bar and another round of shorts was called for. We paid, necked ours quickly and steeled ourselves to bolt. 'Sorry lads, we'd love to stay but we really do have a chicken in the oven.'

'Ah no now! We're barely getting going. Surely you've time for a few more?'

We were already backing out past the rolls of wire, racks of tools and shelves of ironmongery in the shop/front bar of Doyles pub. I stumbled over a lawnmower, and steadied myself by grabbing a strimmer. We'd been down this road at least twice before but this time we really did mean it when we said 'Thanks, enjoy, good luck!' and scarpered.

There was no roast dinner waiting; indeed far from it: we'd already eaten and only popped out for a quick pint in the charming pub to cap off our day walking to and from St Mullins. As if to confirm that Graiguenamanagh is indeed our Swan Island of the south, we were delighted to find the guy who ran the pub was another Pat. It was the perfect space for a final treat and to forget, briefly, the challenges we knew were waiting when we started upstream in the morning.

For much of our run down the river our engine revs were only just high enough for us to steer with. The problem going back was that, while we had a little more control against the flow, we were going to have to use more revs. This wouldn't have mattered on deeper water, but on the shallow Barrow it really made a difference: our having a flat baseplate made these revs likely to pull the water we were floating on out from underneath us, in which case we'd be stuck hard on the bottom, and would only float again once we'd stopped our propeller. If that happened we were going to have to get a tow from the tractor Jim had promised was ready if we needed it. Taking in all we'd hit on our way down the river, not using it seemed unlikely.

While we struggled a bit at the first two locks, we began to fear the river had fallen significantly when we got completely stuck approaching the lock at Ballingrane. Which was odd, for this was one spot we hadn't needed help at on the way down. While it was easy to get a rope from our bow onto the hitch of a WI 4WD, all the tow achieved was to drag us hard against the bank. So the lock gates were closed and the rope passed round where they met in the middle, and then returned to the truck in the hope we could be pulled up to them. It didn't work, and by the smell of things if we had carried on the only winners would have been clutch-plate suppliers. Sensing the distant tractor warming up in readiness to give us a proper beasting, we decided to make one final effort. Somehow, shuffling the rope round various pull points ashore and from bow to midships bollard onboard, we got *Hawthorn* into the lock. We'd only just started and, knowing what lay upstream, at this point our overnight goal of Leighlinbridge seemed an optimistic fantasy.

To our surprise, after all our troubles leaving Borris Lock two days earlier, we got into it without a problem. Though we soon wished we hadn't: the lockkeeper not yet with us, Jill somehow scrambled ashore and got stuck into closing gates and dropping racks to keep us moving. When she went to drop the last rack the WI maintenance men on the bank beside us suddenly got animated. Too late: with a curse from Jill and a loud splash as it hit the water, the rack went in, and the men kicked off. It seemed they were working on the lock's mechanisms and had left out the pins that would have stopped the rack from falling. I couldn't blame Jill, for their absence wasn't obvious.

We got out the two large magnets we keep for such moments, and fished about in 5' of water. Racks aren't light – they're solidly cast metal and weigh two stone – so it was always going to be a struggle. Getting a magnet either end of such a thing when we couldn't see it, let alone then lifting it squarely onto the upturned tines of our keb, took an hour. The only good thing was that working with the maintenance men quickly brought forgiveness.

The pace of the river meant we were often running at 1000 rpm. On the still water of a deep lough that would easily get us along at about 5 knots, whereas on the shallow fast-flowing Barrow it rarely brought us 2, and often not even that. We banged and scraped in places, but by early afternoon we were approaching Goresbridge, and readying for the sandbank we had punched through heading down. We knew we were on it when a sudden drop in speed had us both tilting forward. It felt as if we'd braked, but we kept on going. When the water astern filled with silt we knew we'd blasted through it. While touch and go, that was just a gentle warmer for what lay in wait a mile or so upstream.

Just below Upper Ballyellen Lock was the length of water John had been at pains to warn us of the morning we chatted to him at Slyguff. The river here was shallow and the water raced over the long beds of silt and gravel we'd scraped across. It was one of two spots – the other was the rock gorge above Leighlinbridge – where we feared losing momentum would be particularly painful, and we were a long way from the safety of the lock cut when the scraping started on our way back upstream. The scraping was uncomfortable enough, but that was nothing to the noise that followed when our stern reached the gravelled shallows: all hell broke loose behind us as our propeller ripped the river bed asunder and flung its gravel and stones into our hull. It sounded as if we were being chased up the river by machineguns, and there was absolutely nothing we could do other than keep going and hope we made it. Which we did, though only as far as the lock cut entrance, where we stopped on the sandbar the river's back eddy had deposited across it.

We let everything settle, and then drove gently on, hoping we'd make decent progress to Slyguff, where we'd promised ourselves a few minutes rest. The only downer was we did so on our own, for John was tied up with a TV camera crew and wouldn't be joining us until we got to Fenniscourt Lock a little later.

As we knew from our guidebook, at summer water levels the shallow lock at Bagenalstown restricted passage to boats of under 2' 6" draft. While we'd been willing to be dragged through relatively soft silt and gravel beds if needs be, we couldn't contemplate being hauled over its concrete cill. So we were relieved when John met us at the lock below it with the good news that he'd just measured this crucial shallow and found plenty of water. Though there wasn't plenty on the run up to the bridge just downstream of Bagenalstown, which we only made with a lot more scraping and machinegunning through and over shallows. This was mad, for our being able to get through the shallow Bagenalstown lock meant all the places we'd been hitting the bottom were going to have to be dredged and cleared of countless tons of debris. And we were the only ones who knew this, for we hadn't yet given Jim our increasingly dense report, or suggested that the piles of sand and gravel beside the lock cuts below Bagenalstown and Ardreigh were just the start of what would be needed. Of one thing we were now certain:

we'd made the right decision in getting upstream as fast as possible for, while we'd loved Graiguenamanagh, we suspected its charms would have worn a little thin by October.

Now tiring, it was only John's willingness to work late and our enthusiasm for its striking prettiness that made us press on for the hour it took us to reach Leighlinbridge. We had not seen another boat, either moving or moored, since leaving Graiguenamanagh, so we were not surprised when it looked like we were in for a quiet night on our own there.

With the river being wide, seeing a group of lads gathering round a pack of beer on the far bank was so unthreatening we paid it no attention and, other than the usual noisy bravado, initially we were right. Then it got dark, and the first stone arrived with a clang against our steelwork. A second soon followed. What was it with the Barrow? Other than the brief promise of incoming in Dublin, we'd not had a stone thrown at us anywhere in Ireland, yet here we were being used for target practice for the second time in a few short days. We now needed a dose of Red Ted though, not being gifted in the art of threatening Dublinese, I only managed a solitary 'Oi!' It worked, or at least it seemed to when the shadowy figures on the far bank slunk back into the darkness. I waited and watched, and when all seemed calm went below again. Though not for long as, sitting thinking about the river's pace, the rocks and the weir just downstream of us, I began to fear a later game might involve untying us. So I got up to drop a chain and padlock through the bankside furniture.

I was stepping ashore when the torch went on. It was just a few feet away and was clearly intended to cause me temporary blindness. And then whoever was holding it said 'Can I help you?'

'You can,' I said. 'You can stop bloody blinding me!' The torch went off and a large man stepped into the light spilt from our wheelhouse. He was not wearing a uniform, but he had the confident authority of a guarda. And so he was, and the reason he'd come down was because he'd heard my 'Oi'. He'd guessed it had to come from a tourist, for any local would have shouted 'Hey'. I both appreciated the gesture and regretted my instinctive aggressive response to his earlier blinding. If only things were like this in England! There we'd often had good reason – like the time a petrol bomb was thrown on *Camberwell Beauty's* stern deck one midnight – to call the police when we were moored near Warrington, and if they came at all it wasn't until the following day. So we were surprised by his presence, and very grateful to be given a mobile phone number and to hear he'd be about until the early hours. And then the Garda was gone up the trackway and across the bridge in pursuit of foolish boys. Our chain stayed in its locker.

Our last day on the Barrow was a gentle one. Perhaps we were now getting the hang of things, or it may have been that we knew the hard rock of the downstream sections was now giving way to softer dark-soiled banks and riverbed. With Jill on the bow directing the minor adjustments needed to keep steel and stone apart, even the narrow rocky length upstream of where we overnighted proved simple enough. The day's most disturbing experience was being caught by the silt along the top of one of the weirs: we came to a halt with the drop one side of our wheelhouse more than a little unnerving. As it had done countless times before, our bow-thruster got us out of trouble without recourse to rope and tractor.

Once again WI's lockkeeper at Carlow – John's brother Billy – helped us fold our wheelhouse down just before the run across the wide pool in Carlow's town centre and the upstream push through its arched stone bridge. It was sunny, and as boating with the wheelhouse down is as much fun as dropping the hood on a soft-top car, we went on up the river with it still down, saying we'd rebuild it later. And then Billy had gone, and Noel took us on to Ardreigh, where we passed the mound of drying silt and moored outside *4B*.

It's a good job we're not precious about our boat's paintwork. For *Hawthorn* looked a lot more battered than she had just a few days earlier. Still, we were now very nearly done with the River Barrow and all that remained was half a mile of silted lock cut and a last, very brief, run across the river. It hadn't quite done with us: all I had to do was to pull onto a short jetty just below the first canal lock, yet I misjudged the flow and slammed our home against its concrete.

LOUGH DERG

We left Athy with Jill steering and me reading the English newspaper we'd just bought. It was 7 May 2010, and the United Kingdom was still absorbing the uncertain outcome of the previous day's election that saw no party win outright. It was all a bit a of a mess, and we were both quite happy to watch from a distance while we concentrated on our own, slightly unusual view of the world. For we were now very close to completing our year on Ireland's inland waterways, and the imaginary map of lines in space and time we used to visualise our travels.

In England I'd always imagined those lines were red and, given that a single continuous thin thread across the Irish Sea connected our English past to our Irish present, their remaining red made sense. That single line ran through Dublin and up the Grand Canal as far as Sallins, and then all hell broke loose in our winter's coming and going from Digby Bridge. We had several lines west to Edenderry, and a single one south down the River Barrow to a Graiguenamanagh diving board and back. On that river's narrow boatstream the second line lay atop the first, parallel to the trackway bank. That wasn't true on the Shannon, where wandering was not just possible but a must. And we had wandered: like unfaithful lovers once lured by the rivers Suck and Camlin, Grange and Boyle, we kept leaving the Shannon. How different we'd been on Ree. There, other than a brief flirt with Ted's temptations, scale had scared us into a steadfast conformity we'd maintained on Bofin, Boderg, Key and Grange, and countless other reedbound spaces in between, before Norbert's markings led us astray behind an Allen island. We'd been faithful and direct when returning south to work in Shannonbridge, though once there we'd seized the HBA's offer of a guided tour of Ree's less boated spaces.

With Misfit mates we'd spun our trace across the SEW and round the Erne's countless islands, bays and headlands and returned to thickly coil contentment in a corner of Lough Garadice. Thin again, the line doubled back to Leitrim, and doubled again on returning to the Shannon and up the River Boyle for a last lingering look at Key's perfection. And then we dragged it downstream – with a looping kiss east to embrace Temple Island and the Inner Lakes again – before it found itself again on reaching Shannon Harbour.

We hoped we had saved the best to last but, particularly after all the slack-jawed moments of awe we'd experienced in the last eleven months, it was hard to believe that Lough Derg was going to live up to its oft-lauded promise as the jewel of the Shannon. We'd know soon enough, as long as the run from Athy to Shannon Harbour went without a major hitch.

When we'd left the Shannon for the canal the previous autumn, we'd soon found ourselves feeling frustrated by the slow pace and hard work of barely floating. But after our time on the wild river, being back on the Barrow Line of the Grand Canal in Athy came as a relief: we might not be going anywhere quickly, but at least we should always be going. And it was a little different, with unexpected treats like passing between fields of wheat and barley for the first time since leaving England. A seemingly trivial thing, it goes some way to revealing just how dominated Ireland is by pasture and cattle farming. Though I had to hold my hand up and say that I grew up in Suffolk in the middle of what's known as England's breadbasket, and I had missed seeing an arable landscape. My only regret was we were not there for the golden harvest. I'd never thought I'd miss seeing stubble fields, but then again we'd no idea what it was about England we might miss: it was only on returning there in the winter that Jill and I really took in just how lovely some English villages are.

The canal follows the Barrow's valley as far as Monasterevin, where our last glimpse of the river was as it rippled under the canal's aqueduct, at the far end of which we passed under the new lifting bridge that had we spent most of March and April  waiting to be completed. Knowing we were going to be in the wilds again, we shopped in the town before leaving, and that meant we walked past the front doors of the grand Georgian houses whose large gardens are on the far side of the road, sloping down to the river. The houses are now past their best, but we still loved their lines and huge sash windows, and we guessed both homes and the town itself were at their peak soon after the canal was first opened.

While we could only imagine that, we had the extraordinary experience of seeing how the new-built canal must have looked when we boated through a recently dredged section a little further on. As it had been when we first crossed it a few weeks before, the canal here was almost a portal to another world. For it hadn't just been lightly scraped to give large boats like ours a fighting chance of getting through: over the winter it had been drained and then reprofiled to its original shape. Luckily for us this was a length on the open bog without a lane or a telegraph pole beside it, and all vegetation either side of it had been cut back. Excepting the odd barbed wire fence and occasional distant tree plantations, we felt as if we were looking at a scene little different to what must have greeted the canal's first boaters in the late eighteenth century. We'd enjoyed boating this length when heading south but it was even better the other way when, after hours of slowly grinding along the shallow un-dredged section preceding it, finding our pace soaring to a good walking speed felt like flying.

Once we gained the main line at Lowtown, our flight continued all the way to Shannon Harbour. With Dad now due and our wanting to spend the time on the river rather than the canal, we really did push hard: taking just over a day to make the run from Lowtown to Tullamore we'd spent a week on the previous June. While in the town we called into the WI office to deliver the report we'd made for Jim on the Barrow. It was full of notes of lumps and bumps and scrapings, and we were quietly confident it would keep the maintenance lads in overtime for weeks to come. We stayed a night and then pushed on to spill coffee with Alan at Rahan and to tease his grinning brood. This was our third trip across the Grand Canal and – presumably because its once alien landscape was now familiar – we were beginning to understand why Irish boaters often rush across it.

With many of the boats we'd seen in the autumn now out on the river, there was room in Shannon Harbour for us to wait for my father to join us. We were outside two barges, but fortunately Dad and his wife, Di, were fit enough to cross them without a struggle. As the weather was forecast to be glorious, it seemed they'd arrived at the perfect time.

'It's not all like this, Dad,' I insisted as *Hawthorn* swept between the bright green foliage of two densely wooded islands. It really was wonderful, and so different to the views upstream that I wondered if I'd forgotten or if nobody had mentioned that the Shannon is at its most beautiful between Banagher and Lough Derg. Lined by trees, with frequent backwaters forming islands of all shapes and sizes, it promised several days of adventurous exploring in a dinghy or canoe. We didn't boat far, just the hour or so it took to reach Meelick, where we pulled onto a stone quay and sat looking at the wide slow river, the occasional passing boat and the longest weir we'd seen anywhere in Ireland. Going on the following morning, we boated between dense reed beds and flat and marshy meadows, before the trees and islands returned again for the last few miles to the final obstacle, the swinging road bridge at Portumna. The only crossing on the river to have fixed opening hours, by the time the next swing was due we were one of many waiting craft. And then the lights and sirens of the road's closing kicked in, and the steel and asphalt obstacle barring our progress gracefully eased open. We let the other boats go, and followed them down the last mile or so to where the river banks stopped and Lough Derg started.

Jill and I still hadn't forgotten the impact of first seeing Lough Ree, and knowing Lough Derg was even larger we were curious to see what sort of shock arriving on it would deliver. I suppose we were only ever going to be stunned by the size of the Shannon's great loughs once, and we were glad we'd gone north to Ree first. For Ree's water had extended so far into the distance it fell over the horizon, whereas Derg's dogleg nature meant no single view could ever match that. Not that we discovered this immediately for, just as we'd done on Ree, the first thing we did when arriving on Derg was scarper to the nearest shelter.

Even though our view of it had been limited, we warmed to Derg straight away. For in Castle Harbour we had the town and supermarkets of Portumna a short walk in one direction, and all the woods and lough-side walks of a huge forest park in the other. Hobbes thought he was in heaven, and he wasn't the only one.

We were at it again with our 'It's not always like this!' statements the following morning when we found ourselves boating down a lough so smooth that the bright sunshine bounced off its glass-like surface. Determined to make the most of such a wondrous day, we left the flat ground of the lough's northern shores and headed towards the high hills we could see south of us. That the views were shorter than on Lough Ree turned out to be Derg's blessing, for it meant they were always changing. The lough's width was rarely constant, and there were places where we looked out over several miles of water, and others where the view to port and starboard was limited to just a few hundred yards. There were islands and bays and rocky shores aplenty, and moorings too. Not that we were tempted to put into any, as the lough is big enough to change dramatically with a little wind, and we wanted to experience boating on it when it was truly calm.

We ate our lunch sitting in the sun on our bow in Garrykennedy's very pretty old stone harbour, with a view straight up the lough to the north, and the land rising steeply south of us. Getting in had been a bit of a struggle, and we'd been surprised to find it almost empty. But then most people moored in the brand new facility next door that, not being marked on our gifted but now out of date charts, we'd assumed was private. Not that we minded,

for we might not have seen the walk in the shore-side woods west of us if we'd pulled in there. Not only was it a perfect place for Hobbes, at the far end we arrived on a rocky shore and a proud fisherman showed us the trout he'd just caught.

It was tempting to stop and loiter, to decide a morning's boating was enough, but spending the rest of the day there seemed somehow to risk not making the most of the spell of rare weather. So, once we were clear of the shore's rocky margins, we turned due west and headed for the Scarriff River.

'Honestly, it's not always like this!' Jill and I both exclaimed when Dad and Di were still thinking about the church and round tower on the island to starboard, and looking at the castle rising from the water a little ahead of our portside bow. We had passed a similar castle further north that morning, so we were not surprised they thought this sort of thing was normal. Shortly afterwards we left the lough and wound our way up the rapidly narrowing river between woods and marshy banks and meadows and past a small marina. We stopped on a public mooring half a mile downstream of the town that the river is named after. Which was fine, though it took the owner of the small marina ages to find us. Being in the process of building his own barge, ours passing was a gift he was keen to open. He had a mate with him, and they sat drinking tea and chatting with me in the evening sun. 'That isn't normal either!' I declared to Dad and Di when our callers left an hour later.

The only downer of the day followed when, quite understandably in the evening's heat, the Eastern European men who parked beside us while they walked the banks and fished, stood outside their cars talking loudly into the early hours. The irony is that the only reason they had to shout to hear each other was because their car stereos were already pumping out Europop at excessive volume.

We couldn't understand what had happened with the weather. The lough we returned to the following morning was as smooth and just as sunny as the one we left. While it would be insane to suggest we were close to having explored this vast water, the only length we had yet to see was its southern arm that would take us to the town of Killaloe. At a pace to suit the weather and our surroundings, getting there took three gentle hours. This length was so utterly different to Derg's northern waters it was hard to believe we were on the same lough, as we were now amongst the highest hills we'd seen since leaving Lough Allen. Once in Killaloe we sat outside enjoying the dramatic view of mountain and water, and fully understanding why the Celtic Tiger had brought so many new buildings to the waterside around us. We could see this in our book of aerial photographs; we now had no reason not to flick through the rest of it. For this was as far south as we would be going, and we'd now completed all we set out to achieve on Irish waters. It was a massive moment, but one that was rather lost in all the noise of the relentless traffic crossing the bridge just downstream of us. Given there was no benefit to staying, as we could sit and chat while we boated back north, we got going again. Though little did we know we were about to be doused in a great dying that would deny us any chance of sitting outside.

The weather was perfect for a massive hatch of mayfly, the large membranous winged insects that drove both trout and fishermen wild. While they only lived for just a day, they did so in vast numbers: great clouds of them could be seen hanging over the water, and our roof filled with their dying forms. It was not an experience we'd anticipated seeing, and one that again had Jill and me saying 'It's not always like this.' Watching on, Dad was fascinated: while he was not and had never been a fisherman, he was reminded the experience of a friend, Peter, in Ireland one May day in the late 1960s.

Peter was a psychiatrist and department head in a large hospital near Belfast. Having applied for a then vast sum of money – the figure was something like £500,000 – he was granted two hours to address the hospital's board to present his proposal. Arriving at the meeting, he had just started to make his case when the door opened and a hospital porter discreetly slid in and handed a piece of folded paper to the first of the many men assembled on the far side of a grand table. He opened it, read what was on it, folded it and then passed it to the man beside him. He did exactly the same, and so on down the line. Once they'd read it the men glanced at each other with nervous eyes and hints of nods towards the door. Peter had no idea what was going on, but the meeting's chair stopped him and said they would approve his proposal. The meeting was over almost before it started, and the men headed for the door. A few seconds later Peter was left sitting in wonderment at what had just happened. The piece of folded paper was still lying on the table so he picked it up and opened it to read just two words: 'Mayfly Hatch!'

Hospital directors weren't the only ones excited by what was happening in and on and over the water. For that evening the lough around us was busy with lakeboats dashing to get to the prime fishing spots below the trees most densely crowned with a cloud of dancing mayfly. Dying insects lay all over the water, and the fishermen cast their imitations amongst them in the hope of fooling a feeding trout. Not that I was anything like an expert; indeed all I knew was the tiny knowledge imparted by a kind soul later that afternoon.

On our way into Mountshannon, we'd dropped anchor and set off in the dinghy to have a look at the church and round tower on the island of Inis Cealtra (Holy  Island). We had all gone, and were just scrambling ashore on the low stone jetty when a man, either a farmer or a warden, pointed to a sign that said No Dogs and then refused even to discuss our suggestion that we leave Hobbes on a lead. Seeing there was not even going to be an argument to win, I took Hobbes and Jill back to *Hawthorn* while Dad and Di explored. On returning to collect them

I briefly chatted to a fisherman who had pulled up for a few minutes in the shade and shelter of the island's trees. He talked about the mayfly, and when I said I had a fly rod but no idea what I was doing, let alone a clue of what fly to use, he described what was involved and then opened a little wooden case and gave me one of his. With guests staying, I had no chance of using it, but it was a generous gesture I hope I gracefully thanked him for. Then I begged his pardon and went to catch Dad, who was wandering round old stones and trying to avoid standing in cowpats while he studied faded carvings.

To get to the pub in Mountshannon after we'd moored in its harbour, we went through a small park that felt Mediterranean in the late afternoon's heat. When we returned a few pints later we found an older boater moored beside us. He'd been reading our blogs for months, and the moment we were back he was putting out chairs, opening bottles of wine and encouraging us all to join him. His boating history was so extraordinary it put ours to shame, and we sat listening to all sorts of adventures while the shadows stretched ever further out across the water. It was all very peaceful and, as I'd been telling Dad for days, not exactly normal.

The weather really was outrageous, as was our fortune at having Dad and Di visit here and not on the Barrow. For here Dad was able to steer *Hawthorn* back up the lough the following morning while the rest of us lazed and chatted or, at least in my case, made the most of the lough's glassy sunlit surface to roar about in the dinghy taking photos.

Stopping for lunch at Terryglass we briefly fell in with one of the HBA gang we'd met the previous summer. An M barge owner, he was interested to hear we'd turned *Hawthorn* in the old harbour at Garrykennedy, something his own barge was just a few inches too long to manage. Fair play to him for even going in, for we'd had a bit of a battle getting by the badly moored boat at its entrance: had we been on an M boat we'd probably have spent our lunch break studying the much more difficult task of backing out past it.

Mooring for the night above Victoria Lock at Meelick, we wandered onto the large island between the lock cut and the river, and walked the bank beneath

the trees with a donkey for company. According to the lockkeeper, when the cattle joined him in a few weeks' time he would act as one of them, but until then he thought he was a person. This explained why he not only followed us, but why he insisted on resting his chin on our shoulders. At least I didn't have to tell Dad and Di that this wasn't normal. Being donkey lovers (I'd worry if they weren't) they were delighted; though donkey's charm wore a little thin when he spent half the night braying to a colleague on a farm a few hundred yards away.

We'd only a few miles and about an hour of boating back to Shannon Harbour in the morning. On the way we rang Jason to see if he was about to lend us a hand through the two locks between the river and where Dad had left his car. He was, and we arrived at his lower lock to find the gates open and a smiling Jason leaning on the lock beam ready to whirl into action. We were soon through the second lock and not long after Dad and Di were gone.

And that was that. Our imagined map of red track lines was now complete, and we were even facing Dublin. We were done.

Of course we weren't done, or even considering going back to Dublin to face the perils of the Irish Sea. For once back in England we'd only be living and working and moving about – albeit very slowly on its shallow canals – wherever our fancy took and *Hawthorn's* size allowed. Which is exactly what we'd be doing in Ireland, except it wouldn't be on waters we'd become overly familiar with and wanted to leave, but on the wonderful waterways we'd only just begun to explore,

and in a culture and people we were only just beginning to know. And it wasn't as if our imagined map was anywhere near complete: we'd barely touched any of the large loughs, the Royal Canal was still due to open, and the opportunities for disappearing into backwaters, rivers and streams, with the dinghy and canoe were simply vast. But, above all, we knew what it felt like to want to leave a country, and it didn't feel like this. So I rang Jason again and, after apologising for troubling him so soon and promising it would be months before we were back, we dropped our lines and turned to face the Shannon.

ACKNOWLEDGEMENTS

This book has been a while coming, and might never have come at all without all the encouragement I received from family, friends, and the Irish boating public. I've been spoilt by having two fine editors: my father who encouraged me to get started, read and improved early drafts, and did all he could to maintain any momentum gathered; and in Brian J. Goggin whose extraordinary generosity and attention to detail copy editing my final manuscript saved me countless errors. Any remaining are mine. Alan Lindley, John O Neill and Norbert Eberle kindly took time to read pertinent extracts, and Tom Tuohy generously let me help myself to any of his lyrics.

Both Jill and I are grateful to Di Griffiths for all her advice and encouragement with illustrations.